GW00762540

THE PRAGUE GHETTO

THE PRAGUE GHETTO

Milada Vilímková

Aventinum

Text by Milada Vilímková
Translated by Iris Urwin
Photographs by Pavel Štecha, Vladimír Uher and Miroslav Fokt
Graphic design by Aleš Krejča

English language edition first published 1993

ISBN 80-85277-83-2
Printed in the Czech Republic by SPEKTRUM, Brno
2/99/78/01-01

1/ (Frontispiece)
The interior of the Old-New Synagogue with the *aron ha-kodesh* and the curtain.

Contents

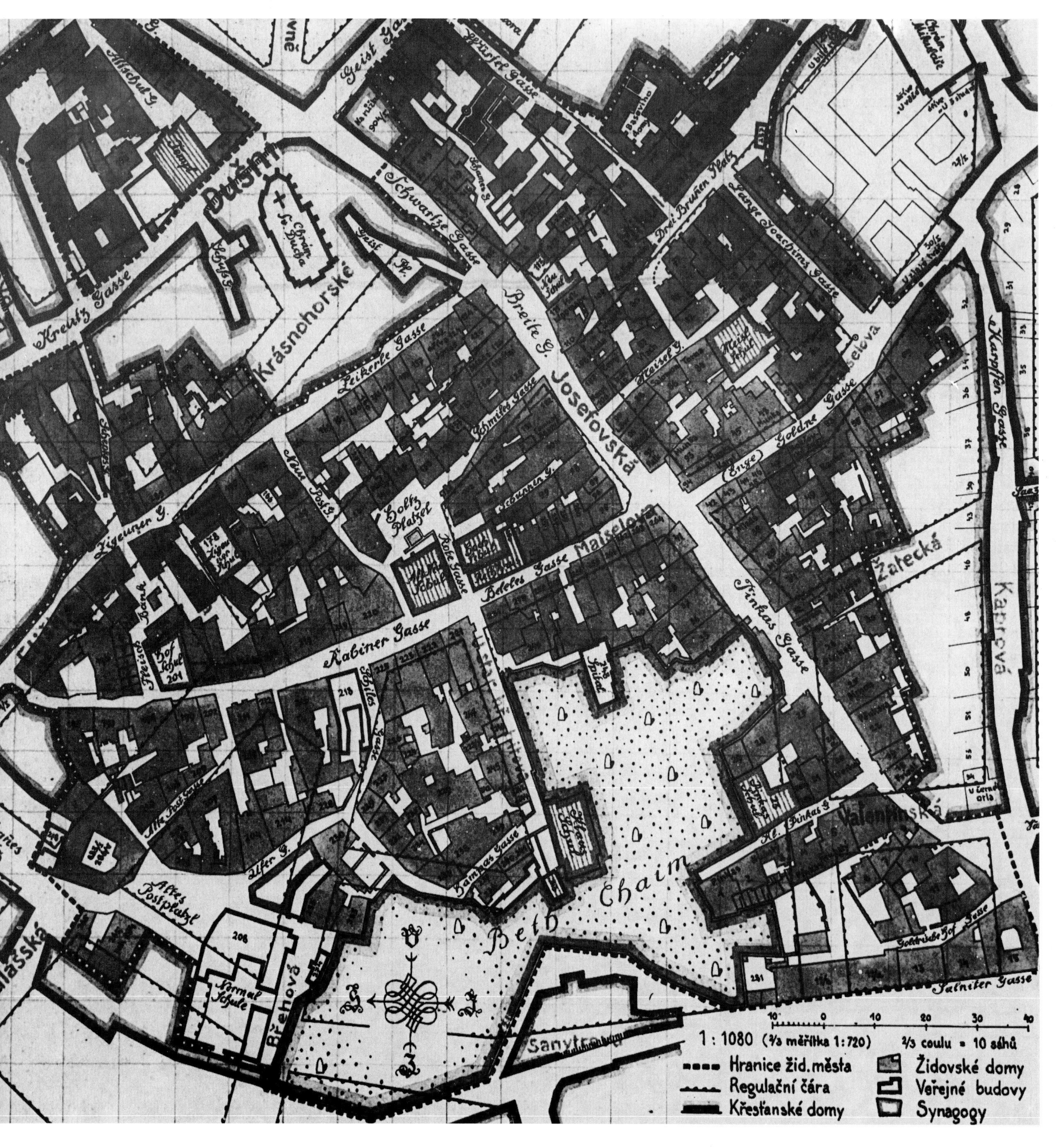

Dušní
Krásnohorské
Kreutz Gasse
Schwarze Gasse
Leikerle Gasse
Breite G.
Josefovská
Drei Brunnen Platz
Lange Joachims Gasse
Meisel G.
Goldne Gasse
Maiselova
Zigeuner G.
Goltz Platzel
Rote Gasse
Belels Gasse
Kabiner Gasse
Hof Schul 201
Pinkas Gasse
Žatecká
Karpfen Gasse
Kaprová
Beth Chaim
Altes Postplatzl
Normal Schule
Břehová
Salniter Gasse
1 : 1080 (2/3 měřítka 1:720)
2/3 coulu = 10 sáhů
10 0 10 20 30 40
Hranice žid. města
Regulační čára
Křesťanské domy
Židovské domy
Veřejné budovy
Synagogy

Foreword

This book about the Prague ghetto came into being partly on the initiative of the publishing house and partly as a way of fulfilling my own obligations to the research papers of my late husband, Dr Otto Muneles, to whose memory the work is dedicated.

Dr Otto Muneles, whose given Hebrew name was Gabriel, came of an old Prague Jewish family that could trace its ancestors as far back as the sixteenth century. He was born on 8 January 1894. After simultaneously attending both the Gymnasium and the Talmud-Torah Jewish school, where the emphasis was on Hebrew Halakah literature, he entered the Arts Faculty of the German University, Prague, in the Department of Classical Studies. At the end of his sixth semester he left, however, and spent the first years of World War I in what was then eastern Galicia, the home of the Hasidic religious movement. For several years he made a systematic study of the Talmud, Halakah and Hasidic literature. In 1921 he was ordained by Eleazar Rokach, the rabbi of Uhnów in Galicia, and his ordination was confirmed early in 1922 by the Chief Rabbi, H. Brody, in Prague. Muneles then returned to complete his university studies, but in the Semitic rather than the Classical Department.

He never took up rabbinical duties, but served up to the outbreak of World War II as an administrator in the Burial Society *(Chevra kaddisha),* and worked as a private scholar interested primarily in Hebrew and Judaic bibliography, and later onomatology. He was an outstanding authority on medieval Hebrew, the Talmud and the Cabala.

During World War II Dr Muneles lost his entire family, and only survived himself by a miracle: in Terezín concentration camp he was given the task of cataloguing all the Hebrew books assembled there by the Nazis and thus his life was spared. After the war he became a research fellow in the Jewish (later State Jewish) Museum, and Chief Librarian. It was during this period that he wrote his major works, *Bibliografický přehled židovské Prahy* (Bibliographical Survey of Jewish Prague) and, together with Dr M. Vilímková, *Starý židovský hřbitov v Praze* (The Old Jewish Cemetery in Prague). A number of important articles followed, published in the *Židovská ročenka* (Jewish Yearbook) and the *Judaica Bohemiae,* published since 1965 by the State Jewish Museum.

Dr Muneles's last work, the MS *Starý židovský hřbitov v Praze* (The Old Jewish Cemetery in Prague), an enlarged and updated version of the earlier book (1955), has served as the basis for the present volume, in particular for the chapters on the spiritual life of the ghetto, on the synagogues, and the Old Jewish Cemetery. Without these and other works from the pen of Dr Muneles cited in the Select Bibliography, I could never have written a book about the Prague ghetto. I have only added material on art and architecture and some general historical background, especially where the life of the ghetto came into contact with the Christian society by which it was surrounded. Most of my facts are taken from contemporary sources preserved in the Central State Archives, the Archives of the City of Prague, and the Archives of the State Jewish Museum. I would like to thank all those who so selflessly helped me to deal with this material and to assemble the photodocumentation, namely Dr V. Sadek, Dr J. Šedinová, Dr B. Nosek, Dr V. Hamáčková, Dr J. Zachová, Dr J. Doležalová, Dr J. Šmejkalová, and Dr A. Pařík, all of the State Jewish Museum in Prague.

Dr Milada Vilímková

2/
The lay-out of the Jewish Town of Prague, according to the cadastral survey of 1842 and a map preserved in the Jewish Museum, Prague, supplemented by the 1895 clearance map. Drawn by E. Kraus, 1896. The proposed new street network is superimposed on the map of the quarter as it was then. Some changes were made later, particularly around the Pinkas Synagogue.

/I/ HISTORY OF THE GHETTO

The slum clearance decree of 11 February 1893 was responsible for wiping the lively urban conglomeration of the Prague ghetto from the map of the historic city, and replacing it with a new modern residential quarter. Only a few isolated buildings were spared: five synagogues, the Jewish Town Hall and the Old Jewish Cemetery. Today the synagogues — once 'a glory of temples' — seem to crouch low between the many-storied Neo-Renaissance, Neo-Baroque and Art Nouveau apartment houses lining Pařížská Street (formerly Mikulášská) and in the immediate vicinity. These florid new buildings covered all traces of a district that had grown in a quite unique manner ever since the Middle Ages. Only a handful of street names survived the rebuilding, and not even they are identical with the original streets of those names in the old ghetto. A few have retained, at least vaguely, the line they originally followed, like Široká (Broad) Street; from the earliest times it was the main thoroughfare, sometimes called Dlouhá (Long) Street or Židovský rynk (Jewish Market Square), while the western end was known as Pinkasova Street. Another such was Maislova Street, as it is now known; earlier on it had three sections: Zlatá ulička (Golden Lane) was the southernmost, Belelesova from there to where it crossed Široká, and then Rabínská (Rabbis Street) down to the bank of the river Vltava. The street now called U starého hřbitova (By the Old Cemetery) follows the route of the earlier Hampejská (Brothel) Street. Behind the Old Town Benedictine monastery the narrow Třístudničná (Three Wells) Lane wandered along to meet Maislova; that ran into Široká and continued on the further side as Šmilesova, with V kůlnách (Among the sheds) and further east Cikánská (Gipsy) Street almost parallel to it. All this has disappeared, overlaid now by the buildings of Pařížská Street.

To the east, around the oldest synagogue in the ghetto, the Old Shul, lay a small separate Jewish settlement cut off from the rest of the ghetto by the Christian enclave of the parish of the Holy Spirit, belonging to the Monastery of St George up in the Prague Castle precincts. All that remains of this settlement is a synagogue built in the 1860s on the site of the medieval Old Shul. Two late Renaissance synagogues were also demolished, Cikánova (Cikán) and Velkodvorská (Great Court), while part of the Old Cemetery had to give

3/
Demolishing houses on the east side of the Jewish Town Hall. Photograph by J. Kříženecký, 1906.

way to the new Sanytrová (Saltpetre) Street (now 17 November Street) and the imposing public buildings on either side of it. Between 1897 and 1901 the Museum of Decorative Arts was built there and later (*c.* 1922) the Faculty of Arts.

At the time there were undoubtedly excellent reasons for demolishing the old ghetto and building a modern residential quarter in its place. The ghetto was overcrowded, dark and airless, with a much higher mortality rate than other parts of Prague, a breeding ground for infectious diseases. It was a run-down poverty-stricken quarter, a slum crying out for improvement.[1)] Practically no thought was given to the alternative of reconstruction, and perhaps that would not even have been possible, given the specific nature of property ownership in the old ghetto: not only might a single house belong to a number of owners, but it was often divided physically between them, each occupying a clearly stated part of it.

For the city fathers the Jewish quarter was an eyesore, besmirching the lovely face of Prague as she tried to take her place among the other great capitals of Europe. They felt even more strongly about it because the subservient position of Bohemia and Moravia within the Austro-Hungarian Empire had long since relegated Prague to the background, far behind the imperial capital Vienna, and since 1867 (after the establishment of the Dual Monarchy) even behind Budapest, now rapidly growing in importance. It was no wonder that the city proceeded to clear the area known administratively as the fifth section so radically that nothing remained but a few buildings admitted to be of such historical value that they had to be preserved. It must be remembered that this slum clearance was not limited to the ghetto, but also affected much Christian architecture in the immediate vicinity, a loss no less regrettable to us today than that of the Jewish ghetto. In a mere 20 years this new part of the Prague Old Town sprang up on the ruins of the ghetto and the nearby Christian buildings. Work began in 1897 and was completed in 1917.[2)]

4/
The corner of Rabínská, Nová and Šilesova Streets. Langweil's model of Prague, 1826—37.

We have started with the disappearance of the ghetto, but we must return to its beginnings, many centuries earlier. Here we come up against two problems that have often been dealt with but never really convincingly solved. The first question, which has troubled many Christian as well as Jewish historians, is: when did the first Jews reach Bohemia, and when did they settle in Prague? The oldest written evidence is a request made by Arno, Bishop of Salzburg, to an unnamed count, to send him a doctor — 'medicum judaicum vel sclavianiscum'. This is usually taken to mean a Jewish doctor from the Slav country, which at that time could only mean Bohemia.[3)] However, the Latin 'vel' (or, at least) places the two adjectives 'Jewish' and 'Slav' on an equal footing, so that it is not impossible that who the doctor asked for could be either Jewish or Slav, rather than both. And since we do not know whom the request was addressed to, nor where he lived, the suggestion that a Jewish doctor from the land of the Slavs is what is meant, is, to say the least, not wholly convincing. More definite evidence is provided by a Raffelstetten customs decree dating from 903—906, which refers to Jewish

5/
The Old Shul and neighbouring houses on the corner of what was then Křížová and Stockhausová Streets. Langweil's model of Prague.

6/
Houses on the corner of Josefovská (now Široká) Street and the former Maislova Lane. Langweil's model of Prague

and other merchants coming from 'those other lands' (that is, Bohemia and Moravia) who are also required to pay duty on their goods.[4)] Here the wording is certainly clearer, yet it still provides no certainty. It could either refer to Jews and merchants settled in the lands mentioned, or to those who had merely passed through them. The often quoted mention of Jews by Ibrahim ibn Jakub in 965 is equally ambiguous. He only refers to Jews who travel with Turks from the land of Turkey, and says nothing of any Jews settled in Prague. Nor is the legend of St Wenceslas and St Vojtěch (Adalbert) any more definite; they are said in this tenth century tale to have bought off the Jews children of Christian and pagan slaves captured during the fighting and carried off to be sold, especially in Hungary.[5)] Those Jews could have been Prague Jews, but they need not have been.

The sixteenth-century Czech chronicler

7/
The Old-New Synagogue and environs, from the north-east. Langweil's model of Prague.

Václav Hájek of Libočány has a more interesting story, which he sets in the year 995, of Jews helping the Christians in their war against the pagans. According to Hájek, in reward for this aid, the Jews were allowed to build a school *(shul)* in the Little Quarter of Prague, below the Monastery of Our Lady on the bridge.[6] It can be said of Hájek that he invented and prettied up many things in his chronicle, and that his information has often proved unreliable, but as a rule there is a grain of truth in what he puts forward. If Hájek says that the Little Quarter synagogue stood somewhere below the Convent of St Mary below the Chains, as was told in his day, he is probably right. We learn from the chronicle of the Monk of Sázava in the twelfth century that when the Prince of Znojmo, Conrad II, besieged and took Prague in 1142, the synagogue in the outer bailey of Prague Castle was destroyed by fire.[7] At that time the Little Quarter was the outer bailey of the Castle. We know perfectly well that it was not until 1160 that the Church of St Mary and the hospice of the Knights of St John of Jerusalem attached to it were founded, but this makes no difference to the degree of probability we can attach to Hájek's statement. The synagogue may well have stood on part of the large estate donated to that monastic order. It is of course not clear exactly where: it may have been 'below the convent' towards the river bank, or 'below' in the sense of 'lower down the river' following the course of the Vltava. The existence of the Jewish settlement to which this synagogue belonged is also attested by the fact that early in the eighteenth century, the Jewish community in the Old Town paid for the bones of their forefathers to be carried across the river from the Little Quarter. It is interesting that just at that time the Thun Garden (in the region of what is now Míšeňská Street) was broken up into plots on which houses were rapidly built. It is not impossible that the Little Quarter Jewish Cemetery lay somewhere hereabout. Unfortunately we do not know whether the Jewish settlement here ended when the synagogue was burned in 1142, or whether it survived much longer. It is not insignificant, however, that its existence was still widely remembered as late as the early eighteenth century, and the exact site of the cemetery was also known.[8]

There are several more references to the Jewish settlement in the Little Quarter in Hájek's chronicle, some of them much later.[9] He recounts that many Jews moved into Prague in the year 1067, asking Prince Vratislav to allow them to settle there, and bringing him great gifts. They made the same request to the Bishop of Prague and promised to pay heavy taxes. The prince allowed them to purchase 12 small houses on Újezd Lane. Seven hundred Jews are said to have settled there; then the prince ordered half of them to cross to the other bank, to the Greater Town, where again they were only allowed 12 houses. Perhaps we may see in this story the beginnings of Jewish settlement close to the Church of the Holy Spirit. References in Czech medieval chronicles make it clear that Jews had settled on the right bank of the river Vltava even before the Little Quarter synagogue burned down. In the chronicle of Cosmas (1045—1125) Jewish settlements were said to exist, by the year 1090, both below Prague Castle and on the right bank of the river Vltava, along Vyšehradská Street *(vicus vyssegradensis),* which led presumably from the Vltava ford opposite what is now Kaprová Street, its probable route being Valentinská, Husova and Spálená Streets, across the bottom of Charles Square towards Vyšehrad.[10] According to Cosmas they lived quite well.[11] This is very important personal testimony by Cosmas. Soon, however, the position of the Jews deteriorated.

The Jewish community suffered persecution at the time of the first Crusade in 1096. As the soldiers of the Cross passed through Prague on their way to the Holy Land, they attacked the Jews, forcing them to be baptised and murdering those who resisted. Both Czech and Hebrew sources confirm that the Jews of Prague did resist conversion; after their forced baptism they returned to their own faith, and many moved away to safer parts, mostly to Poland and Hungary.[12]

A story from the chronicle of Cosmas illustrates the insecurity of Jewish lives: the Jew Jacob Apella, who stayed on in Prague and acquired great wealth, became an adviser to

8/
The Old-New Synagogue, western façade, looking towards the Jewish Town Hall and the former Belelesova Lane. Photographed *c.* 1890.

Prince Vladislav I (d. 1125) and accepted baptism, turning the *shul* in his house into a chapel with an altar. Later he returned to his old faith, knocked down the altar and threw the sacred relics into the privy. This brought about his fall. His friends are said to have saved him from execution by paying a large ransom.[13)]

In the region of what is now Vladislavova Street, which still bore the name 'the Jewish Garden' (Na zahradě židovské) early in the last century, there was a Jewish cemetery (the 'garden'), and, as late as the fifteenth century, five Jewish houses. This cemetery was older than the one in the Old Town. The Jews probably built their houses there soon after the New Town had been founded, since Charles IV gave them permission to settle there.[14)] It would appear that these houses, along with several Christian ones, were built right up against the cemetery wall. Permission to create this cemetery is said to have been given by Přemysl Otakar II in the year 1254. The privilege he granted the Jews in that year regulated their standing, their duties and rights in the Czech kingdom, but does not mention the cemetery, which must have been treated separately. The existence of a cemetery certainly implies the existence of a settlement, although it may not have been in the immediate vicinity. The New Town Jewish cemetery continued to exist for over 200 years; it was abolished by King Vladislav Jagellon in 1478. The ground of the cemetery was apparently not built on for a long time, for as late as 1706—10 the Jewish Burial Society paid for bones to be exhumed there and carried over to the Old Jewish Cemetery. It would seem that large-scale building was then beginning on the site. Later, fragments of Gothic gravestones were taken from the New Town cemetery and built into the revetment of the *nefele* mound behind the Klaus Synagogue.[15)]

As yet we do not know when exactly the Jews finally left the Little Quarter. If what Hájek's chronicle tells us of the location of the synagogue there is correct, they may have left the settlement as a result of the foundation of a hospice there by the Order of St John of Jerusalem, in the 1160s.[16)]

There is another point to be considered, when trying to date the foundation of the Jewish settlement on the right bank of the river Vltava and the rise of the ghetto. Sometime between 1158 and 1172 the Judith Bridge was under construction, built of stone, to replace the wooden bridge destroyed by floods about the middle of the century. This new bridge, however, was not built where the earlier one is believed to have stood, but further south, where a ford crossed the river higher up. Inevitably this new link between the two banks of the river must have meant moving the main roads and trade routes which used it on either side. What had been a busy route leading to the wooden bridge, located somewhere near the present-day Široká and Kaprová Streets, seems rapidly to have lost its importance. In our opinion it would hardly have been thinkable for the Jews to settle in the busy centre of a Christian town; if that centre is to be located near the two streets suggested above, then the Jews were likely to settle a little further away — which would correspond to the site of the early independent settlement round the Old Shul, in what is now Dušní Street. Only later, when the main routes moved further south, after the new bridge was built, could Jewish settlement cover the area of the future ghetto. Nor is it impossible that the left bank Jewish settlement moved to make way not only for the St John's hospice, but also for the new road leading to the Judith Bridge.

It is assumed that the Jews came to Bohemia from two directions, from Byzantium in the east, and over the Alps from Bavaria in the west. Those who came from the east are believed to form the older stratum of Jewish settlement in Prague, which was concentrated over a small area round the Old Shul between present-day Dušní and Vězeňská (Prison) Streets. Indeed, until its modernization in the nineteenth century, the rite in use at the Old Shul was a special one with some marked oriental features. The second wave of settlers, coming from the west, occupied a larger area round the Old-New Synagogue. It is possible that to some extent this western influx was connected with the settlement of Germans in Bohemia and Moravia in the thirteenth cen-

tury. It is extremely difficult to form any idea of how the ghetto grew. We have too little source material for the early Middle Ages, and no archeological study on modern lines was ever carried out. The Old Shul was demolished, even to its foundations, and replaced by the modern building known as the Temple. We do not know whether the Old Shul was a Romanesque or a Gothic building. At the time of the slum clearance nobody was interested in how old the masonry was that was doomed to destruction, nor what the cellars looked like — that is where the clearest marks of the age of a building are to be found, as cellars usually escaped the ravages of fire.

Even so, we have some more definite in-

9/
The Old-New Synagogue and environs, from the south-east. In the background, the Old Jewish Cemetery. Langweil's model of Prague.

formation, starting from the second half of the thirteenth century, although it is necessarily of a general nature. In the privilege issued by Přemysl Otakar II in 1254 we find some interesting details. No dues were to be paid at the frontier when the Jewish dead were taken from one community to another, one province to another, or even one country to another, for burial. Another paragraph sets out the penalties for desecrating Jewish cemeteries. Deliberate damage to Jewish 'schools' (that is, synagogues) was also punishable. When minor conflicts were being settled, Jews were to take the oath at the entrance to a synagogue.[17)] The privilege speaks of both cemeteries and synagogues in the plural, so that there must have been a number of each not only throughout the country, but in Prague itself.

The reign of Charles (Karel) IV, too, was a time of peaceful prosperity for Jews throughout his domain, and in Prague itself. When he founded the New Town he allowed Jews to settle there with their families and their property, under his protection. Jews were to enjoy the same tax rebates as Christians.[18)] The *Maiestas Carolina* civil code of 1355 (later rescinded) even allowed Jews to hold villages in fee, handing over the taxes to the royal coffers. The sale of such villages, when they came into Jewish hands as a result of non-payment of debts, was only possible with royal consent.[19)] Two years later Charles IV confirmed the privilege issued to the Jews by Přemysl Otakar II. The Jews were regarded as 'servants of the royal chamber' and Charles IV explicitly recognized 'the useful services rendered to him [by the Jews] in earlier times, and which they did not cease to perform for the royal chamber'.[20)] The privilege gave the Jews a guarantee against unjustified attacks by Christians. Before the law Jew and Christian were equal, although the terms in which the law is couched make it quite clear that the Jews were the property of the monarch.

During the reign of Charles's son Wenceslas (Václav) IV things seem to have deteriorated. For unknown reasons, in 1385 Jews were ordered to be seized during the night and thrown into jail, while their property was to be sealed at the king's pleasure. The reason for this order is incomprehensible, for most of Wenceslas's measures were relatively favourable towards the Jews. Nevertheless, when he was absent from Prague in 1389 a pogrom broke out, said to have been provoked by some Jews throwing stones at a priest carrying the sacrament to a sick man. Whatever the true reason, the event illustrates the contradictions between rights on paper and in real life. It seems to have been Catholic preachers who roused the mob to fury; they then overran the ghetto, setting fire to houses and murdering whoever tried to escape. Many Jews who took refuge in the Old Shul were killed. A Latin manuscript entitled *The Passion of the Prague Jews* (in the St Vitus Chapter Library) recounts the tragedy, as does the *selicha,* a Hebrew elegy by the rabbi and poet Abigdor Kara. The king is said to have confiscated five tons of silver, which were robbed from the Jewish Town and then returned to the Old Town Hall. It may have been in consequence of this pogrom that King Wenceslas again ordered the Jews in the cities to be imprisoned and safely guarded, while their property was confiscated and removed to safety.[21)] Such measures were perhaps intended to protect the Jews from further such catastrophes. In 1410 Wenceslas confirmed the privilege given to 'the Jews, servants of Our chamber', to use their cemetery in the New Town and the houses adjacent to it, 'for ever and ever'. The citizens of the New Town of Prague were not to obstruct them in any way in their use of the cemetery.[22)]

The legal position of the Jews remained equally uncertain during the Hussite Wars. There is a report from the year 1422 of the mob looting not only the aldermen's houses in the Old Town, but those of the Jews as well, because they 'were trying to please both the Catholics and the Utraquists'. Jewish homes in Prague were again looted in 1448, when the city was taken by the army of George (Jiří) of Poděbrady, in spite of strict orders that there was to be no looting whatever. Robbing and looting had always been part of warfare, however, and we can assume that those Jewish houses were not the only ones to suffer.[23)]

We also have some information about individual houses in the Prague ghetto at around this time, although it is very fragmentary. In his *Základy starého místopisu pražského* (Materials for the Early Topography of Prague), W. W. Tomek lists 143 buildings in the ghetto area, giving them their Hebrew numbering. Medieval towns were usually so small that the Jewish settlement could be considered a town, at least in size. Even compared to other Jewish settlements of the time, like that in Frankfurt am Main, thought to have comprised 20 houses in 1439, the Prague ghetto was unusually large. At the end of the nineteenth century there were 279 houses, and on Jüttner's plan of Prague in 1811—14, on which Tomek based his topographical study, the numbering of the Jewish houses goes up to 264. This means that Tomek was able to find medieval evidence of over half those buildings.[24)] Until 1577, when separate Jewish records were instituted (the *Libri albi Judaeorum*), Jewish properties were recorded in the books of the Old Town of Prague. Of the 143 buildings listed by Tomek, up to the year 1435 when his record ends, only 33 were temporarily or permanently owned by Jews. This of course does not mean that there were only 33 Jewish families in Prague at that time. Not all houses, nor all changes of ownership, were entered in the city records. Yet even these few details can tell us something about the way the settlement of the ghetto progressed. We can exclude the places where the houses of Christians stood before the year 1435: those on both sides of Jáchymova Street (which corresponds roughly to the street of the same name today), on the east side of Třístudničná, the west side of Dušní, the west side of the northern end of Rabínská, and the southern side of Černá (Black) Streets, and finally the northernmost houses, close to the Monastery of the Greater Cross on Jánské náměstí (St John's Square). There was also a small group of houses on the north side of the Church and Monastery of the Holy Spirit. The fact that Tomek found no references to the remaining houses in the ghetto does not mean that some of them, at least, were not already standing. Judging from the location of those houses which were recorded in the city books, we could put forward the hypothesis that medieval Jewish settlement in the fourteenth and early fifteenth centuries was concentrated around the Old Shul, in the group of houses on the eastern side of the Holy Spirit Convent, probably along both sides of what was Pinkasova Street and Široká which ran into it, and in the groups of houses on both sides of Rabínská, except for its northern end. It would appear that the earlier settlement around the Old Shul was already stagnating, probably having never expanded, while the later settlement centred around the Old-New Synagogue grew in all directions during the Middle Ages. Tomek gives similar limits to the medieval ghetto in his *Dějepis Prahy* (History of Prague).[25)] He believed that Jews were settled mainly around Pinkasova and Široká Streets, around the Old-New Synagogue, along about half of Rabínská Street and the three lanes which led from it to the Old Cemetery. Southwards settlement followed Golden Lane (now Maislova Street) up to the vicinity of St Nicholas's Church.

The entire area was separated from its Christian surroundings by gates and posterns which governed access to the medieval ghetto. The written records refer to them as 'portae Judaeorum', and explicitly mention six. The first was situated at the western end of the principal Jewish thoroughfare, near the Church of St Valentine. The second gave access to Golden Lane, while the third was at the corner of a little street behind what is now Meisl Synagogue. The fourth was placed at the end of the main street — Široká — close behind the enclave of the Monastery of the Holy Spirit; this gate is still shown on Jüttner's plan of Prague in 1811—14. The fifth gate stood more or less across the middle of Rabínská Street, while the sixth closed a byway going down to the river bank. These last two gates were known as 'closer to the Brothel' (Hampejz). Tomek thought that Jews rarely succeeded in purchasing property outside these gates during the Middle Ages. Later on they spread over a much larger area, especially to the north, to the west towards the river, and to the east, as well as southwards beyond the jurisdiction of the Holy Spirit Convent, and south towards the Church of St Nicholas.

The Gothic ghetto was a small built-up area with its main street and its side streets. It was called 'V židech' (Among the Jews), which was undoubtedly a literal translation of the Latin 'inter Judaeos'. Similar Jewish settlements are known from medieval Spain, Portugal, France and Italy. The designation 'ghetto' was not common before the sixteenth century, when the Jews were moved to a new location in Venice in 1516; this 'getto nuovo' was called after the Venetian quarter 'Gietto'. The areas around the ghetto were known in Prague as 'V podžidí' (Around the Jews) — again from the Latin 'in subjudaea' or 'sub Judaeos' — and also as 'Za židy' (Beyond the Jews). The former referred to the area bordering on the Holy Spirit enclave, and the latter to the less dense settlement in the direction of the river bank. Both were originally occupied by Christians.

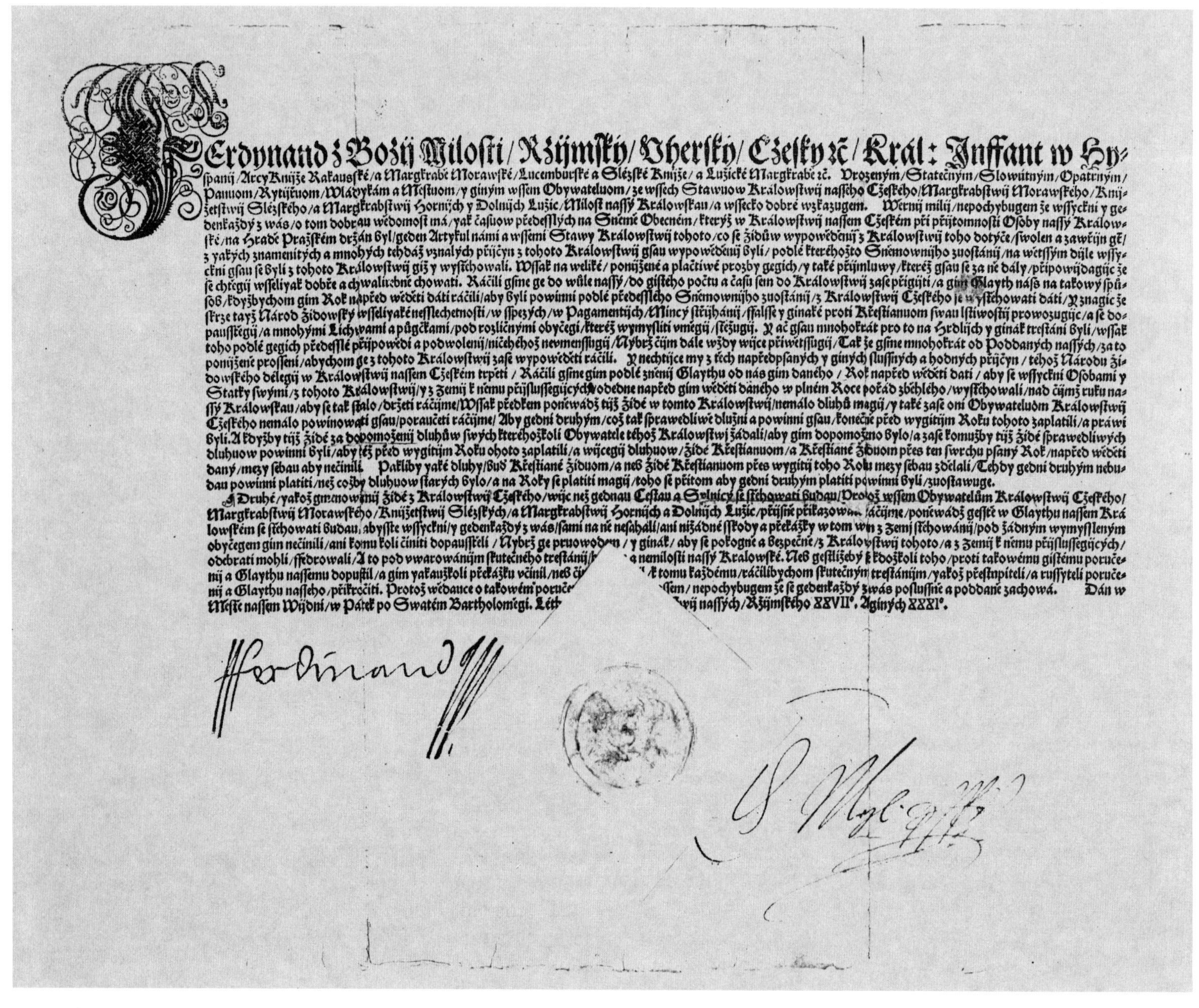

Ferdynand z Božij Milosti / Ržijmský / Uherský / Cžeský rc. / Král : Jnffant w Hy-

10/
The Emperor Ferdinand I expels the Jews from Prague and the Lands of the Czech Crown, for the second time. The decree of 28 August 1557.

At first sight it would seem that the location of the gates meant that the limits of the ghetto were firmly fixed, but that was not absolutely true. Especially on the edges of the ghetto, property changed hands between Jews and Christians, both ways. We know that in 1366 Charles IV donated the house of one Lazarus, a Jew, situated behind the Church of St Nicholas, to the college of Charles University, which occupied it until 1386. Later the building reverted to Jewish ownership. Then in the fifteenth century part of the building was purchased by a Christian physician, Mauricius Bučina.[26)] The house bearing the number 87, known as 'U věže' (By the Tower), behind the Meisl Synagogue, tells the same story: the property of a Jew, Pinkas, it was given by Wenceslas IV to his illuminator, Frán, in 1404. The house facing the Monastery of the Holy Spirit passed from Jonah the Jew to the hands of Squire Smil of Sulevice, and later belonged to the burgher Osvald Roll. Wenceslas also gave the house of the Jew Michael, by the gate to 'Hampejz', to his secretary Jan of Smržov, who in 1404 acquired three more of Michael's houses by the St Valentine gate.

We should not imagine, though, that the king simply took Jewish property away from its owners to give it to his Christian officials or favourites. The Latin document concerning the transfer of Michael's house contains the highly significant word 'olim', meaning formerly, in earlier times; from the legal point of view this clearly implies that the Jew Michael was no longer alive. He undoubtedly died without heirs, and so at his death his property passed to the king. The same rule applied to the king's Christian subjects. The house of Lazarus the Jew is also described as 'formerly belonging to Lazarus', and it was two years later that the king gave it to the university. It would be therefore wrong to assume, as some writers have, that the king simply treated Jewish property as his own and did what he liked with it. He could only dispose of this property when it became his on the death of the owner, and this was equally true of houses owned by his Christian subjects.

In his *History of Prague*,[27)] Tomek also mentions the house called 'U erbů' (At the Coats of Arms), where there was a *shul* recorded in 1519 and still there in Tomek's own day. In 1446 the house of the Jew Jonah passed back to the Jewish community for non-payment of taxes; it was then given to the rabbi Elias of Landa. The interesting thing about this entry is that the Christian owner of a house in the ghetto seems to have been obliged to pay taxes to the Jewish community, and when he failed to fulfil his obligations his property reverted not to the Old Town of Prague, but to the Jewish authorities.

To the west of the ghetto there were two gardens belonging to Christian owners, which were bought in 1430 by the community for a new Jewish cemetery. This was enlarged in 1440 by the purchase of a house and garden 'opposite the brothel' (hampejz).[28)] The New Town Jewish cemetery may have been abolished in 1478 because there was a new burial ground available in the Old Town, which was subsequently enlarged. In 1526 the community added another garden, acquired by purchase. It is thus clear that there were smaller Christian houses in this area, towards the river and towards the Convent of the Holy Cross and that of the Holy Spirit, towards the east. All Prague brothels were demolished in 1419, at the outset of the Hussite Wars, but one of them was long remembered in the name of the little street running north from the Old Jewish Cemetery, Hampejská.[29)]

Towards the end of the fifteenth and in the early sixteenth century Jewish settlement in Prague was not confined to the ghetto alone; we know of many exceptions. After 1478, for instance, there was for a short time a Jewish settlement in the New Town, in the street called 'V jámě' (In a pit). They were even allowed to build a synagogue, but the settlement soon dispersed.[30)] There were several Jewish houses in the Little Quarter at that time, too. In 1489 King Vladislav allowed his personal physician, the Jew Angelin, to buy a house in Strahovská (now Nerudova) Street, so that he could be near at hand. Angelin owned the house until he died in 1497, when it passed to his brothers, who sold it to a Jew, Isaac. It did not pass back into Christian hands until 1509. There are many such cases, but by 1516 all formerly Jewish-owned houses in the Little Quarter were again in Christian hands.[31)]

King Vladislav Jagellon issued an edict in 1499, by which the Jews of Prague were subordinated to the court judge, and the Jews elsewhere in his kingdom to the royal chamberlain. Vladislav was a weak ruler, however, and lower authorities were often found interfering in Jewish affairs, especially in the towns. The burgomaster and aldermen of the Old Town of Prague, for instance, took upon themselves the right to control the election of the elders of the Jewish congregation. In 1502 the council of the New Town of Prague voted that Jews would no longer be allowed to remain there. They were only permitted to enter for a time, and that only in very limited numbers.[32] On the whole, the atmosphere of the time was very unfriendly towards the Jews. Although the aldermen were constantly reminded from above that it was their duty to prevent attacks on the Jews, several cities expelled them. Even the Old Town of Prague won the king's promise, in 1507, that they would be allowed to expel the Jews within a year. While Vladislav Jagellon did confirm his promise, he nevertheless put the Jewish Town of Prague in the charge of Squire Zdeněk Lev of Rožmitál and Blatná and the burgomaster of Prague, Jindřich Tunkel, the following year. If a Jew left Prague without the royal permission, his property would pass to these two men, and to Albrecht Libstein of Kolowrat, the supreme chancellor of the kingdom of Bohemia. That same year (1508) the king revoked the promise he had made to the aldermen of the Old Town, and two years later (1510) renewed the privilege given to all Jews in his kingdom, explicitly stating that they were never to be expelled. It is reported that in 1513 a decree protecting Jewish cemeteries was issued, for they were often the target of Christian hatred.[33]

In spite of these measures, animosity towards the Jews continued. In 1514 a pogrom was organized but prevented in time. The expulsion of the Jews was again discussed in 1517, due to the furriers and shopkeepers who feared their competition. It took some time, but in 1518 it was decided that the Jews could stay. In 1522 King Louis Jagellon confirmed Squire Zdeněk Lev of Rožmitál in his office as protector of the Jews of Prague. This powerful and extremely competent gentleman certainly gained a great deal from his position.[34] It was not humanitarian feelings that moved the king to change his mind. During the reign of the Jagellon kings, just as later, there were economic motives in the background. Those Jews who were expelled from Prague sought refuge with country magnates, and those who sheltered them then drew benefit not only from their activities, but also from the taxes they paid. Zdeněk Lev of Rožmitál was the supreme governor of the castle of Prague, and thus the first man in the kingdom, after the king himself. If the king gave the Jews into his care, that he might profit from the office, then he was indeed well rewarded for his services to the monarch.

In 1526, after the Jagellon line had died out, the Austrian Archduke Ferdinand I, a Hapsburg married to Anna Jagellon, came to the throne, and Fortune showed an ever less favourable face to the Prague ghetto. However, the first fifteen years of his reign were fairly calm, and this showed in the urbanistic growth of the ghetto. New plots were not built up, but existing houses were extended and new wings added to them. The Jewish Town Hall was finished in 1541, a new bath-house was opened in 1537, while in 1530 the Jewish hospitals attached to the Old Shul and to the Old-New Synagogue were extended, as new buildings were purchased. In 1535 Ahron Meshullam Horowitz rebuilt and enlarged a small, late Gothic synagogue next to his house, and had a new prayer house built for his family, in the late Gothic style but with some features of Renaissance architecture.[35] Soon after this building was completed, however, the situation of Prague Jewry changed radically.

In the early years of the reign of Ferdinand I the animosity of the Christians toward the Jews found occasional expression in efforts to have them expelled. The monarch either refused, or postponed a decision. The Czech Chamber (the regional authority) was more or less favourably inclined towards the Jews, for financial reasons. It was their duty to cultivate and multiply the royal property in the Lands of the Czech Crown, and for them the Jews represented primarily a source of

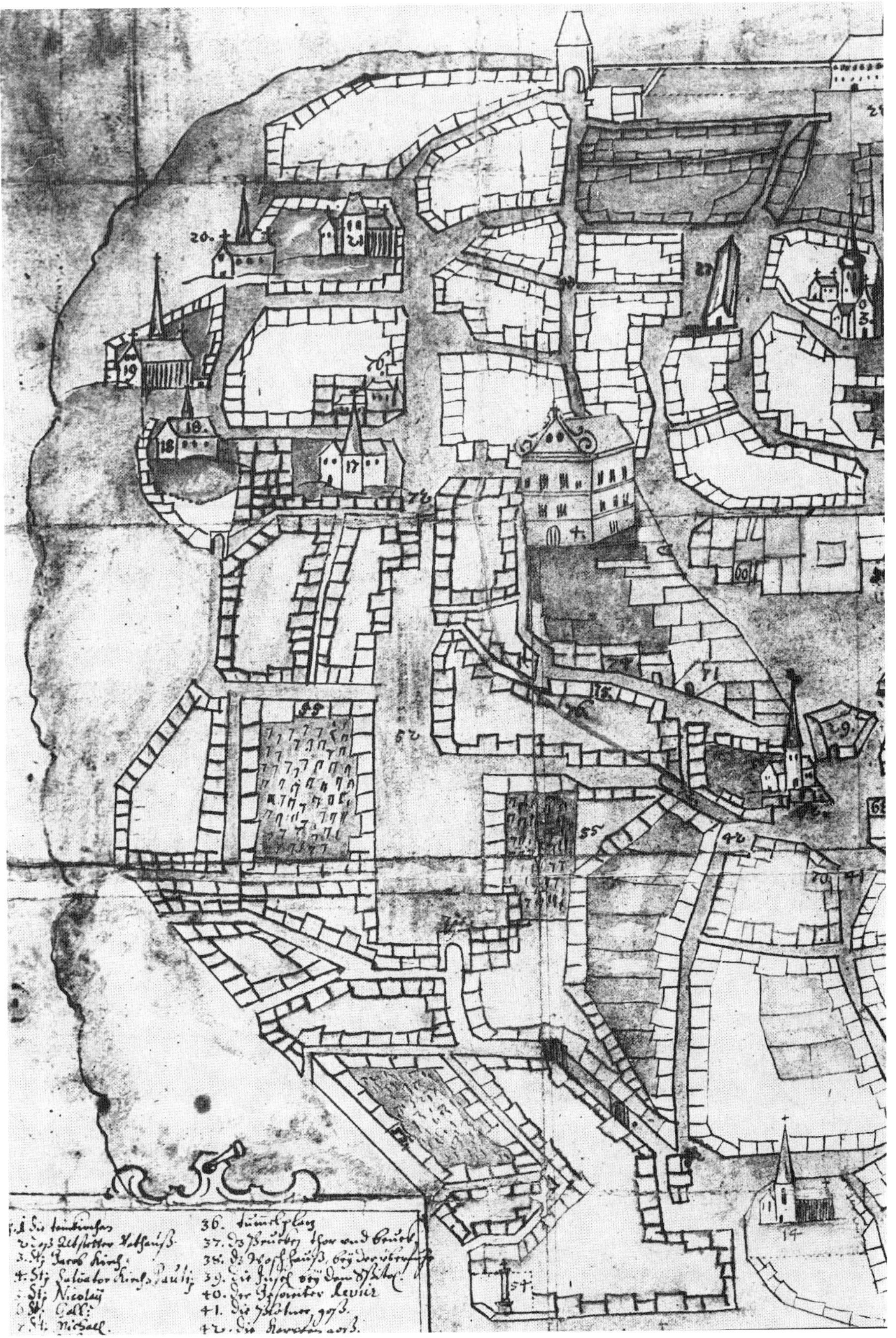

11/
The Jewish Town of Prague as shown on a map of the Old Town, 1628—35. Probably drawn up by Matouš Unger, monk of Strahov.

12/
The Jewish Cemetery in Žižkov, established during the plague year 1680. At that time it formed part of Olšany. Overall view.

income. During the early years of his reign Ferdinand I more or less kept his word as given in the privileges he renewed for the Jews in 1527. Very naturally he tried to limit the influence of the burgomaster and aldermen of the Old Town of Prague over the election of Jewish elders. It cannot be said that the monarch's wishes, nor the ideas of the Chamber, were given much weight. There were plenty of complaints about interference in Jewish affairs by the aldermen of the Old Town of Prague. It even appears that there was an element among the Jews themselves that would have welcomed their freedom from the restraints of the Czech Chamber — according to the Chamber councillors this trend was led by Zalman Munka Hořovský (Horowitz).[36] It is difficult to say why Zalman Munka should have worked for this end; the people of Prague were not particularly well inclined towards the Jews, as we can see from the fact that the Czech Chamber in 1533 asked the king to order the 'Praguers', i.e. the Old Town burgomaster and aldermen, to protect the Jews against attacks by 'tradesmen and others' who were beating them and throwing stones.[37] It would seem that Zalman Munka, at that time the richest man in the Prague ghetto, dropped the idea of freeing his fellow Jews from the yoke of the Czech Chamber. In 1534 Ferdinand I granted special privileges to him and to his family, such as were once granted by Louis Jagellon, concerning the election of the Jewish elders.[38]

Still, complaints by the Czech Chamber that the 'Praguers' were always interfering in Jewish affairs continued, and on the other hand there were increasing complaints that the Jews did not respect the conditions of privileges granted to them, and often confirmed, and especially that they 'debase the currency' and export silver from the country. Finally King Ferdinand let himself be convinced that the Jews were spying for the Turkish enemy. In 1541 he put before the Czech Assembly a proposal to expel the Jews from Prague and from the Lands of the Czech Crown. The Assembly discussed the matter between 12 and 19 September, and decided that the Jews should move out by the feast of St Martin, i.e. 11 November of the same year. However, legal questions were involved, for property was at stake, and the date set was too early. The time for the expulsion from the capital was then postponed several times. According to the royal edict to the secretary of the Czech Chamber Florian Griespek, the Jewish houses were to be occupied by tradesmen and craftsmen. But the Jews kept asking for postponement, so that Ferdinand gave them papers, known as 'gleit', allowing them to remain in Prague at first until the end of 1542, and then renewed several times. Those Jews left in Prague without 'gleit' moved out in April and June of that year; the majority moved to Poland. Although all landowners were forewarned that the Jews must be allowed safe passage, there were many incidents, as the report from Beroun, 23 June, suggests: the Jews were robbed and 'done to death'. There were also many who did their best to turn the expulsion of the Jews to their own advantage.[39] The people of Prague, nevertheless, soon began to complain that with their 'gleit', the Jews were becoming too numerous in Prague, and that not all those who did not have the 'gleit' had gone. The situation remained confused, and in 1546 lists were drawn up of those who had permission to remain in Prague, and those who had no such authority.[40]

In 1546 the Schmalkalden War, with the active opposition to Ferdinand I of Prague and other royal towns, and even some of the Protestant nobles, broke into this unresolved knot of problems. The king had never been popular with his Czech subjects, and at this critical moment the Jews seemed useful. They supplied his army with blankets and horse-rugs, for example. For a time, probably because he had other things on mind, the king forgot all about the need to expel the Jews. And when the Schmalkalden Union was defeated in April 1547, the king strengthened his position in the Czech Lands at the expense of the opposition nobles. By limiting the rights of Prague and other cities, it was natural that for a time the Old Town burghers did not dare to complain about the Jews. Even if the Czech Chamber accepted their complaints, the monarch was not likely to listen to them.[41]

In 1551 Ferdinand I issued an edict that all Jews in Austria as well as in the Lands of the Czech Crown should wear a mark distinguishing them from Christians. A yellow circle sewn on to their garments was decreed. The Czech Chamber came to the aid of the Jews, pointing out that if Jews were to wear such a mark they would be in danger of attack by wicked people.[42]

After ten years of relative quiet, the Jews were again threatened with expulsion. This was the work of Archduke Ferdinand, the younger son of Ferdinand I, who held the office of vice-regent of the Lands of the Czech Crown. The Archduke was well-educated and high-minded, and undoubtedly of a humanist turn of mind, but the constant complaints about the Jews 'debasing good currency' by cutting and filing coins, melting down the silver and taking it out of the country, thus damaging the economy, led him to propose to his father in May 1557 that he expel the Jews. The burgomasters and aldermen of the three Prague towns hastened to support the proposal, but appealed to the Archduke, not to Ferdinand himself. They presented a long document showing how their rights had been limited by the privileges issued to the Jews in 1548, and how their interests had been damaged by it. Ferdinand granted his son's demand and at the end of August issued a decree ordering the Jews to leave the kingdom. This decree also rescinded the 'gleit' allowing some of them to remain and others to return. The authorities immediately began to plan how to use the ghetto; the houses were to be bought from their owners and sold to Christian tradesmen, while the smelting workshop and those of such trades as represented a danger of fire were to be moved there from the Castle — especially the smithies, the locksmiths' and wheelwrights' shops. And the ghetto might offer better room for the cannon for which there was no armoury in the Castle precincts.

In spite of all this, the date of the expulsion was again and again postponed, and 'gleit' were again issued allowing certain Jews to stay on. This was usually because influential people spoke for them, such as the Archduke Maximilian, heir to the throne, or his wife Maria, or even the vice-regent Archduke Ferdinand himself, for it was to him that the Prague Jews appealed. And once again, many who had no permission to stay on simply did so. When Ferdinand I died in 1564 the expulsion of the Jews from the Czech kingdom was still an open question, and after his death it quietly subsided without any decision being taken about who should be allowed to stay, or which of the expelled Jews should be allowed to return.[43)]

The uncertainty surrounding their future had a negative effect on building projects in the ghetto from 1541 to 1564. According to the tax records probably drawn up before 1540, that is to say before the first mass expulsion, there were 171 taxpayers in the ghetto. They can be classified in three groups, according to the value placed on their property. The city records of the time show 94 of these taxpayers, 81 of whom owned houses. This is certainly not a complete record, for it was not obligatory to enter sales and other legal property dealings in the city books. Sometimes the entry was simply postponed, sometimes there were legal drawbacks, sometimes the owners tried to avoid registration, which involved paying a certain sum. All records of alterations and additions to buildings in the ghetto date from before 1541, after which date there are practically none. Nevertheless houses were still bought and sold, inherited and — most important — divided up. The purchases of property were primarily by those who had a 'gleit' permitting them to live in Prague, while those who had none and were forced to leave were the sellers. By that time houses were physically divided not only when inherited by more than one heir, but also when bought and sold. It was not at all unusual to divide a house between a considerable number of owners, but in the Jewish ghetto this division was a real one, not simply one of the legal value of the property. Each owner had his own, carefully marked out part of the house, and lived in it.[44)]

The reign of Maximilian II (1564—76) ended the time of uncertainty in the Czech kingdom and brought more favourable conditions for the Jews. Judging from an order sent by Archduke Ferdinand, who remained vice-regent for a time, to the burghers of Kolín, dated July 1566, that Jewish houses bought by Christians should be returned to their original owners, we can assume that similar orders were also issued in Prague.[45)] In 1567 Maximilian II confirmed the privileges granted to Jews settled in Prague and throughout the kingdom, with the exception that apart from those settled Jews allowed to trade, new immigrants, unknown Jews from other lands, would not be allowed to settle without the emperor's express permission. Another limiting regulation concerned those towns where silver was mined. Jews were not allowed to settle there.[46)]

Under Rudolph II (1576—1611) things became even better. The strange personality of this monarch, delighting in curiosities, was undoubtedly attracted by the Jewish religion,

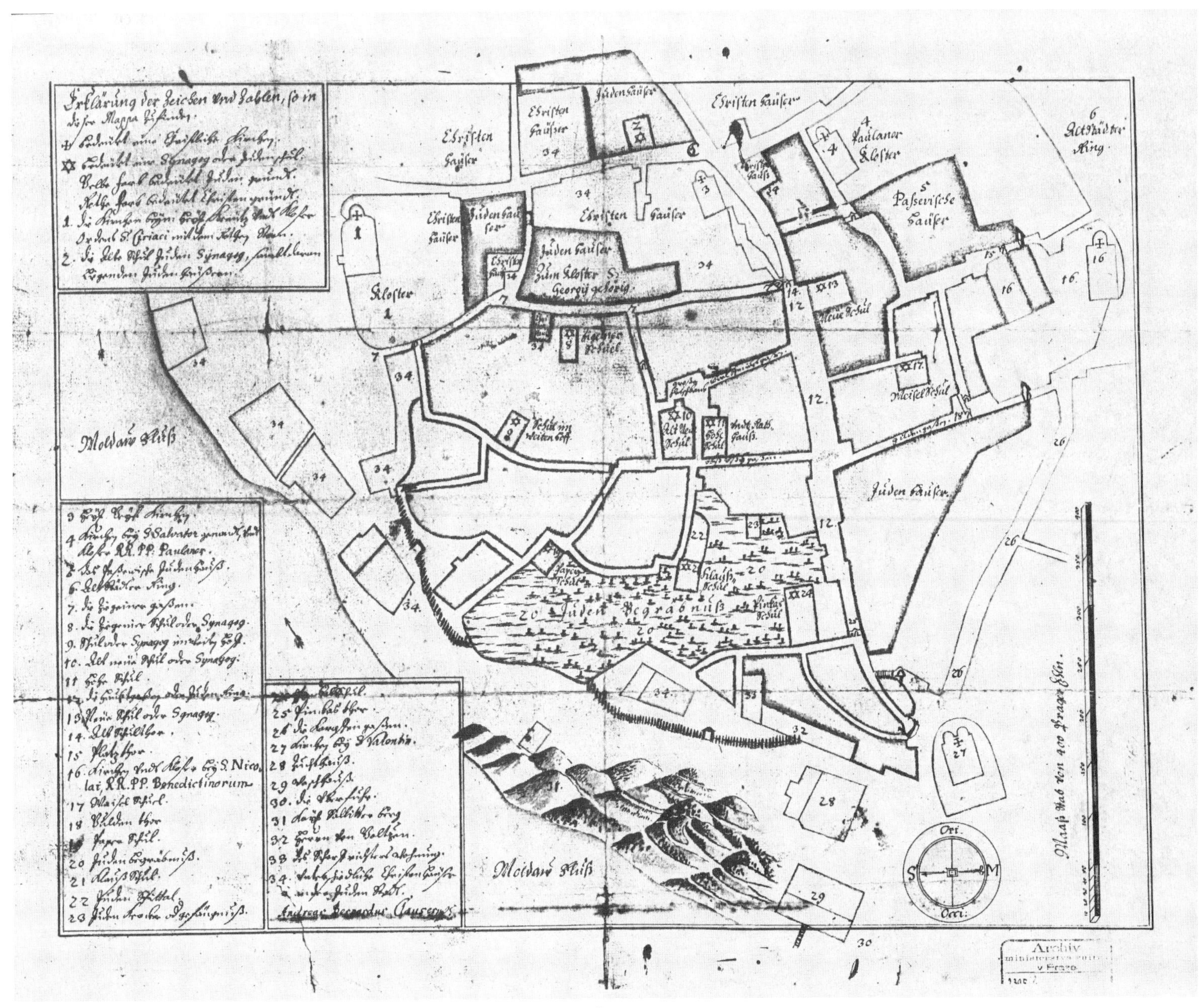

and by Jews as such. And although like his predecessors he made good use of the Jews as 'servants of the Czech Chamber', his orders are couched in calmer and more peaceable terms. In the privileges which were renewed in 1577 the Jews were assured that in the future they would not be expelled either from Prague or from the Czech kingdom. As we have already mentioned, it was in that year that separate city records were instituted for the Prague ghetto — *Libri albi Judaeorum*; they were kept in the Old Town Hall, and all records of property were entered there. Rudolph II also issued many decrees protecting

13/
Andreas Bernard Klauser: Survey of the Jewish Town after the fire of 1689.

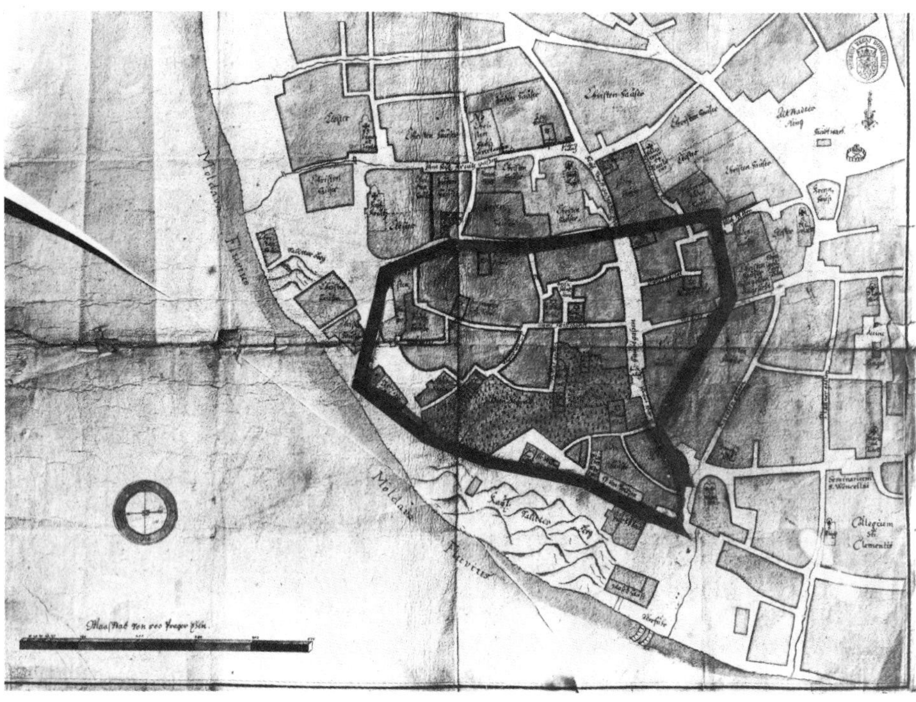

14/
Proposed reduction of the Jewish Town of Prague after the fire of 1689. Unsigned, probably the work of A. B. Klauser.

Jewish traders, especially in the three towns of Prague. On several occasions he allowed independent election of Jewish elders, without official permission from higher authority.[47]

The reign of Rudolph II was a good time for architecture altogether, and favourably influenced the expansion of the Jewish ghetto, which gradually expanded beyond its medieval limits. This is attested, for instance, by the contract signed between clerks of the St Nicholas parish and Jewish owners of houses in the parish which had passed from Christian to Jewish hands. This agreement is dated January 1590, and concerned 11 houses. The Jewish owners had to pay the relevant taxes to the parish. There was a similar agreement signed in 1601 between Jewish owners and clerks of the parish of the Greater Cross.[48] In 1595 there were 150 houses in the ghetto, and yet there must have been incredible overcrowding. We have already mentioned the custom of physically dividing up house property, and these 'parts' of a house were sold for high sums of money. A room with a cubby-hole cost an average of 200 to 300 bags (of three-score) Meissen groschen.[49]

Attempts to expel the Jews from the Old Town of Prague were not entirely dropped even under Rudolph II. In 1601 the burgomaster and aldermen of the Old Town presented the emperor with a long explanation of why the Jews should be expelled. They were accused of not keeping to the terms of the 'artykule' issued by Maximilian II in 1567, allowing those who were still in the country to remain. The Old Town authorities were particularly annoyed because Jews were coming from elsewhere and settling in the ghetto without permission, and also because in spite of the legal prohibition of such deals, Jews were buying Christian houses in the immediate vicinity of the ghetto and thus extending the ghetto not only close to certain churches, particularly the Church of the Holy Spirit, but even almost to the Old Town Square. There were other complaints about Jewish trading, but this long document does not seem to have been welcome at the imperial court.[50] The Jews were still a worthwhile source of revenue, thanks to the Jewish taxes, the war taxes and various loans and other forms of financial 'aid' demanded of them by the Czech Chamber. In spite of opposition from the Old Town authorities, Christian houses were still being purchased. In 1605, for instance, the Jewish hospital was enlarged by the purchase of Matthew Blovský's house for the sum of 350 bags of Czech groschen. In 1610 Jacob Bashevi, later head of the Jewish community and the first Jew to be elevated to the nobility, bought a Christian house in the parish of St Nicholas, for 1,000 bags of Czech groschen.[51]

In 1611 King Matthias (1611—19) confirmed the privileges given to the Jews by his predecessors, although without enlarging or improving on them. This document is dated 15 August, and shows that another request by the Prague authorities to expel the Jews had not been granted. It was presented by the Czech Assembly in April of that year.[52]

From time to time we learn something of the hygienic conditions in the ghetto. At that time things were no better anywhere in Prague, complaints about 'dung and other refuse' being made daily in all four Prague towns. It was not surprising that in 1613 the Jewish elders asked for a commission to be sent to look at the 'filthy dirt thrown into their baths by the bath-house attendant', and asked for an end to be put to this mischief. At the same time the Jewish community asked for permission to dig three wells 'in their Jewish street', to be used in case of fire. One well was to be dug in front of Abraham Frenkl's house 'on the way to the Old Shul'; the second 'in the square in front of Samuel Bassev's house' and the third 'near Simon Brandeis's house, towards the Holy Spirit gate'. It would seem that these three wells later gave its name to Třístudničná (Three Wells) Street.[53)]

Towards the end of the sixteenth and in the early seventeenth century the number of synagogues also increased. In 1592 the new Meisl Synagogue was finished, and in 1599 the Munk Synagogue, later called Wechsler's, was built on the south side of Židovská (later Široká) Street, in the houses at the eastern end. The synagogue called Cikánova (Cikán), after its founder Salomon Cikán, was founded before 1613.[54)]

The defeat of the army of the Czech Estates in 1620, in the Battle of the White Mountain, and the Thirty Years' War that followed brought many changes to the whole of Prague and no less to its Jewish quarter. Both positive and negative, these changes meant that the Jewish quarter suffered even more than the rest of the city, when foreign troops occupied it. The allied and imperial armies passing through were equally given to looting and pillaging, to destroying houses and even asking for levies. The local troops were no less unscrupulous than those of the enemy. The war also brought epidemics with it, and the plague of 1639 undoubtedly decimated the population of the ghetto. When the Swedes besieged Prague in 1648 the people of the ghetto took an active part in its defence, the men digging earthworks and keeping them in repair, and patrolling the streets, while the women, the old men and the children were on alert to put out fires that might be caused by enemy gunfire.[55)]

On the other hand, the situation was now more favourable for the Jewish quarter to expand. Many houses were left deserted in Prague, by those who had taken part in the rising of the Estates (1618—20), and by those who preferred exile to conversion to the Catholic faith, which was the only religion accepted in the Czech kingdom after the defeat of the White Mountain. The houses of the former were confiscated and managed by the Czech Chamber, while the latter were usually sold quickly and cheaply. The Chamber officials soon realized that without repair and maintenance the confiscated buildings deteriorated and lost in value. In the end these houses were sold to anyone, and cheaply, before losing all their value. In this situation, and certainly in no small degree due to the services of Jacob Bashevi, the court Jew raised by Ferdinand II (1620—37) to the ranks of the nobility, permission was given for 39 Christian houses in the vicinity of the ghetto to be purchased by Jews. Permission was given in 1622 and the purchase effected from 1622 to 1623. Since an important role in this transaction was played by the then vice-regent for the Czech kingdom, Prince Karl of Liechtenstein, these houses were later referred to as the Liechtenstein houses. In 1623 Ferdinand II then issued a new highly significant privilege that resulted in a greatly improved status for the Jews: they were now allowed to learn a trade and to carry it on.[56)]

It would be wrong to imagine, however, that Ferdinand II was in any way inclined to favour the Jews. The Hapsburgs were not in the habit of handing out privileges for nothing, and as he was placed at the end of the Thirty Years' War Ferdinand would not even have been able to indulge such a fancy. Behind his decision lay 240,000 Rhine guilders lent to him by the Jews, to continue the war after the Battle of the White Mountain. The Jewish community did not have such a sum at its disposal, and was forced to borrow elsewhere at high interest.[57)] It is thus difficult to imagine any great building activity in the ghetto — apart from the purchase of the houses mentioned above — up to the middle of the seventeenth century. Only the wealthiest of the wealthy could afford to build in those days. In Prague itself Albrecht of Waldstein, and in the ghetto Jacob Bashevi, were the only ones who could rebuild their houses as Renaissance palaces with arcaded courtyards. The latter even put up a new synagogue on the northern edge of the ghetto in 1627, known as the Velkodvorská (Great Court) Synagogue.

After the Peace of Westphalia (1648) the Jewish ghetto was impoverished, the population decimated, and heavily in debt. At that time there were 2,090 inhabitants, 598 of them children.[58] It can be assumed that building in the early Baroque period was not very brisk. We know what the ghetto looked like then, because two plans have survived, one dating from 1628—35 and attributed to Matouš Unger, and one in the archives of the Crusaders with the Red Star dating from close after the middle of the century. In Unger's plan the Jewish Town is shown in yellow, and already includes the Liechtenstein houses on the outer fringe. There were 18 small groups of houses, of irregular shape and size. To the west the ghetto ended in a group of houses outside the original gate leading towards the river. The houses near to Kaprová Street were Christian on the southern and Jewish on the northern side, separated by big yards or gardens. On the east side the Jewish houses were close to the Churches of the Holy Spirit and the Greater Cross, while to the south they came close to the parish Church of St Nicholas, thus bringing the ghetto very close to the Old Town Square. Two green patches more or less in the middle of the ghetto represent the cemetery, surrounded by houses and separated from each other by a grey-green area which may have meant land that was not yet built up. To the south-east the Jewish houses lay up against the Pauline Church of St Salvator. Of the synagogues only the Old Shul behind the Church of the Holy Spirit, and the Meisl Synagogue, are shown; the others are not marked.

The other plan may have been drawn up on the initiative of the Order of the Cross with the Red Star. It shows the drains of the eastern part of the Old Town, which entered the Vltava close to their hospital. It is more accurate than Unger's plan, although the buildings are shown in elevation. The ground plans of those groups of houses which remained unchanged up to the time of clearance in the nineteenth century agree with what is shown on later and more accurate plans. On the plan of the Order of the Cross the Jewish quarter is not distinguished by any special colour, nor is it shown in its entirety, since the map ends on a line with St Nicholas Church to the east. The original area of the cemetery is shown clearly, divided into a western and an eastern part by a line of houses. The southern edge of the cemetery comes up to the Pinkas Synagogue, shown with three windows in the west façade. The little houses on the opposite side of the street are probably the 'klaus' built at the instigation of Mordechai Meisl. Where the Old-New Synagogue stands there are two buildings shown, side by side, with parallel saddle-back roofs; the larger, to the south, is that of the synagogue itself, the smaller, more northern, is the lobby. A long building with a double saddle-back roof can be equated with the Meisl Synagogue. It is not possible to pick out the Cikán or the Great Court Synagogue in the group of buildings between Rabínská and Dušní Streets. As a whole the plan gives a good picture of the Prague ghetto in the early years of Baroque, with small, low, densely placed buildings. This is of course still the Renaissance picture.[59]

In 1624 the Emperor Ferdinand III (1637—46) issued a decree by which the Jews could not be expelled without imperial consent. Conditions throughout the kingdom, however, were far from consistent, for there were estates from which the Jews were expelled, in spite of this decree.

The first years after the Peace of Westphalia (1648) were fairly peaceful for the Jews of the Prague ghetto. The Jewish Town probably progressed like the other parts of the city, but it is likely that it was more a question of repairs, additions and reconstructions, and where really new building was undertaken, this was of minor importance and called for less investment. One thing is certain, that in the ghetto there was no purchasing of more houses at once, to build a palace or extensive ecclesiastical houses, such as was typical for the other Prague towns at this time. The population of the ghetto must have grown fast, since in 1680 the authorities began to consider reducing it. There was the suggestion to transfer the Prague ghetto to Libeň, outside Prague. A small Jewish settlement existed there probably since the second expulsion of the Jews from Prague, in 1557. At the time Libeň belonged to Albrecht Brykner of Brukstein, who was well inclined towards the Jews. He even gave them permission to build a synagogue in 1592. However, the settlement suffered a great deal from frequent floods. Before the 'reduction of the Jewish population' could be decided, an outbreak of plague in 1680 undoubtedly afflicted the overcrowded ghetto far worse than the other Prague towns.[60)] The Jewish elders bought a piece of land at Olšany (now Žižkov) for a plague burial ground, and built an infirmary alongside it.[61)]

The plague was not the last blow to fall on the Jewish Town in the last quarter of the seventeenth century. In June 1689 a fire broke out in the Christian house At the Black Eagle,

15/
The Jews leaving Prague at the end of February and beginning of March, 1745, following the expulsion decreed by the Empress Maria Theresa, 18 December 1744. Anonymous copperplate engraving.

in the Old Town, and spread with such rapidity that almost the entire ghetto — 318 houses at the time — was burned down. Another 382 Christian houses in nearby streets of the Old Town were also destroyed. A hundred and fifty people died in the ghetto. It appears from contemporary documents that the fire was started by men recruited and paid by French spies, which is why it is sometimes called 'the French fire'.

This was not the first fire to rage in the ghetto; there had been serious conflagrations in 1561, 1567 and 1603, but this is the first about which we have detailed information. The burgomaster and aldermen of the Old Town were not slow to suggest that it was high time to do away with the ghetto altogether, and to settle the Jews outside the city walls. The Emperor Leopold I (1657—1705) was in favour of this solution, and a location for the new Jewish town was discussed. One suggestion was the 'Big Island' (now Štvanice), another the river bank opposite Libeň. Both suggestions were turned down, the sites being subject to floods. It was not possible to dig foundations, and the houses would have had to stand on piles. There was still plenty of room in the New Town, but the authorities there were not anxious to see the Jews building there. New houses would cost far more to build than would the repair and renovation of the burnt-out houses in the ghetto, which had solid foundations and cellars, and where the ground floors had not been seriously damaged so long as they were vaulted. Nor were the Jews likely to want to move away from the synagogues they had built with such care. Then, too, it was in a Christian house that the fire had started, so why should the Jews be punished by having to move? That was the view of the Czech Chamber, put before the emperor for his immediate information.

Leopold I allowed himself to be convinced, but made considerable demands on the way the ghetto was to be rebuilt. Stone and bricks were to be used, and not timber as before the fire, although even then this was only partly the case. That was a sensible condition. More serious was the demand that the streets should run in a straight line, and be broad. A wall was to be built along the river bank, and a stone rampart was to divide the ghetto off from Christian houses. Several gates were to be placed in the wall by the river, to allow access to the water in case of fire. The number of houses was to correspond to the number of Jewish families in the ghetto, and was not to be increased in the future. The number of synagogues and cemeteries was to be fixed, as well as the number of slaughterhouses and meat shops. Proper lavatories were to be installed, with drains running into the river. The houses were not to have more than two storeys, and were to be numbered. This meant the Jewish Town had to be surveyed, a task given to the Chief Surveyor, Samuel Globic. He is said to have fallen ill on account of the terrible filth in the burned ghetto, and the work was carried out by a regional surveyor, Andreas Bernard Klauser, in 1690.

Both the plans showing the state of the ghetto at the time, and those for the proposed reconstruction have survived. The ghetto was to be smaller than before; several peripheral areas were to be excluded, as was the group of houses by the Church of the Holy Spirit, and a broad street was to separate the Christian from the Jewish houses. To make up for the loss of this part of the ghetto, where the Old Shul stood, the Jews were to be given ground on the river bank, and they were to purchase Christian houses to make up for the loss of their own. Family houses were to be built in place of the seven (out of thirteen) synagogues which were to be abolished. The plan came up against great difficulties at once. If the streets were to be made regular, the reliable old foundations could not be used, and building would be much more expensive. The Christians were said to be asking exorbitant sums for the conveniently placed houses the Jews were to buy. And naturally the Jews fought to retain the Old Shul, which was built of stone, with a tiled roof, and had escaped major damage by the fire. Only one corner of the women's gallery had suffered, and part of the roof over it that had already been repaired. Nevertheless the Old Shul was closed down and officially sealed, and was not to be reopened.

The situation was very complicated, with the Czech Chamber insisting on the cheapest

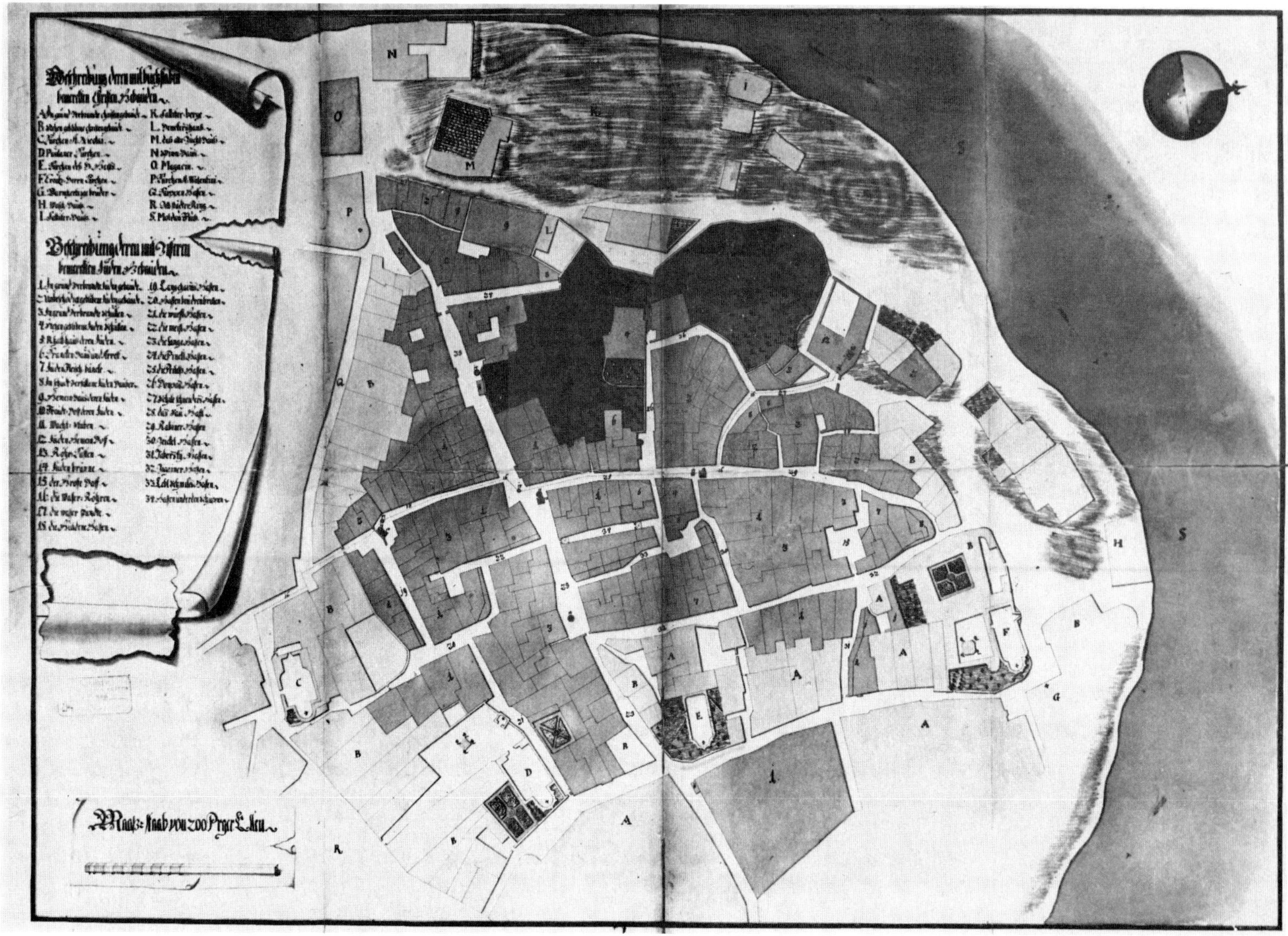

reconstruction, which meant using the old foundations and ground plans. The Emperor Leopold I was reluctant to agree, and it was the Archbishop of Prague who intervened. He considered the situation dangerous from the point of view of the Church. For as the upper storeys of the burned houses were uninhabitable, Jews were living in Christian houses. There was not much room to be found in the Old Town, itself severely damaged by the 'French fire'. 1,115 people from the ghetto were living in the New Town, in burghers' houses and even in palaces, like the Piccolomini and Kolowrat palaces. Naturally the Jews arranged prayer-rooms in some of the houses, and Jan Bedřich of Waldstein, the Archbishop, pressed the emperor to put an end to this dangerous cohabitation of Jews with Christians as soon as possible. In the end practically nothing remained of the ambitious programme of rebuilding the ghetto. By 1690 it was practically decided that the old ground plans would be preserved, and in a short time the Jews of Prague had put up faithful copies of their former homes. The question of gates took longer to decide, and was still being dis-

16/
J. F. Schor: Survey of the Jewish Town of Prague after the fire of 1754.

cussed in 1702. The final decision was for six gates, with slight changes in their location. It is also clear from the sources that the Jewish houses were already numbered.

It was many years, however, before agreement was reached about the Old Shul. At first Leopold, supported by the Archbishop, was adamant, but the Jews would not relinquish their oldest synagogue, and finally in 1703 they offered to pay 20,000 Rhine guilders to have the building preserved and reopened. The money was quite welcome, among other things it enabled the emperor to pay what his daughter, Archduchess Josepha, owed to the merchant Planckner. And so, after the Jews agreed to the Archbishop's demand that they brick up two windows which gave on to the Church of the Holy Spirit, move the entrance to the other side of the synagogue, and raise the surrounding wall, the order to abolish the synagogue was rescinded.[62)]

Another survey of the ghetto was made in 1714, by the Castle master mason Jacob Anthony Canevalle and Paul Ignaz Bayer, but the plans have been lost.[63)] This was again a time when the reduction of the numbers of Jews in Prague was called for; there were now many more than in 1680. In 1703 the ghetto had a population of 11,517, while all four quarters of the Old Town were inhabited only by 11,618. King Charles VI (1711—40) again ordered a commission to be set up to study the question and submit proposals on how to reduce the Jewish population. This was to run concurrently with the campaign to determine how many houses there were in the towns of Prague, how large they were, in what condition, and also the number of inhabitants and their trades.

In actual fact the survey of the Jewish Town did not take place until three years later, and the forms used were somewhat different. There was no space for a description of the houses, doubtless because the whole ghetto was to be measured again. The plan was to be drawn in detail, including the arrangement of each floor of each house, as well as the ground plan. Both the houses and the apartments in them were to be numbered, as were the synagogues, schools, cemeteries and other buildings. The survey was indeed begun, under the regional surveyor František Antonín Leopold Klose, and groups of houses were entrusted to Prague builders, among them Kilian Ignaz Dientzenhofer and Thomas Haffenecker. Five plans have survived; they were published twice, but the originals have been lost. The draft list has also been preserved, and gives us a good idea both of the size of the population of the ghetto, and their trades and social stratification; in 1729, 10,507 people were living in the ghetto, in 333 out of 367 houses, 34 being uninhabited. Families were to be classified according to whether they had been settled in Prague before 1618 or had arrived later, and in particular it was to be noted which persons had moved into the ghetto after the reduction of the population ordered in 1661, of which we have no detailed information. According to the report on the survey of 1727, Klose was to receive 450 Rhine guilders for running this scheme.[64)]

Although some of the measures proposed — and indeed put into effect — were drastic enough, like the limitation of marriage to the eldest of the sons, there were many lesser ignominies to endure in the ghetto. As we shall see, the reign of Charles VI was one of relative peace for the Jews. Maria Theresa (1740—80) soon showed herself much more radical in her views. It is difficult to distinguish all the reasons behind the expulsion of the Jews from Prague and from the kingdom of Bohemia, in 1744, by a decree of 18 December. Her aversion to the Jews may have had a religious background, and been encouraged by the Jesuits whose position at court, especially as confessors, was very strong. Maria Theresa, in any case, was convinced that the expulsion of the Jews was good in the eyes of the Lord. There may also have been financial considerations. For several decades the economic situation of the ghetto had been weak, and the Prague Jews owed vast sums to the treasury in unpaid taxes. For years various committees had tried to find ways and means of getting these arrears paid. The financial profit to be made from the Jews was decidedly less than had been expected, and in addition there were sums owing to private creditors. It is probable that loans taken to rebuild the ghetto after the fire of

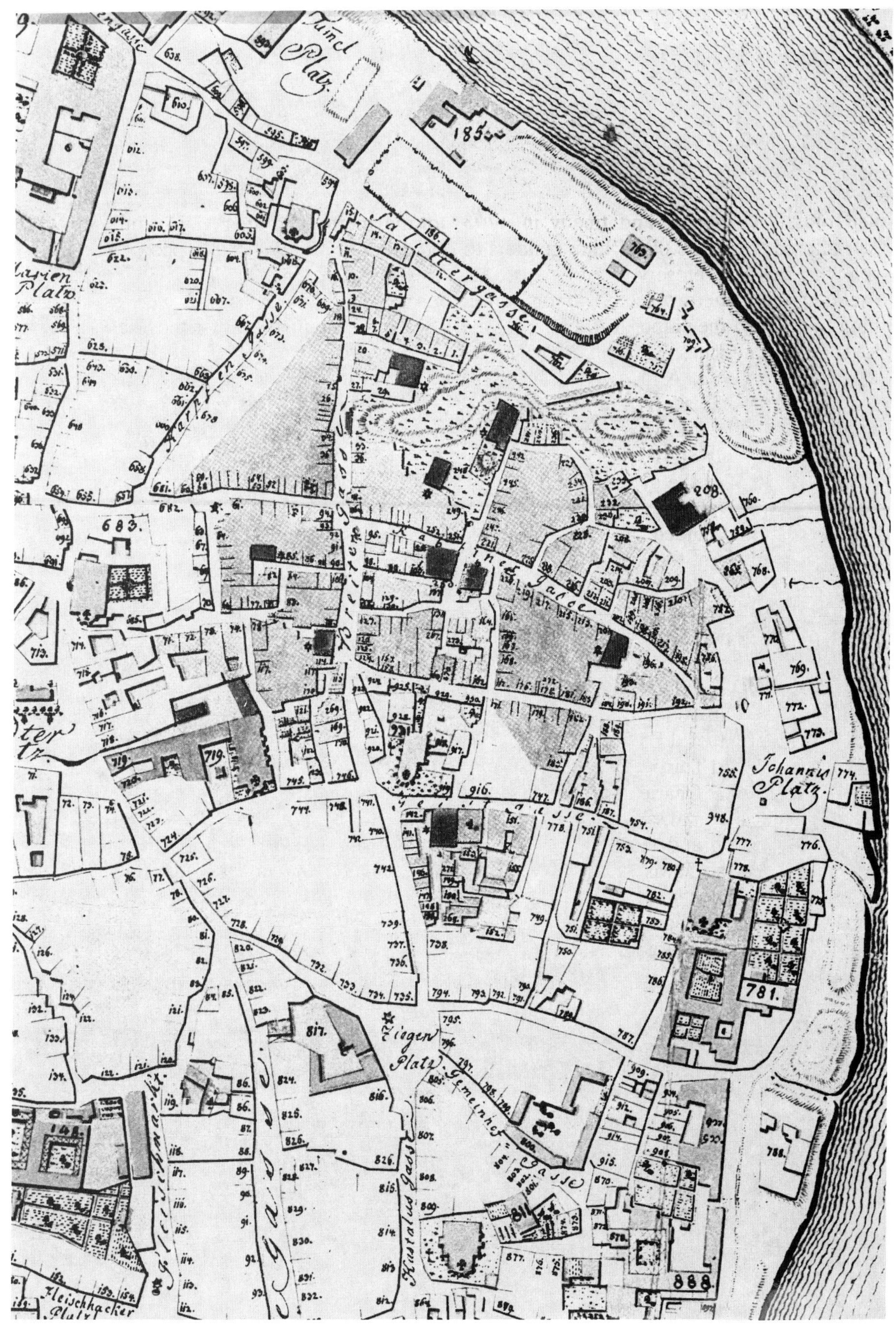

17/
F. A. L. Herget: The Jewish Town on a map of Prague dated 1790.

Johannes Platz
Salpeter Anlage
Platz
JUDEN
V
Breite Gasse
Stockhaus Gasse
Schwarze Gasse
Niklas Platz
Großer Ring

1689 were largely to blame. It is also possible that some Jews collaborated with the invaders during the Bavarian-French occupation of Prague in 1741, or at least were accused of doing so. That was something Maria Theresa was rather sensitive about. While the Prague Jewish community presented Maria Theresa with a 'donum gratuitum' of 90,000 Rhine guilders at the time of her Prague coronation, this had little effect. The Jews were ordered to leave Prague by 31 January 1745, and to leave the kingdom of Bohemia by June 30th of the same year. The order was clear, but to carry it out was more difficult. There were financial obligations on both sides that had to be dealt with, and so the original six months' term became six years, and in the end those Jews who had left came back to Prague.

The Czech Chamber took a firm stand against their expulsion, and many written reports sent to Vienna point out the financial losses brought about by this measure, losses not only to Prague, but to the whole kingdom. The auditors of the Czech Chamber worked out the figures in detail, and they added up to a considerable sum: for Prague 2,519,646 Rhine guilders annually, and another 1,880,633 for the countryside. This sum did not include unpaid taxes, nor the losses to trade as a result of the expulsion of Jewish customers. The value of Jewish property in Prague was assessed at 170,000 Rhine guilders (houses and synagogues), while it was stressed that in spite of the prohibition of 1690 many houses had again been built of timber, and that after two years of exile, they were derelict in 1747. Of course the furnishings had long been stolen from all these houses. Often there was only one entrance to four or more, even seven houses. Sometimes there was only one kitchen and one lavatory for two or three houses. The value of such buildings was of course much lower than the original assessment, and the Czech Chamber put the sum as low as 60,000 Rhine guilders. The Chamber also reminded the monarch that the Jews had lived in the kingdom for many centuries, with the permission of the monarch, and had been granted many privileges. And since the Czech Chamber could be very active and inventive, when it wanted to attain some end, a device surprising for the time was invoked — a public opinion poll. Questionnaires were sent out to the heads of the Prague trade guilds and merchant societies, asking what they had got against the Jews, whether the presence of the Jews in Prague threatened their business or not, and whether they wanted the Jews to remain in exile. The results showed that only a few trades, and not the most important, thought it was to their benefit that the Jews had gone. The embroiderers, haberdashers, glovers, wig-makers, hatters, brush makers, tinsmiths and locksmiths represented trades where the Jews offered competition either with their own production or by importing goods. On the other hand, the big trades like the bakers, butchers and building trades (bricklayers, carpenters, cabinet makers, locksmiths, house painters, potters, stove makers and others) were convinced that the expulsion of the Jews had meant a loss of trade. They were in favour of letting the Jews return. Finally Maria Theresa allowed herself to be convinced. She rescinded the expulsion order and the Jews were allowed to return to Prague after not quite four years of exile.[65)]

We do not really know where these Jewish families spent those four years. Some may have stayed in Libeň, but there was not much living space there; at the turn of the second and third quarter of the eighteenth century the settlement consisted of 38 Jewish houses which sheltered 135 families.[66)] At the time 1,500 families were forced to leave the Prague ghetto, and most of them must have travelled further on, for one of the conditions attached to the expulsion of the Jews was that they must not settle less than two hours' distance from Prague.

The first 58 families returned to the Prague ghetto towards the end of August 1748. In October of the next year another 918 families came back. They came back to homes that were derelict and looted, without any basic conveniences and often on the point of collapse. Hardly had they carried out the most needful repairs, when the ghetto again went up in flames, in 1754.[67)]

Tradition has it that this fire, too, was deliberately started, but it was never discovered

18/
J. Jüttner: The Jewish Town on a map of Prague, 1811—15.

by whom. The fire was said to have started in one of the Christian houses facing the Old Shul, but at the same time fire broke out in Cikánská Street and near to the Great Court Synagogue. 190 buildings were burned down in the ghetto, about two thirds of all those standing. The only parts of the ghetto which were not touched were those round the Old Cemetery and by the river. Again we must remember that those buildings where stone and brick had been used were less damaged than those of timber. Their beams and ceilings might burn, but the stone vaulting survived. The ceiling of the Cikán Synagogue was preserved, for example, although it stood almost at the centre of the conflagration. The stucco ornament of the ceiling survived. In the High Synagogue, too, the wooden roof burned but the solid vaulting resisted the flames. Greater damage was caused in the neighbouring Jewish Town Hall, however, where the upper storey was certainly not vaulted. Although it was forbidden to build timber houses after 1689, nevertheless there were many, and they could not be saved. The Jewish hospital and the orphanage were thus burned down.

The architect Johann Ferdinand Schor was charged with elaborating a plan for the reconstruction of the ghetto. He was told to take care that the streets would be wide enough. In the narrower streets the houses could only have three storeys, while four were allowed where the street was broader. The uppermost storey was to be built of stone, not of wood, and the roofing was to be of tiles and not of shingles. This order was not consistently adhered to, either in the ghetto, or elsewhere in Prague. As late as the 1840s there were many Prague buildings with shingle roofs.[68)]

A plan dating from 1758 shows the state of the ghetto after the fire of 1754. It is clear that once again the fire did not remain within the confines of the ghetto. Many Christian houses burned down, especially to the south and north of the Old Shul, and to the north of the Church of the Holy Spirit.[69)]

The Jewish community of Prague, ruined by expulsion from the city from 1745 to 1748, and by the cost of repairs to the buildings that were then dilapidated, was unable to meet the cost of rebuilding the ghetto. Loans had to be arranged, from the government and from private creditors. The Bank of Vienna made a loan of 200,000 Rhine guilders, while 185,000 guilders were lent by private creditors. Czech aristocrats, ecclesiastical institutions and burghers also gave funds. There are lists of the damages to buildings and to the furnishings, amounting altogether to 800,444 Rhine guilders. The money provided by the loans was distributed to 159 victims, from 40 to 3,000 guilders according to their damages. These were probably those left homeless, needing rapid repair to their homes, or those left with loss of furniture.[70)]

As the Prague ghetto was rebuilt after the fire of 1754, architecture had entered the phase of late Baroque and early Neo-Classicism. Only one building has remained to illustrate this phase — the Jewish Town Hall, rebuilt by Joseph Schlesinger in the late Baroque style. Building was completed in 1763, and a commemorative document was placed in the clock tower, referring to the loan of 200,000 guilders which made it possible to repair, rebuild or build anew from the foundations of both public and private buildings. Of the public buildings we must name not only the Town Hall, but also the principal treasury, the prison, the hospital (which was moved for a time to the plague infirmary by the Olšany Plague cemetery), the rabbi's home, a new well and a broad new gate. In the 1770s the Jewish community bought a house which had once belonged to Karl Goltz, knight, and had it made into an apartment house according to plans drawn up by Ignaz Palliardi. At the end of the eighteenth and in the early nineteenth century many well-known Prague architects worked in the ghetto, among them Alois Palliardi, Karl Schmidt, Jan Prachner, František Heger and Jindřich Hausknecht.[71)]

What the Jewish Town looked like as built between 1754 and 1756, can be seen from the cardboard model of Prague put together by Antonín Langweil, a miniature painter and graphic artist, who created this model in 1826 to 37. It would seem that the Jewish Town was not yet the poverty-stricken slum that it became in the second half of the century.

19/
The banner of the Jewish Town of Prague, donated by Mordechai Meisl.

20/
The houses on both sides of the former Rabínská Street, looking north. Langweil's model of Prague.

As the rebuilding of the ghetto was gradually being completed, the first waves of enlightenment, as seen by the Emperor Joseph II, came to touch it. In 1792 and 1797 decrees were issued which put the Jewish population — previously considered inferior — on an equal footing with other citizens. In the ghetto itself, views were divided. There were those who accepted the new spirit and would have the Jews adapt themselves to their Christian environment. And there were the conservatives, led by the rabbis, who clung to the old traditions.

In the ghetto, as elsewhere in Prague, rebuilding in the Neo-Classical manner meant poorer quality, especially when it involved new wings built at the expense of courtyards which often were reduced to dark ventilation shafts. Although the ghetto itself was no longer a sternly separated enclave, since the last gate was done away with in 1822, conditions for living went from bad to worse. Except for a few wealthy homes like that of the Wedeles, or the nearby Mosheles house with its terraces, the grand Renaissance house built by Bashevi, or the house of Samuel Hönig of Hönigsberg, all the buildings were overcrowded, with insufficient sanitation. Early in the nineteenth century the houses and apartments were counted several times, giving an idea of what it was like to live in the ghetto. In 1801 there were 274 houses, divided into 1,191 actual living quarters. 1,790 rooms in these houses could be heated, while 1,204 were without any source of warmth, as were the 276 cubbyholes, 201 cellars, 1,198 kitchens and 356 attics with windows for the feast of *Succoth.* In 1806 there were 278 houses, arranged more or less on the same principle; 1,629 families lived there, numbering 6,298 individuals. We have a fairly clear idea of the state of these houses from a list drawn up in 1826, showing the apartments and the changes made up to 1835. At that time there were 276 houses, two fewer than in 1806. At least 80 buildings were in such a state that the Prague authorities constantly urged the owners to carry out urgent repairs and have their plans passed by official circles. Undoubtedly many houses were indeed rebuilt during this time, for the authorities were indomitable and their fines were cruel. Yet the limited area of the ghetto allowed little chance of improving the situation. The Neo-Classical style of architecture was more utilitarian than earlier styles, with the result that the first half of the nineteenth century shows us the worst possible solutions — unless we are dealing with an ambitious building where there was no need to save money. The homes now built were remarkable for the way they divided rooms again and again until the space was exhausted, only to gain more apartments. This was the case throughout Prague, and so we can assume that in the ghetto things were even more so. Building higher houses, another characteristic feature of the time, meant that the streets of the ghetto were narrower than ever, and that the sun rarely penetrated there.[72)]

It was no wonder, then, that the wealthier Jews sought to escape from the overcrowded ghetto with its constant threat of infectious diseases. Up to 1806, 89 houses were acquired outside the ghetto, housing 181 families, or 760 individuals. For the most part these houses were in Kaprová and Dušní Streets, near Stockhaus (today Vězeňská) and on St John's Square. This region did not belong to the ghetto proper, and was referred to as 'beyond the rope', because it was marked off from the rest of the Old Town by a wire fence which showed how far the Jews were allowed to walk on the Sabbath. By 1811, 28 more houses had been acquired in the vicinity of the Church of the Holy Spirit, but later the regional authorities forbade the purchase of houses outside the limits of the ghetto. Nevertheless, in 1812 an area 'beyond the new rope' was acknowledged and by 1836 another 53 houses had been added. At this time a further 42 houses had been built in the Jewish town itself; 22 houses had been rebuilt and four demolished. Not that there were no problems and difficulties as the Jewish Town expanded. From time to time it was forbidden to purchase Christian houses and in 1846 the Prague authorities tried to have Jews moved back into the ghetto, where they already lived outside it. Such views were opposed with the argument that elsewhere in Europe the Jews could live where they wished, and that ghettos no longer existed except in Prague and the Orient. It was not until after the revolutionary year 1848 that this question was finally settled. In 1849 the Jewish Town of Prague was made one of the city's quarters, called Josefov. In 1861 it was finally freed of its inferior status and the Jews became not only formally but in fact equal with other citizens and free to settle where they wished.[73)]

That the Jews could settle wherever they wished meant that the ghetto became a slum, and not only a Jewish but a Christian slum as well. Not only within, but beyond it too, the fifth quarter of Prague began to change. The banks of the Vltava were still threatened by constant inundation, built on in an unplanned and mostly impoverished manner; the exception was the short strip from Charles Bridge to the north. From the middle of the nineteenth century the picture began to change. The first urbanistic project (1841—45) produced the Smetana Embankment, with its statue of Franz I, and regulations about the permitted height of the buildings. Twenty years later the Lažanský Palace was erected on the corner of the embankment and what is now Národní (National) Street. A few years later, in 1868

21/
The houses on both sides of the former Rabínská Street, looking south. Langweil's model of Prague.

to 1871, the Prozatímní (Temporary) Theatre was built on the opposite corner, followed by the National Theatre on the same site, completed in 1881. Almost at the same time the northern end of the river bank began to develop. The Rejdiště (Roadsteads) facing the houses between Platnéřská and Kaprová Streets and the vast area of saltpetre and timber warehouses that Langweil's model shows as almost constructivist architectural forms, were replaced. In 1876—84 the Rudolfinum was built, originally as an art gallery for the Society of Patriotic Friends of the Arts (now the House of Artists). When this was finished, the Neo-Renaissance School of Applied Arts went up across the square. The slum clearance law was already on the horizon. Since 1856 legal, technical and financial aspects of the plan had been under discussion, and in 1889 the areas to be cleared were specified. There were two main sections of the town: the whole of the fifth quarter (Josefov), with those parts of the Old Town that were integrally a part of it, and part of the New Town. Between 1882 and 1886 the Town Council had been inviting projects for the rebuilding of these areas.

When the law came into effect, the area to be cleared was divided into 38 sections. Clearance and rebuilding began at once in the north-east part of the ghetto, between Josefovská, Dušní and what is now Pařížská Streets, and the Old Town Square. In spite of the practical difficulties, and against the protests of all those who wanted to preserve buildings of historical and architectural value, from 1897 to 1917 the slum clearance scheme went forward and nothing was allowed to stand in its way. The Prague ghetto and the neighbouring parts of the Old Town were demolished, and in their place a new residential quarter was built. Of the important historical buildings outside the ghetto that fell victim to the plan we should remember particularly the Benedictine Monastery of St Nicholas, designed partly by F. M. Kaňka, partly by K. I. Dientzenhofer. Only the church was preserved, and a not very successful copy of the prelate's building was then put up alongside it. The houses along the northern side of the Old Town Square were demolished, as well as the outstanding monument of Kren's house which closed off the square to the north-east.[74)]

During its long life the Prague ghetto proved extraordinarily resistant, intractable, and capable of surviving all threats to its existence. There were natural catastrophes, like the fires which raged with far worse effect than in Christian parts of the town, where building was of better quality and there was less overcrowding. From time to time there were great floods, a menace to the Jewish quarter as to the other Prague settlements on the river banks. Until the eighteenth century the ghetto suffered epidemics of the plague, particularly drastic where the people were crammed together in unhygienic conditions. And over all, as we have shown, there were the repeated attempts to reduce the population of the ghetto, or to get rid of the Jews entirely by expulsion. All these troubles were overcome again and again, at great financial sacrifice. What proved an insurmountable obstacle to survival, however, was the situation in the late nineteenth century, created by the so-called 'emancipation' of the Jews. They could now settle outside the ghetto, an advantage only for the wealthy. The historical entity of the Jewish population was thus broken up, while at the same time the houses they lived in (in the ghetto) became more and more dilapidated, as no-one bothered about the future of the property. This gradually created the conditions leading to the slum clearance, wiping the Prague ghetto off the map of the city at the turn of the century.

Yet even after these drastic changes, the synagogues which survived — the Old-New, High, Klaus, Meisl, Pinkas, the Temple (also called the Spanish Synagogue) — and the Jewish Town Hall remained the spiritual home of Jews not only in Prague but throughout Bohemia and Moravia. The Nazis broke this tradition for a time, as the Jews were deported to Terezín and other concentration camps. The administrative and religious function of the Jewish Town fell into abeyance. Nevertheless — and today it seems a miracle — unlike the historical Jewish centres in Germany, like Worms or Frankfurt, in Prague not one of these architectural monuments was destroyed. The synagogues were preserved,

and the Old Jewish Cemetery, too, escaped devastation. All that was of value in the synagogues or homes in the Protectorate was carefully collected and listed. This applied to books, too, and from the libraries collected in Terezín from the whole of Bohemia and Moravia it was possible to regenerate the tradition of Jewish learning. The historic buildings of what had been the Prague ghetto could again fulfil their function as religious and administrative centres. The Old-New Synagogue is once more the Jewish religious centre, while the Jewish Town Hall serves the Jewish community in civic life. The other buildings are used as museums, displaying the rich heritage of synagogal and domestic vessels, the imposing Hebrew library. The Prague ghetto lives on where it used to be, still alive although only in a few historical buildings.

22/
J. Minařík: Demolition of the houses in Rabínská Street during the 'slum clearance' of the Jewish Town. Oil on canvas.

/II/ LIFE IN THE PRAGUE GHETTO

It is impossible today to evoke the life of a society long dead, which lived on generation after generation in the same small area. Rarely does a tombstone in the Old Jewish Cemetery recall in flowery phrases one of those tens or even hundreds of thousands of lives. Here and there an outstanding Jew may be mentioned in contemporary sources, while the most distinguished were honoured with an inscription in the Memorial Books of their synagogue. All we know about life in the Jewish Town of Prague is what can be gained from looking in at it from outside, and that cannot suffice to show the breadth and depth of that life, in its daily details and in its moments of exaltation. Nevertheless we must try to build some kind of a picture from the very varied and often fragmentary information at our disposal. It might be thought that the Jews, living enclosed in the ghetto and separated from their Christian neighbours by walls and gates, could carry on their own way of life without hindrance. Yet that was not so. Friction between the Jews and those around them was not restricted to social life, but was created in the sphere of religion as well, and indeed far more often.

We must say at once that the ghetto lived a double life, an inner and an external one, which were markedly different, and yet interwoven. The inner life of the ghetto, like that of Jewish communities today, was regulated by the Jewish religious calendar, and from cradle to grave hedged around by innumerable rules, commands and prohibitions, drawn partly from the Old Testament, especially the Pentateuch — the Torah, and partly from oral tradition as codified in the Mishna, made more precise by the Talmud and supplemented by interpretations of individual cases discussed in the commentaries, additions to the commentaries and by rabbinical decisions from the time of the Exile until after the destruction of the Temple in Jerusalem in A.D. 70.

These interpretations and decisions were continually repeated, expanded, and made more precise. The rabbinical authorities either accepted each other, or took different stands and argued with each other; the ensuing polemics were the basis for more and newer decisions. These rules, commands and prohibitions touched on every aspect of Jewish life, as can be seen from the very titles of the six 'orders' *(sedarim)* of the Mishna. The first, *Zeraim* (Seeds), deals with interpersonal relations, agricultural tasks, and the things of everyday life, religion expressed through prayer. The second, *Moed* (Festivals), gives the rules for the Sabbath, for festivals, and the Jewish calendar. The third, *Nashim* (Women), covers marriage and the regulations for betrothal, divorce and connubial life. The fourth order, *Nezikin* (Damages), deals with civil and criminal law in Jewish society. The fifth, *Kodashim* (Sacred things), covers religious services, temple offerings, ritual animal sacrifice, in which the rules for kosher slaughter are rooted, while the sixth order, *Tohorot* (Purification), deals with ritual purity and uncleanliness. The Mishna became the core of the Talmud, supplemented by the *Gemara,* further interpretations and discussion of the matters dealt with by the individual orders, arranged in tracts and chapters. Two versions of the Talmud came into existence, one in Palestine, where Jewish culture survived even after the destruction of the Temple, and one in Babylonia, where some rabbinical authorities had settled when they left Palestine. While the Mishna is written in Hebrew, both versions of the Talmud are written in western and eastern Aramaic (the Palestinian and Babylonian versions respectively). From the second century A.D. Aramaic began to supersede Hebrew as the language of Jewish literature. In both versions of the Talmud, the Halakah — systematically arranged regulations — are interspersed with historical tales and anecdotes, the Haggadah.

The prime religious duty enshrined in the Talmud is that of prayer — morning, afternoon and evening prayers are obligatory for men. The members of the community meet for communal prayer in the synagogue, especially on Monday and Thursday, and of course on Saturday both in the morning and the afternoon. The principal part of the Sabbath services is the reading of the Torah, divided into 54 sections *(sedarim)* so that the whole Torah is read in the course of a year.

Another obligation is that of preserving ritual purity both in food and in sexual matters. Only the flesh of those mammals that chew the cud and are hoofed may be eaten, and only those fish that have both scales and fins. A list of birds that may be eaten was drawn up. Then the creatures must be killed ritually, their throats cut with a sharp knife so that their blood is all drained off, a form of slaughter that was already common in ancient Egypt. Naturally all venison is forbidden, for shooting does not comply with the regulations for ritual slaughter, and the flesh is not kosher. The Jews had and still have their special butchers *(shochet)* trained in the traditional manner of slaughter. Even when ritually killed, however, the flesh need not be kosher; the presence of any anomaly in the animal's organs makes the flesh unclean. This explains why Christians would cheaply buy meat from Jewish butchers, a habit which caused many riots in Prague. The Church authorities did not like to see Christians buying meat from the Jews on a Sunday. Another prohibition forbids the eating of meat and milk foods at the same time. A conservative Jewish home had two separate sets of vessels for these two types of food, and separate cloths to wipe them.

In sexual life, ritual purity forbade intercourse during a woman's menstruation. At the end of her period a woman had to go to the ritual baths, the *mikvah,* for purification.

The Jewish religion has never preached celibacy, as Christianity did from the outset. Life as the Talmud sees it is based on marriage, and to marry and found a family is a sacred duty. The wedding ceremony took place beneath a *chuppah,* a canopy that symbolized that the bride (*kala*) was freely entering upon marriage. The symbol of the marriage is the ring which the bridegroom *(chatan)* places on the bride's first finger, in the presence of two witnesses, while repeating a *kiddush* (blessing). Reading the *ketuba,* or marriage contract, was also part of the ceremony. It set out the rights and duties of both parties, and the husband bound himself to provide his wife with a certain standard of life in case of divorce or widowhood. After the contract had been read seven marriage blessings were read over a glass of wine, and at the end of the ceremony the bridegroom broke the glass, in memory of the destruction of the Temple in Jerusalem.

The arrival of children meant that the marriage was fulfilled. A woman who bore no children for several years could be divorced, so important was the question of progeny. Eight days after birth a boy is ritually circumcised, by which act he becomes a member of the Jewish community. Tradition has it that only a boy born of a Jewish mother is a Jew, whether circumcised or not. The children of a Jew and a non-Jewish mother are not Jews. At thirteen a boy reaches religious maturity with the celebration of his *bar mitzvah.* Now he has to fulfil his obligations, praying with the *tefillin* (phylacteries), and called to read the Torah in the synagogue. This was not as difficult as it might seem, since boys began to learn their letters as soon as they began to speak. Girls reached religious maturity at twelve, but fewer concrete religious duties were laid on them since their purpose in life — to bring forth children — is in itself a holy one.

The regulations concerning the Sabbath and festivals were binding for men and women, and were strictly adhered to. Saturday, the seventh day, was a day of rest, on which it was forbidden to work, to engage in trade, or even to travel or take arms — except in cases of mortal danger. The Sabbath was devoted to religious duties and charitable works. The community met in the synagogue for prayer, and individuals visited the sick to show their charity. The arrival of the Sabbath — thought of as a bride — was celebrated by lighting at least two candles and pronouncing a blessing over a glass of wine. There was more to eat on the Sabbath, but it had to be prepared the day before. The holy day ended with another blessing over a glass of wine and the candles, or wax braids neatly plaited.

The Jewish year begins in the autumn, on

23/
J. G. Hartmann — J. Hiller: Procession of Prague Jews to celebrate the birth of an heir to the throne, Prince Leopold, in 1716. Copperplate engraving. (The Jews chose this way of celebrating the happy event in the royal family, along with triumphal arches, illuminations and fireworks displays.)

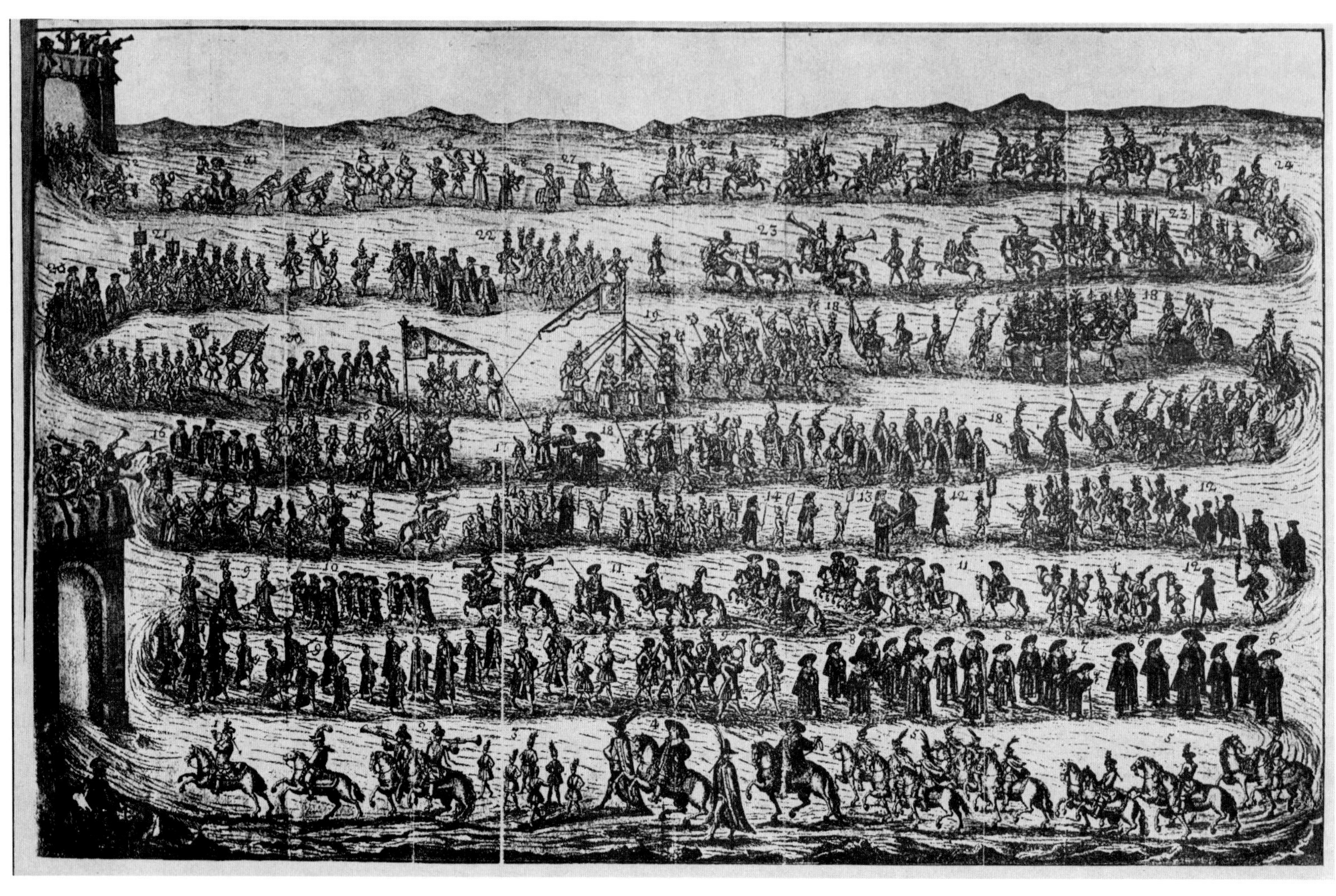

24/
Procession of Prague Jews to celebrate the birth of an heir to the throne, Prince Joseph, in 1741. Copperplate engraving.

the first day of the month of *Tishri,* which may fall in either September or October of the Christian calendar, since the Jewish year is a lunar one, and therefore moveable. The New Year is not only a commemoration of the creation of the world, but the beginning of a ten-day fast and period of repentance, of settling accounts with the Lord. This is encouraged during synagogue services by blowing the *shofar,* the ram's horn that is blown in three different ways: *tekio* (single notes), *shebarim* (broken notes) and *teruo* (powerful, long and loud). On the tenth day of Tishri this period comes to an end with the Day of Atonement, *Yom Kippur.* This is a day of strict fasting; everyone must be reconciled on this day, and forgiveness asked for all offence caused. The orthodox Jews spend the whole day in the synagogue at prayer. The final service, with the prayer 'May we enter into Thy gates', ends with 'The Lord, He is God', repeated seven times.

Almost immediately after the Day of Atonement comes the fifteenth of Tishri, again either in September or October, when the festival of *Succoth* is celebrated. In Bohemia this Festival of Booths was also known as 'Under the green'. Originally an agricultural festival, Succoth celebrated the end of the harvest and especially the end of grape-gathering. It lasts for seven days, and is symbolized by a bunch of palm, myrtle and willow twigs, the *lulav,* and an *etrog,* a fragrant lemon. The palms and lemons for the ceremony were brought to Bohemia from Calabria. The lulav was waved in processions moving into the synagogue for thanksgiving services. Throughout the festival meals were eaten in special booths set up in the open air, but in the Prague ghetto these booths were usually permanent wooden structures incorporated in the roof. The ninth day after *Succoth* begins is the *Simchat Torah,* dedicated to the Torah, and called 'the joy of the Torah'. On this day the year-long reading of the Torah comes to an end, and a new beginning is made, starting with the first page. All boys who are not yet thirteen years old may be called to read on that day. Succoth is both the first major festival in the Jewish New Year and the last in the agricultural year, which naturally begins in spring.

Later in the autumn there is another eight-day festival, at the end of the month of *Kislev,* the third month from the beginning of the Jewish year. It falls in November or December of the Christian calendar. This is the festival of *Hanukkah,* the Feast of Lights. It is not derived from the Bible, but was instituted in memory of the victory of the Jews over the Syrians in 165 B.C., when Judas Maccabaeus led his countrymen to free the Temple of Jerusalem. The lights commemorate the reconsecration of the Temple: on the first day one candle is lit, in a special candelabra kept for the occasion, a second is lit the next day, and so on until the full count of eight is reached on the last day.

There is a long pause after these festivals, broken only by *Purim,* a joyful festival celebrated on the fourteenth day of the month of *Adar,* which in the Christian calendar falls in late February or in March. This is indeed a merry occasion, reminding the Jews of the story of Esther. Historical Czech sources call it the 'Jewish carnival'. Chapters of the *Book of Esther,* inscribed on special scrolls, and often illuminated, the meggilat Esther, are read in the home, telling how Esther, the niece of Mordechai, married to King Ahasuerus, saved the people of Israel in Babylonian exile from the dreadful fate prepared for them by Haman, the king's favourite.

The first festival of the ancient agricultural year is that of *Pesach,* an eight-day event which begins on the 19th of *Nisan.* It falls in March or April, more or less at Easter time, since the events of the last days of Christ's life took place during this festival in Jerusalem. Pesach commemorates the deliverance of the Jews from slavery in Egypt, and is also known as the 'Feast of Unleavened Bread'. Pesach begins with a religious occasion in the home, the festive evening meal *seder* (order). Unleavened bread, bitter herbs to eat with it, and wine are prepared. The youngest child present asks four questions, the first of which is: Why is this night different from all others? The answer describes the Israelites being led out of Egypt by Moses, read from the *Pesach Haggadah* which is often beautifully illustrated and describes events in the history of Israel. While the Temple in Jerusalem was still standing a lamb was eaten on this evening. All four Gospels give the same description of this meal — the Last Supper. In the diaspora a mutton bone takes the place of the Easter lamb. Another symbol is hidden in the bitter herbs dipped in salt water, representing the sufferings of the Jews, and the eggs, in place of the offerings made erstwhile in the Temple. A special mixture of crushed apples, raisins, nuts and figs is eaten *(charoseth)* to commemorate by its colour the bricks made by the Israelites in Egypt.

Seven weeks after Pesach comes another agricultural festival, *Savuot.* Originally celebrating the wheat harvest, this two-day festival (outside Israel itself) also commemorates Moses on Mount Sinai, receiving the tablets of the Law, with the Ten Commandments.

Among the lesser festivals, *Tisha B'av* is of importance. It falls on the ninth of *Av,* that is to say in July or August, and commemorates the first and second destruction of the Temple in 586 B.C. and A.D. 70. The time when the dead are remembered, it resembles the Christian All Souls Day. Thus from one Sabbath to the next, one festival to another, from birth to death, life in the Prague ghetto went on. The last things of man were looked after by the *Chevra kaddisha,* the Burial Society which was founded in Prague in 1564 — or perhaps reconstituted after the uncertain years of exile. Its members had the duty to visit the sick, watch over the dead, prepare the bodies for burial and perform the funeral rites. For eleven months the *kaddish* prayer is said by surviving children, and every year on the anniversary of the death. The prayer includes a call for the kingdom of God to come.

This brief survey is intended for readers who do not know much about the Jewish religion. It may seem oversimplified to scholars, but without these basic facts it would be difficult to understand the grounds for conflict between the people of the ghetto (governed by Christian civil authorities) and the Catholic church or their Christian neighbours, which will be dealt with in this chapter.[1)]

Naturally relations between the Jews of the Prague ghetto and the rest of the city varied a great deal. They could be neighbourly, where Christian and Jewish houses stood side by side, or where a Christian house stood in an enclave in the ghetto — this was less frequent. It is difficult to say what this meant in practice. The church authorities wanted to limit social contacts, and Jews were forbidden to invite Christians into their homes and offer them hospitality. How far these prohibitions were observed, we cannot say. There were of course financial, commercial relations. The Jews lent money to Christians, at interest (usury), on bonds, or on pawned goods. These financial undertakings were not as one-sided as many people believe. The Jews did not only lend money to Christians, becoming their creditors, but they also borrowed money from Christians and became their debtors. Nor were these transactions conducted in secret. Great sums were often involved, and valuables pawned, so that records were kept on both sides. Many are still to be found in historical archives today.[2)] Later trade began, the Jews importing luxury cloths, in particular, brocades, velvets and damask, furs, spices and other exotic goods. Second-hand clothing and other items were also sold, not only along the main street of the ghetto, but also in the Jewish 'tandlmark', or Flea Market, in Havelská Street, as we shall see later. In time Jews also began to carry on trades. It is interesting that as early as the beginning of the sixteenth century we learn of Jewish glassblowers who counted Christians, and even church institutions, among their customers. Soon there were goldsmiths and embroiderers among the Jews, still remembered in the surnames Goldschmied, Goldstücker or Perlstücker. They were later joined by braid makers, wigmakers, hatters, brushmakers, glovers, saddlers and even tinsmiths, and other trades we shall be dealing with later.

The daily contact between the ghetto and its surroundings was not left to chance, but grounded in a certain order, ruled by certain regulations, as was life within the ghetto. Not only in Prague, but throughout the Lands of the Czech Crown, Jewish society was based on royal privilege. There was the first privilege granted by Přemysl Otakar II in 1254, mentioned above, which was renewed and somewhat broadened for the Jews in Brno in 1268. It consists of thirty-three paragraphs of which the first seven deal with money lent to Christians for goods held in pawn. Different kinds of discord which might arise are set forth. The Jews' oath is given full validity and in case of disagreement it is not enough for one Christian witness to give evidence against a Jew. There must be one Jewish as well as the Christian witness. For civil cases this privilege made it clear that Jewish disputes were not to be settled by the city courts, but by the royal or the Chamber court. Four paragraphs dealing with criminal law guaranteed the health and safety of Jewish subjects. There was a fine for killing, wounding or beating up a Jew. In the first case confiscation of property, in further cases big fines to be paid to the Royal Chamber and to the victim (twelve marks in gold to the king, twelve marks in silver to the victim, plus the cost of his medical care). The Jews were permitted to cross the frontiers freely, although bound to pay duty on any goods they carried. They were also allowed to carry their dead from one community to another for burial, and if any toll-gatherer charged them for passage, he was to be punished. The desecration of a Jewish cemetery carried the death penalty, while damage to a synagogue was punished by a fine payable to the Jewish court.

The subsequent paragraphs deal with relations between Jews. Fines were inflicted for false witness at trial by duress, for refusal to appear before a Jewish court, and for wounding a neighbour. Only in serious cases was it allowed to swear on the Torah. Paragraphs 21 and 22 again deal with criminal law. In cases of secret murder aid was guaranteed in tracking down the culprit. If a Christian laid hands on a Jew by force, his hand was to be cut off. The final paragraphs deal with conflicts between Jews to be judged by a Jewish court, and the indemnity to be paid for pawned goods. Christians were to pay interest on their loans. It was already forbidden for Christians to accept Jewish hospitality. Indemnity for

25/
The Clementinum, the first seat of the Jesuits in Prague and the centre for their attacks against the Jews and their attempts to make converts from Judaism. The western façade.

landed property given in security was to be obtained by the sale of movable property. Anyone carrying off a Jewish child was to be punished as a thief. If goods given in security were not redeemed within a year and a day, the Jew could treat them as his own property. The Jewish Sabbath was not to be disturbed for redeeming pledges, and taking pawned goods by force was a punishable offence. Judgment over Jews was to be delivered only in the synagogues (the shul), and only the king had the right to bring Jews to judgment. In accordance with the Bulla of Pope Innocent IV (1243—59) issued in 1253, the Jews were not to be suspected of using Christian blood for their rites. If a Jew was accused of killing a Christian child, three Christian and three Jewish witnesses were required before he could be convicted. If he proved innocent, the man who accused him falsely was punished.[3)]

26/
The tombstone of Simon Abeles in the Týn Church, Prague.

27/
Simon Abeles, frontispiece to the book recording the trial of his father and supposed murderer, Lazar Abeles, published in 1728.

It is clear from the content of these thirty-three paragraphs in the privilege granted to the Jews by Přemysl Otakar II that in the Middle Ages the Jews were primarily engaged in lending money against securities, for this subject takes up most of the text. By that time, however, they were already acting as importers of undefined goods for Bohemia, and paying duty on their wares. No trades are mentioned in the privilege, however. The Jews had their own system of justice which decided their internal conflicts and was responsible to no lesser court than the Royal

Chamber and the king himself. They had their own houses, schools and cemeteries — mentioned in the plural. The two bullas issued by Pope Innocent IV in 1253 and promulgated by Přemysl Otakar II the following year were intended to protect the Jews in their religious and their civil life. They were not to be forcibly baptised, violence was not to be allowed against them, and their cemeteries were not to be desecrated. In the paragraph which deals with the accusation that Jews used Christian blood in their rites, Innocent IV pointed out that the Old Testament specifically forbade the Jews to use any blood whatever, let alone human blood, and yet this accusation lived on almost to our own day. In 1268 Přemysl Otakar II added two more paragraphs to this privilege, one of which forbids the Jews to accept as security goods which they suspect may be stolen; the other paragraph commands them to pay one quarter of the cost of repairing the city walls and moats.[4)]

Understandably, the criteria set out in the privilege issued by the Přemysl king, and in the bullas of Pope Innocent IV, bear the sign of the times. Nevertheless they sound reasonable, and demonstrate a human attitude toward the Jews. However, to issue such regulations was not enough. To carry them out was the job of higher and lower official institutions at the regional level. When the monarch and his central government were strong, as Přemysl Otakar II certainly was, then all could go well. Every such privilege ended with the death of its author, and his successor had to be asked to renew it — a matter of no little financial burden. To be fair, we must say that it was not only the Jews who paid for their privileges, but Church institutions as well. It would seem that each monarch, in turn, confirmed the privileges given to the Jews, although not all documents have survived. Some monarchs broadened the privileges, and improved their conditions, but not all ruled with a strong enough hand to guarantee these privileges throughout the kingdom and thus ensure the security of the Jews. We may assume that Wenceslas IV (1378—1419) also confirmed these privileges, as his father Charles IV had done in 1356, and yet it was in Wenceslas's reign that the bloody events of 1389 took place, as described in the previous chapter.

If the government was weak, there were other consequences, too. The Prague Jews had their autonomous authorities, but in matters of property they were not independent. The sale or purchase of Jewish-owned houses, legacies, wills, bills of change and such like were not recorded in the books kept in the Jewish Town, but in the relevant records of the Old Town. Understandably, the burgomaster and aldermen took this to mean that they had certain rights as regards the Jewish Town, rights which they enforced all the more strongly when the central government was weak. In 1393 Wenceslas IV gave the Jews the right to be judged only by royal officials, but this privilege did not last long. Many things changed during the Hussite Wars, and as early as 1440 the Old Town aldermen incorporated many paragraphs giving them rights over the Jews, in their charter. Once again these rights were concerned with money-lending, duties on imported wines, Jewish courts of law, and even the clothes to be worn by Jews. Later, King Vladislav Jagellon, who ruled in Bohemia from 1471 to 1516, issued a number of regulations concerning money-lending, on the whole favourable to the Jews, allowing them to charge a higher rate of interest. Nevertheless many city councils issued their own regulations, disregarding the privileges granted and confirmed by successive monarchs. The aldermen of the New Town of Prague, for instance, issued their own rules in 1503.[5)]

Almost all the records and regulations, as well as court cases, deal with money. Originally, as the 'servants of the royal chamber' *(servi camerae),* the Jews paid an annual fee to the monarch himself. In 1487, however, the Czech Assembly decided that extra taxes should be levied, from which they would profit. Such extraordinary taxes increased with the years. The amount of interest Jews could ask on loans was fixed. In the sixteenth century they were no longer allowed to lend money on security, but only on pawned goods. Extra taxes and 'special aid' was called for, in addition to the annual royal tax. This was paid half by the Jews of Prague, and half by those Jews settled on provincial estates. The 'special aid' demanded by the king for his own use was a frequent issue. In 1540, for instance, the Jews were called upon for 2,000 Rhine guilders, when a garden was to be set up near by Prague Castle.[6] The subject of various accusations brought against the Jews — rightly or wrongly — was always money: counterfeit coins, melting down of the silver coin of the realm, exporting silver, illegal loans, and so forth. Later it became an obligation for the Jews to offer considerable sums of money at every coronation, or other royal celebration. It must be said, however, that the same was expected of Christian institutions. In the seventeenth century the Jews paid 45 per cent of the taxes due to the Czech Assembly, whatever the number of the Jewish

28/
Buildings near Pinkasova Street, with part of the Old Jewish Cemetery, to the east of the Pinkas Synagogue. Langweil's model of Prague.

population. Each year the sum differed, and the Jewish quota was divided so that the Jews of Prague paid two thirds, while those settled in the country paid one third. The Prague Jews naturally thought this unjust, and in the eighteenth century they tried to have their quota reduced to three fifths, leaving two fifths to the country Jews. Considering that the rate of tax was fixed in 1653, we must judge it more or less appropriate, for at that time there were 2,090 Jews in Prague, including 598 children, while there were only 1,127 adults and 372 children elsewhere in the country. Later the relative numbers changed, and there were more Jews settled in the countryside.

During the Thirty Years' War the Jewish population declined, and was financially ex-

29/
Houses along what was then Cikánská Street, towards the river Vltava. Langweil's model of Prague.

31/
Jáchymova Street with the Meisl Synagogue in the centre background. Langweil's model of Prague.

hausted, so that they were unable to meet their tax obligations. The unpaid taxes grew from year to year. From the early eighteenth century there were innumerable committees set up to deal with the problem; naturally, the Jews themselves were not represented. In 1702, for example, a list was drawn up, showing what tax the Jews should pay on certain goods. The list covered everything: food, drink, textiles, clothes, trades, property ownership, the fees paid to the Burial Society, fees for use of the ritual baths, and even taxes on luxury goods actually forbidden to the Jews. A committee set up in 1740 allowed a special tax for Jews who wished to wear silk, velvet or damask, with silver and gold jewelry (all forbidden by the law of 1702).[7)]

We have already mentioned the medieval autonomy of the Jews. In the sixteenth century five elders acted in the interests of all the Jews in Bohemia, while the Jews of Prague were represented by five elders and the Jewish mayor. The Jews were allowed to elect their representatives, but the list of names had to be presented beforehand to the Czech Chamber (after Ferdinand I stiffened the royal power) and the elections were supervised by officials from the Chamber. In the first half of the sixteenth century, the 'primas' was not yet acknowledged the leader of the elders, who took

30/
The bank of the river Vltava, with timber floated down for the sawmills, north of the Jewish Town. Langweil's model of Prague.

turns to head the body for four weeks at a time. The Jewish judges were elected on the same lines. Nevertheless, the Jews chose their own rabbi, although the names of those elected were also sent for confirmation to the central authorities, who sometimes asked the archbishop to give his opinion. Elections were secret, but the electors were limited in number. Earlier, the council of elders was elected every year, but later, towards the end of the sixteenth century, it changed to only every third year. The elders had to pledge their oath to the monarch that they would serve loyally, in truth and justice. Towards the end of the sixteenth century the office of 'primas' became acknowledged, and by the middle of the seventeenth century the governing Jewish body was gradually enlarged. There were still only five elders representing the community as a whole, but each community elected six, while there were four official scribes, one mayor and eight observers.

The Jewish court consisted of five lawyers of the first rank, five lesser lawyers, five of the lowest rank, and two candidates. The administration also included six ecclesiastical elders, six street inspectors, six inspectors for the Jewish market, and five who were to supervise Jewish students. Besides these elected officials the Jewish community in Prague employed a treasurer, a chief accountant and an assistant accountant called the 'Gegenhändler'. They kept separate books, which were compared when the books were balanced. There were several other treasurers, responsible for the many taxes and duties levied on the Jews. The community also had a scribe and a servant attached to the Týn market, which from about the twelfth century had provided foreign merchants with hospitality and storage space. After paying duty on their goods they were allowed to sell them in the city. The Jewish community paid its own employees from its own funds, as well as interest on loans, the cost of street cleaning and similar items. The Jews were also required to pay an annual sum to the mayor of Prague and to the military commander of the city, for their 'protection'. In addition, local custom required New Year gifts to the heads of the many ecclesiastical orders around. The community also paid for their 'Easter and autumn fruits', which must have been the fruit and branches for *Succoth* and perhaps for *Pesach* as well. The Jewish elders were also paid for their services. It is of interest to note that the community sent pike to the monasteries as a New Year gift. There can be no doubt that the major part of the annual taxes found its way into the treasury of the Czech Chamber, through the channels of the 'rentmaster's' office.[8)]

It could be thought that while such care was taken over the election of the Jewish elders and even of the rabbi, when the commercial life of the ghetto was so well controlled, that private life was free. That was not the case, however. Not only were the Jews forbidden to wear luxury garments, not only did they have to sport special badges from time to time, they were not free to move about especially during Christian festivals and on Sundays. The authorities even interfered in matters one would consider private. There was a regulation that Jews could only invite forty guests to a wedding, twenty from the bride's side and twenty from the bridegroom's. Only twenty guests could be invited to celebrate a circumcision. These restrictions are to be found in the 'regulations for the Jews' of 1702, and were apparently meant to induce sobriety, so that debts to the state could soon be paid.[9)]

It was not only in the sphere of civil rights that conflicts between the Jews and the Christians occurred. The Jews were not full citizens, because they did not fit into any of the historical categories. Their rabbis were not accepted as members of the clergy, and there was no place for the rest of them in the citizen ranks. Great care was taken to see that no Jew, becoming rich, tried to pass himself off as a burgher.

Another sphere of possible conflict was that of religion. The Catholic church in the Middle Ages was a militant church, in reality as well as in theory. It was the Church's mission to convert the heathen, and as often as not, by using violence. The Jews were the worst heathen of all, for it was they who had caused Jesus of Nazareth to be crucified, and thus bring salvation to all mankind, except for the obstinate Jews who refused to recognize him as the Messiah. There were times when the Jews were left alone in their 'Old Testament heresy', but occasionally there would be an upheaval, and they were persecuted or converted by violence to the 'true' faith, i.e. the Catholic church. In the Middle Ages this was usually a forced conversion, while later on the Church proceeded more carefully and systematically. On the whole there was not much trouble of this kind in Bohemia, until the second half of the sixteenth century. The Hussite Wars had so reduced the old medieval monastic orders that the few monks left in their monasteries had a hard time of it keeping the order going, and no energy to spare for the heathen Jews. They were more concerned with what the Hussite Wars left behind — the Unity of the Czech Brethren, and later the Lutheran church. Things changed, however, when the Jesuits were brought into the country, and settled at the Church of St Clement in 1555. The Jesuits were a militant order with the mission to convert both the heathen and non-Catholic Christians. Although they were sent for to deal primarily with the Protestants, the Jews did not escape their attention. This happened remarkably soon, although the Jesuits had troubles of their own during their first years in Prague. Nevertheless, true to their calling, they soon set to work on the Jews in the ghetto close at hand.

In 1560 the Emperor Ferdinand I appointed 'men learned in the Hebrew tongue' to check all Jewish books, which were said to contain things insulting to the Catholic faith. It has been said that this idea originated with a converted Jew, one Jehuda of Modena, but since the Jesuits were trained in the knowledge of Hebrew, we believe that they may have been behind it. The Jewish books were indeed all sent to Vienna, but returned to the community that same year, on the emperor's orders. There can be no doubt that the Jesuits actively intervened in life in the ghetto the following year, 1561. Doctor Jindřich Blyssenius, who taught theology and Hebrew in St Clement's seminary, was given the task of preaching to the Jews every Tuesday in St Clement's. He preached in German and in Hebrew, while one Father Wenceslas preached to them in Czech in the Church of the Holy Spirit. The enterprise had little success. Those who were forced to go to church are said to have stopped their ears, and very few were persuaded to convert. In time these sermons were discontinued, and the Jews left in relative peace until the Battle of the White Mountain, when things changed radically. While, as

32/
A *tallit* (prayer shawl, white with dark brown stripes, and fringes) and the *tefillin* (phylacteries, parchment with passages from the Torah, bound on the forehead and left arm during prayers).

33/
J. Minařík: Jewish butchers' shops. Oil on canvas.

we have seen, the period after the White Mountain was favourable for the Jews in some respects, it was of course primarily the time of the Jesuits. The Archbishop of Prague, Cardinal Arnošt Harrach, who took office in 1623, was a very energetic man, and his goal of re-catholicizing the country was not confined to heretics alone. The Jesuits worked hand in glove with him, and of course there was always someone in their midst who taught Hebrew in their schools, and therefore knew at least something about the subject. In 1630 the civil and the ecclesiastical administration again decided, at the highest level, that the

Jews would have to be preached to on Saturdays, in the Church of St Mary by the Pond (na Louži). The sermons were to be given by a Jesuit well versed in Hebrew, and 80 to 100 Jews from the ghetto were to attend. It soon became apparent, however, that the Jesuits' Hebrew was not such that the Jews could understand it, and indeed, it may have seemed comical to them. It was then decided that the sermons should be delivered in German. This enforced attendance at Catholic sermons was absolutely contrary to their own Jewish rules for keeping the Sabbath and cut right across their most sacred beliefs. The people of the ghetto went to the synagogue on the Sabbath, but to leave the ghetto and listen to a Catholic sermon was desecration of the Sabbath.[10)] Unfortunately we have too little information about how this new rule was respected by the Jews of Prague, but there cannot have been much of a congregation to listen to the sermons in the Church of St Mary by the Pond, on a Saturday. The Jesuits were most concerned to convert young Jews to Catholicism. A special fund was established and a house known as 'Bělohrad' (White castle) was bought for the young converts — neophytes — opposite the Church of St Václav (Wenceslas).[11)]

That this worthy attempt to convert young Jews might end badly is illustrated by the tragic fate of twelve-year-old Simon Abeles and his family. The father, Lazarus Abeles, is said to have killed his son when he learned that the boy wanted to be baptized. He paid for this crime with his life, after being tortured and convicted. He left a widow and three younger children. Much in the court proceedings is unclear, particularly the figure of a converted Jew, Franz Kafka, who drew the boy to his own house, refused to let him return to his father, and later disappeared. The whole affair arouses suspicions that all was not as it appeared in the official version which was later circulated in 1696, after the trial, in Czech, German and Latin. Young Simon was originally buried in the Old Jewish cemetery, secretly and with no funeral rites. Exhumed and examined by the medical coroner, he was ceremonially reburied in the Týn Church, where his tombstone can still be seen.

34/
Jewish butchers' guild emblem.

The Catholic authorities were most outraged, however, by Jewish books, whether printed in Prague or imported from neighbouring countries, mainly Poland. The Archbishop's consistory worked in close collaboration with the Jesuits in the censorship of Jewish books, and reported proceedings to the Czech Chamber and the Vice-regent's of-

35/
The Old Jewish Cemetery and environs, from the south-east. In the background part of the cemetery which was done away with during the clearance of the 'fifth quarter of Prague'. Langweil's model of Prague.

fice for Bohemia.[12] There is a great deal of material concerning the censorship of Jewish books, in the archives of the former Jesuit seminary of St Clement's. For the most part it was the Jesuits who initiated the confiscation of books in the ghetto and in Jewish printing presses. An exceptionally active Jesuit in this respect was Father Wolfgang Preissler, regarded as a Hebrew scholar, active in Prague towards the end of the seventeenth century.

In the early 1690s a great affair blew up. At that time none but Jewish scholars read or understood the Jewish books printed in Hebrew, and Preissler himself obviously understood them only partially. The books could have influenced no-one, yet they were confiscated from the rabbis and other scholars. Judging from Preissler's lists, where the Hebrew titles are often distorted, practically all the books in general use were confiscated

— the Talmud, various books of interpretation, prayer books and cabalist literature. According to Preissler, the Talmud contained many insulting references to Christianity, as did the book of *Zohar* — a cabalist work of Jewish philosophy, ethics and law — one of the basic works of Jewish mysticism. The list includes the most popular and most widely read Halakah works, such as the *Schulchan aruch* of Joseph Kara and the writings of the Prague rabbis, *Orach le-chayyim* by Shelomo Ephraim Luntshitz and *Lebushim* by Mordechai ben Abraham Jafe. That was not all — the rabbis of Prague were forbidden to preach during synagogue services. The Jewish community tried to defend itself, demonstrating that Jewish books had been allowed for centuries without censorship, and that when a similar confiscation took place in 1669, it was agreed that the books dealt only with Jewish religious matters and had nothing to do with Catholicism. Then, the Jewish books were returned to the community, but Preissler did not give up so easily. He kept on presenting evidence that the confiscated Hebrew books were dangerous and heretical, and even drew up a list of quotations such as 'a Jew should do neither good or ill to a pagan, but he should try to kill a Christian'; or 'if a Jew sees a Christian on the brink of an abyss, he should throw him down'. Even 'if a Jew wants to kill a Christian, and kills a Jew by mistake, his act should be forgiven'. Many such nonsensical sentences were included, and the long reply by the Jewish community's leaders showed clearly that Father Preissler was not the Hebrew scholar he claimed to be. Preissler also proposed that Jewish rabbis should send a written copy of their sermons a week in advance, to be censored.

The Jews protested that this interfered with their religion, and that it was not usual for the

36/
Unknown artist: Annual banquet of the Jewish Burial Society (*Chevra kaddisha*). Oil on canvas, first half of the nineteenth century.

37/
Unknown artist: Members of the Burial Society praying at the tomb of Rabbi Loew. Oil on canvas, first half of the nineteenth century.

rabbi to prepare his sermon beforehand. Nor had it ever been heard of that Catholic priests should censor Jewish sermons. The heads of the Prague ghetto demanded that experts from abroad, from Leyden, Basel, Leipzig and Wittenberg, should be called in before a decision was made. In the ensuing correspondence the heads of the Jewish community suggested that although 'Father Preissler may be a very learned priest, he cannot understand Hebrew and Chaldean (Aramaic) speech as well as a rabbi or a Jewish scholar'. The Jewish scholars were not slow to translate and explain all those passages in the Jewish texts that Preissler had found disturbing. Thus they showed up his ignorance and lack of understanding. Finally they presented a long list of 'imprimatur' i.e. permission to print, given by the archbishop's consistory. Father Preissler wrote yet another invective attacking the Jewish texts, but his arguments were very weak.

How the whole affair ended is not recorded in the archives of the St Clement's Jesuits but we can assume that the archbishop's 'imprimatur' was a strong enough argument, and that the Jesuits returned the confiscated Jewish texts. Censorship continued, however, and was particularly strict concerning books to be printed in the Prague Hebrew presses. In 1715 the chief rabbi, David Oppenheim, was told to 'pre-censure' Jewish texts. He declined, pointing out that he would not then be able to carry out his duties as Chief Rabbi, in a long letter dated August 1716. His letter mentioned the inconsistencies involved, such as a book allowed to be printed, but not reprinted. A Jewish censor was then appointed, one Simon Jaiteles. It still happened that Hebrew texts were confiscated, so David Oppenheim did not dare to keep his great collection of rare books in Prague, but left them in Hanover with his kinsman.[13)]

Censorship and the confiscation of Hebrew

texts represented the most serious interference with the religious life of the ghetto, but from time to time regulations were issued which had a direct or indirect effect. After the fire of 1689, for instance, it was decided that not all of the twelve synagogues would be restored. Four of these (according to the lists of 1670) were in private houses. Only six were to be restored, and the Old Shul was not among them, as we have seen in the last chapter. The Jews had to fight hard and long for the re-opening of the Old Shul, and paid heavily for it. Ever since the Thirty Years' War there had been objections to these private prayer rooms, some of which were study circles (*bet ha-midrash*) while others were temples. The ghetto was constantly checked for such transgressions. In November 1716, for example, the Little Quarter governor who was not responsible for the Jewish Town over the river, but could be asked to inspect it, reported 'illegal' Jewish 'schools' which ought to be forbidden, except for those prayer rooms arranged for the sick. The religious services conducted in the prayer rooms of David Karpeles and Moses Glazer were to be moved to the Old-New Synagogue, while the illegal 'study circle' in Anshel Günzburg's house was to be liquidated. The community asked, then, for the prayer rooms in Karpeles' and Glazer's house to be permitted to remain, since they served old people whose weak health did not allow them to go as far as the 'Big Shul'. To make a just comparison, let us look at the situation in Christian circles; the Archbishop's consistory had to approve the building of any shrine, but this was rarely withheld.[14)]

Jewish religious life was affected by some administrative measures which were not on the surface so aimed, although their effect was to conflict gravely with the basic principles of Jewish life. We have already mentioned that the population of the ghetto was seriously re-

38/
Unknown artist: The rabbi speaking at a burial in the Žižkov Jewish Cemetery. From the series 'The Prague Burial Society'. Oil on canvas, first half of the nineteenth century.

39/
The dead-end street behind the Meisl Synagogue. Photograph by J. Eckert, *c.* 1898.

duced by the Thirty Years' War, and although many died in the plague of 1680, there were many births. In 1703 there were 11,517 inhabitants of the ghetto, of whom 2,816 were adult males who could bear arms. In the half century that ensued, the population of the ghetto rose to five times that number. During the plague that devastated Bohemia in 1713, the ghetto suffered much, but even so, the population did not sink to the level of 1653. At the request of Charles VI a special commission again discussed how to reduce the Jewish population. The purpose of the lists then drawn up, as we have already remarked, was to set the limit to the number of Jewish families allowed to settle in Prague, and to prevent this number being exceeded. Jewish families from the countryside were strictly forbidden to settle in the ghetto, and the people there were constantly checked. The 'reduction committee' came up with an idea which was absolutely contrary to the basic principles of Jewish family and religious life.

40/
The south side of Široká (former Josefovská) Street, looking east. Photograph by J. Eckert, *c.* 1898.

41/
Šmilesova Lane leading to the Small Timber Square (Dřevný plácek). Photograph by J. Eckert, 1896—1905.

A law of 16 October 1726 allowed only the eldest son of Jewish parents to marry. Younger sons were not condemned to celibate life, but they could only marry outside the kingdom of Bohemia. The younger sons of Jewish families, then, had to choose between celibate life or exile. Severe physical punishment, and exile from the land, was the threatened consequence.

Once we realize that the meaning of life for the Jews was the family, and children, we can imagine what such a measure meant for them. Of course they protested and tried to defend their view of life, but this was in vain for a long time. Not until 1734 was this inhuman regulation somewhat lightened, and in addition to that of the first-born, seven marriages were allowed in each region.[15)]

From time to time regulations and prohibitions were issued, reflecting the Christians' dislike of their Jewish fellow citizens. Under Rudolph II, for instance, in 1587, the Jews

42/
Looking down Rabínská Street towards the north. Photograph by J. Eckert, *c.* 1890.

43/
Three Wells Square (Třístudniční plácek) at the junction of Maislova, Kostečná and Jáchymova Streets. Photograph by J. Eckert, *c.* 1898.

were forbidden to celebrate their 'carnival', that is to say, the festival of Purim, at the same time as the Christian feast of Easter.[16]

The third sphere in which the people of the ghetto met and often came into conflict with the Christian population, was that of their livelihood. As we have seen, during the Middle Ages almost the only calling allowed to the Jews was that of money-lender, and the rates of interest were high. By a decision of King Vladislav Jagellon in 1497, the Jews were allowed to charge double the interest demanded by Christian money-lenders, because they were obliged to pay taxes on this money to their patron, the king, as well as to the authorities, and a yearly tax from which the Christians were exempt. The loans were all entered in the books kept by the chief burgomaster's office in Prague, and in the municipal books of other towns, and were written down in the presence of the debtors' guarantors. Since at that time Christians could charge 10% interest, Jews were allowed to ask 20% per year. However, the surviving records show a much higher rate being charged by Jewish usurers. At first money was lent on bond, and on goods in pawn, usually jewelry or luxury clothing. Stolen goods presented a problem, since the man holding them as security usually only found out that they were stolen when the victim discovered his lost property in the ghetto, and demanded its return. This meant a heavy loss to the Jew who had lent money to the thief. King Vladislav Jagellon finally allowed loans on the security of stolen goods, on the assumption that things would work themselves out when the victim found his property and settled matters both with the Jew and the thief. Understandably, this led to frequent and serious trouble. There was more trouble when the Jew demanded more than the rightful interest on his loans, and again when debtors did not pay up on time and then refused to pay the compound interest.[17]

Towards the end of the fifteenth century Jewish trade began to look up. A decision by

44/
Jáchymova Street, looking towards Three Wells Square (Třístudniční plácek). Photograph by J. Eckert, *c.* 1898.

were no longer kept by the chief burgomaster's office.[18])

The form of oath used by the Jews undoubtedly had to do with usury and the high rates of interest. Even late in the seventeenth century they recalled the spirit of the early Middle Ages. The Jew had before his eyes a book with the Ten Commandments inscribed in it, and the Christian requiring his oath would do so in the following words: Jew, I adjure thee by the only true and living God, on this book of the Torah and its Law... The Jew was first called upon to make sure that the book he was swearing on was indeed the right one. As he gave his oath he put his hand into the book, and called down upon his head all penalties and curses if he swore falsely. In the Middle Ages Jews were forced to stand on a pig's skin while taking the oath.[19])

The importance of trade grew rapidly. By 5 October 1538 the Czech Chamber cited trade as the principle livelihood of the Jews in the

45/
Looking along V kůlnách Lane towards the southern vestibule of the Old-New Synagogue. Photograph by J. Eckert, *c.* 1890.

46/
The corner of Jáchymova and Úzká Streets. Photograph by J. Eckert, *c.* 1890.

the Moravian regional court in Olomouc, dated 1500, allowed the Jews to 'hold fairs and keep shops' in the towns, but not in the villages. However, regulations differed from city to city and region to region. In the New Town of Prague, for instance, we read in 1503 that besides lending money, though that only for pawned goods and not for bonds, Jews were allowed to sell 'new and second-hand clothes' at markets set up for the purpose. They were not allowed to sell at Christian markets, nor to compete with Christian tradesmen. Later this was changed, to allow Jews to lend money on security bonds but not to sell new goods, either of cloth or leather. Second-hand goods and old clothes, however, could be sold. This change came in 1515, when Vladislav Jagellon entrusted the administration of the Jewish ghetto to the burgomaster and aldermen of the Old Town of Prague. Loans were not allowed to exceed 300 score Meissen groschen, except with special permission from the burgomaster and aldermen. At this time the records of loans

47/
J. Minařík: Little Pinkas Street, looking towards the Old Jewish Cemetery. On the right, the western façade of the Pinkas Synagogue. Oil on canvas.

48/
J. Minařík: Hampejská Street, looking towards the Museum of Decorative Arts. Oil on canvas.

Czech Lands. Money-lending for securities was no longer permitted. The people of Prague, however, did all they could to prevent the Jews prospering, and confiscated their goods. The expulsion of the Jews from Prague in 1541 meant the end of Jewish trade until after the death of Ferdinand I in 1564, when they were allowed to return. Maximilian II and Rudolph II were both favourable to the Jews, and trading was allowed everywhere except in mining towns, undoubtedly for fear the Jews would get their hands on the silver and carry it out of the country. The Jews were still expert and successful financiers, and even the Czech royal Chamber began to use their services. In 1569 they helped when the cur-

1731

49/ *(Page 72)*
The yard behind a house near the Old Shul. Photograph by J. Eckert, 1905.

50/
The courtyard of the big Renaissance house of Jacob Bashevi. Photograph by J. Eckert, *c.* 1900.

51/
The courtyard of a house in Červená Street, the Cikán Synagogue in the background. Photograph by J. Eckert, *c.* 1900.

rency was changed from small to standard larger coins — a very difficult business, since all manner and sizes of coins were in use in the realm.[20)]

Jewish trade also grew fast because the Jews were to a considerable degree cosmopolitan, travelling a great deal. They soon began to import goods from abroad, especially rare and precious cloths from Italy and the Far East — silk, brocades, velvets and damask, as well as luxury furs and spices. By degrees individuals were given permission to become artisans. At first these were isolated cases. In 1577, for example, the Emperor Rudolph II issued an open patent to the Jew, Joseph de Cerui (Coref), allowing him to carry on the trade of goldsmith in the four towns of Prague and even in the Castle itself. In the sixteenth century there were already embroiderers in the ghetto, 'perlstyckers' who not only made

52/
The corner house belonging to the Wedeles family and that of the Mosheles family in the former Nová poštovská Street. Photograph by J. Eckert, *c.* 1900.

curtains and Torah covers for the synagogues, but worked for Christian customers and even ecclesiastical institutions. Gradually Jews were allowed to buy and sell at Christian markets and fairs.[21)]

By the end of the sixteenth century the Jews of Prague were trading not only in luxury cloths and furs, but in tailoring, wool, wine, unguents, horses, cattle for slaughter and all sorts of other goods. The furriers' guild complained of Jewish competition in 1593. In 1595 Rudolph II forbade the Jews to work furs in secret, but they were allowed to sell such products because they often acquired them as security for loans which were not repaid.[22)]

At this time Jewish traders were no longer confined to the ghetto, to occasional markets or the house-to-house peddling which was always a cause of trouble; they now had their own regular market inside the Old Town, known first as 'tarmark' and later as 'tandlmark' (Flea Market). This Jewish market was in Havelská (Gall) Street, on the north side of the Church of St Gall. Jews had rooms or cellars rented from Christians, to store their goods, and set up their stalls under and round the covered walk in front of the houses. They must have paid a high rent for all this, and there was a tax to the Old Town authorities for the right to sell in the 'tandlmark'. The sale of furs, clothing and other goods was permitted by various privileges mentioned in a decision by the Emperor Matthias, settling in 1617 a conflict between Christian merchants, shopkeepers, tailors and furriers, and their Jewish rivals. The Jews had the right to sell clothes and furs, but not to make them; that was to be left to Christian artisans.[23)]

The Jewish 'tandlmark' gave rise to innumerable conflicts. The stalls and little shops in Havelská Street were very close indeed to the church, which belonged to the Carmelites after 1620. The monks were constantly complaining to the Czech Chamber about the noise made by the Jews and their market, disturbing church services. The Jewish merchants had rented quarters in nine houses, on the ground and lower floors. In 1715, certainly instigated by the Carmelites, the Chamber began to consider moving the market elsewhere, and in that year practically all the little shops in front of the covered walk along those nine houses were demolished. It was not only the Jews who protested, but also the owners of those nine houses, who had certainly enjoyed considerable financial profit. Finally a compromise was arrived at, by which a lane was to be left clear between the market and the church, to a width of three to three and a half metres, closed off by a wall. From the proceedings of the many commissions set up to deal with the problem, we learn that the Jews had shops and storage space rented elsewhere in the city as well, mostly in the vicinity of the market. One site was in what is now Melantrichova Street. Thus the 'tandlmark' was not

53/
The east façade of the Meisl Synagogue, looking into the former Maislova Lane. Photograph by J. Eckert, *c.* 1898.

54/
A second-hand shop in the ghetto.

abolished, although it continued only on a smaller scale.[24)]

By the early eighteenth century the Jews were trading in practically everything that could be bought and sold. The police issued special regulations for Jewish traders in 1702, which quote precious and base metals, jewels, wool, flax, leather, furs, clothing both old and new, feathers, drinks including wines and spirits, foodstuffs and spices, horses, cattle of all kinds, poultry, wax, oil, unguents and leather goods, especially saddles.[25)]

Up to the late 1620s it was still the exception for a Jew to be allowed to learn and carry on a trade, but it is clear from the source materials that they often did so in defiance of the regulations. The furriers and tailors were those who most often complained. It was not until 1628 that Ferdinand II issued a privilege allowing the Jews to learn any trade — perhaps excepting that of armourer — and to carry on business, but only for fellow Jews. They were forbidden to take on Christian apprentices or journeymen, or to employ persons not entitled to work at the trade. It cannot be said that the Jews were attracted to all trades alike. We have already named the goldsmiths, embroiderers, glass-blowers, shoemakers, tailors and furriers. Later lists show that there were also glovers, tanners, saddlers, hatters, comb and brush makers, button and dice makers, dyers, tinsmiths and even stocking and wig makers, in the ghetto. Some of the trades had their own guilds, separate from those of the Christians; they were allowed in the last quarter of the seventeenth century. The study of public opinion mentioned in our last chapter, which took place in 1745, and the earlier census of Prague Jews taken in 1729, both show that the building trades were not then represented. There is no mention of Jewish bricklayers, carpenters, stonemasons, smiths, fitters, coppersmiths and farriers, not even cabinetmakers or stove builders. We know that (according to the articles of the stone-cutters' guild of 1741) the tombstones for the Old Jewish cemetery were cut by Christians, and doubtless they also served the other Jewish cemeteries. At the end of the seventeenth century there were isolated cases of permission for candlemakers and wax refiners. The Jews certainly had their own bath attendants. The only 'independent' profession they were allowed to take up was that of physician. Jewish doctors enjoyed an excellent reputation among Christians, too. Only one Jew was allowed to study medicine at Charles University before the enlightened Joseph came to the throne. That was in 1719, and he was Moshe Solomon Gumpertz. From 1774 Jews were allowed to study medicine at the university on condition that they would only practice among their fellow Jews.[26)]

In the last quarter of the seventeenth century we learn of Jewish artists in the Prague ghetto. Two members of the painters' guild in the Old Town complained that the Irish monks of the Franciscan monastery had not only entrusted Jewish painters with the painting of the refectory, but even with a painting of St Francis for the altar, which — according to the plaintiffs — was very badly done. The Jews were accused of trying to force their paintings on the burghers of Prague. One of the accused, Loebl Brandeis, defended himself by saying that according to a privilege granted by Ferdinand II in 1628, he had the right to carry on the trade of painter. Contemporary sources tell us no more. Whether he was allowed to go on painting or not, we do not know, but we can assume that having commissioned and paid for paintings from him, the Franciscans did not go to the trouble of having them painted over, and that the work of Loebl Brandeis continued to adorn their refectory until the monastery was disaffected under the Emperor Joseph II (1780—90).[27)]

It is less surprising to read of the good reputation and great popularity of Jewish musicians, who were often called upon to play for high society. In 1580, for instance, when Petr Vok of Rožmberk was married, Jewish musicians were brought from Prague to play at his wedding. In 1650 the Archbishop of Prague, Cardinal Arnošt Harrach, permitted Jewish musicians to play not only at Christian banquets, but even at Christian weddings and christenings — after the religious part of the celebration was over. Naturally, again, their great popularity gave rise to many complaints

55/
J. Minařík: The former U Staré školy Lane, looking towards the east façade of the Temple. Oil on canvas.

1911.
Minaří

by their Christian rivals. The musicians of the Prague ghetto had their own guild, with very strict rules to ensure that they did not compete too sharply with their Christian competitors. A Jewish musician was allowed to teach only two of his children to play an instrument, and new members could only be accepted into the guild when an existing member died or became so ill that he could no longer play. A special inspector was appointed to keep a check on them. A list of the musicians playing in the ghetto in 1651 has survived. There were eleven members of the band, playing on an 'instrument' which probably meant a portable organ, with a descant of violins, a double bass and cymbals.[28)]

In the seventeenth and eighteenth centuries the ghetto was very different from that of the sixteenth century. The population was more numerous, but the community as a whole much poorer. The tax records show that in the thirties and forties of the sixteenth century there were 171 families in the ghetto, ten of whom owned property worth more than two thousand guilders. Sixteen families were worth more than one thousand guilders, 66 were middling prosperous families worth from 200 to 999 guilders, and seventy-nine poor families worth less than 200. A similar list dating from 1748 shows 766 families in the ghetto, but only six of them were worth more than 10,000 Rhine guilders. There were eight families in the 5,000 to 9,999 guilder bracket, thirty-two worth 2,000 to 4,999 guilders, a hundred and six in the 500 to 1,999 category. The great majority, six hundred and ten families, the poor, were not worth more than 100 to 499 guilders. The Prague Jews were no longer the wealthy financiers who could lend money to kings and emperors and take goods from burghers and noblemen as security for their loans. They were now frequently their debtors (although they had occasionally borrowed from Christians, too, in the previous century). They not only owed a backlog of taxes to the government, but were in debt to private individuals and to institutions, especially to church bodies. In 1744 the greatest creditors of the Jewish ghetto were the Dominican monks of St Mary Magdalene in the Little Quarter, St Giles' in the Old Town, Jablonné v Podještědí in northern Bohemia and Cheb in western Bohemia. They were followed by the Jesuits of St Bartholomew's Monastery, and then the Augustinians of St Thomas's Monastery. As for debts owed to private persons, the ghetto as a whole owed the considerable sum of 160,100 Rhine guilders, although this was before the fire that devastated the ghetto in 1754. It is perhaps surprising to see church institutions lending so much money to the Jews, especially the Jesuits who did all they could to make life hard for them. Simon Schürer, the Superior of their convent, lent the Jewish community 5,000 Rhine guilders in 1677, at the current rate of 6% interest, while the Jesuits of St Clement's lent them another 3,000 guilders in 1695. These figures show the immense complexity of relations in and around the Prague ghetto. They should not be judged one-sidedly, whether from the Jewish or the Christian point of view.[29)]

57/
The former chapel and mortuary of the Old Jewish Cemetery, built in Neo-Romanesque style by the architect Gerstl, 1911—12, to replace the earlier mortuary. This is the only religious building to have been erected in the ghetto at the time of the clearance. Today it forms part of the State Jewish Museum.

56/
J. Minařík: Žatecká Street. Oil on canvas.

/III/ PERSONALITIES OF THE GHETTO

Life in the ghetto was not only a matter of greater or lesser day-to-day vexations interspersed with the joyous hours of the Sabbath and the holy days. It was a life underpinned by the ancient spiritual traditions of Judaism. The ghetto had its spiritual leaders. Very often they were remarkable men, rabbis who not only preached to the Prague community (described, like other large communities, by the biblical epithet: 'a city and a mother in Israel' (*ir va-em be-Jisrael*). They were also scholars in the specifically Jewish sense of the word. The Prague ghetto had its poets and writers, its famous doctors and scientific thinkers, many of whom are buried in the Old Jewish cemetery and will be mentioned again in that context, together with their epitaphs. Not all of them, by far, were born in the Prague Jewish Town where they later became famous, and not all of them lived out their days there. For some of them, Prague was only a shorter or longer episode in their lives.

It was not only the rabbis and the scholars who influenced the spiritual life of the Prague community. There were always a few energetic, prosperous individuals in the administration who, as members of the Council of Elders, had a considerable say in the choice of a rabbi. They often headed one or another of the synagogues, especially when they themselves, or their forbears, had played a major part in its establishment.

The Sanhedrin, the Jewish Council, ceased to exist in Palestine early in the fifth century, under the Emperor Theodosius II (A.D. 408—450). A little later the persecution of the Babylonian Jews began, and resulted in stagnation in the once famous centres of Jewish learning there, which never regained their former glory. Nevertheless the Babylonian Talmud became the foundation on which the religious, ethical and philosophical ideas of Jewry in the diaspora evolved, a foundation which was continually being refined, polished and perfected, in repeated re-interpretation of individual passages. No doubt the new interpretations reflected the changed times and the changed way of life of the Jews in the diaspora. New environments and hitherto unknown situations must often have led to moments of uncertainty, and it was essential to find new ways to apply the old rules. For Jews in the diaspora the Jerusalem Talmud was less meaningful than the Babylonian, since it reflected Palestinian conditions, which were very different from those the Jews encountered in exile. The most important commentary was that written by Shelomo ben Isaac, known as Rashi, in the eleventh century. The 'tosafot' school in northern France, from the word 'tosafot', meaning 'additions', based its arguments on Rashi's commentary; it attempted to overcome the conflicting attitudes found in the Talmud by using casuistics. Later generations of rabbis and scholars followed this line, so that new interpretations and new decisions were constantly appearing. In the twelfth and thirteenth centuries such scholars were already active in Bohemia, some of them explicitly saying of themselves that they came from Prague or Bohemia. Jacob ha-Laban, the 'white one', whose 'additions' found their way into many Talmudic collections, was a 'tosafot' scholar. One of his manuscripts is preserved in the Munich Library. Another was Isaac ben Mordechai of Prague, who headed a school; yet another was Eliezer ben Isaac.

In the thirteenth century Bohemia already had its Jewish writers, one of whom, Jekutiel ben Jehuda ha-Cohen, known as the 'Punktator', wrote the *Reader's Eye.* This manuscript has survived, and was published early in the nineteenth century. Abraham ben Azriel also wrote in Bohemia. His exhaustive commentary on synagogal poetry, *Arugat habosem* (A Bed of Basil), preserved in manuscript, was prepared for publication in 1939. The work of Abraham Isaac ben Moshe, known as *Or Sarua* (Light shed wide), from the title of his work, is of great interest to students of Slavonic languages. He deals with specific Talmudic tracts, adding the views and decisions of various authors, and many notes in Old Slavonic, Old Czech. *Or Sarua* speaks of Old Czech as 'our language, the language of Canaan'.[1)]

Rabbi Abigdor Kara is the first poet who is reliably known to have lived and died in Prague. His gravestone is the oldest one to survive in the Old Cemetery. According to David Gans, the sixteenth century chronicler of the Prague ghetto, Rabbi Abigdor wrote an elegy on the tragic events of 1389, when the rabble was incited to attack and loot the Prague ghetto, killing many of the inhabitants. The elegy begins with the words: 'Who can describe all our sufferings, who can

58/
The guild emblem of the Prague Hebrew printers. Woodcut. From the Pentateuch published in Prague in 1530.

recount them?' and forms part of the prayers read in the synagogues of Prague on the Day of Atonement. The father of Abigdor, Rabbi Jizchak Kara, is referred to in contemporary sources as a martyr, and it is thought that his son, then a small child, lived through that tragic experience and witnessed his father's death.

In the second decade of the fifteenth century Rabbi Abigdor was a member of the 'bet din', the rabbinical court, in Prague. Fragments of his traditional religious writings have survived: notes on the Pentateuch, a fragment of the book *Eben sappir* (The Sapphire Stone) devoted to allegorical explanations of the Bible, a short lexicographical work and the manuscript of *Kodesh hillulim* (The Sacrament of Praise), a cabalist commentary on the last psalm. He is much better known, however, for his synagogal songs, of which he composed many more besides the elegy mentioned above. He seems to have been the last of the medieval synagogue poets. Since his name does not figure in the Memorial Book of the Old-New Synagogue, it is thought that he was the rabbi of the Old Shul, a small congregation founded by Jews from the east which (according to some historians) was attended by Jews expelled from Spain and Portugal. According to one of his contemporaries, Rabbi Jacob Möln, Rabbi Abigdor was a favourite at the court of Wenceslas IV, who liked discussing religion with him. Rabbi Abigdor is even thought to have had some influence on Master Jan Hus. In contemporary Latin sources — the city chronicles of the 1430s — he appears several times under his Latinized name of Magister Victor. He found his way into Czech literature as one of the characters of Alois Jirásek's three-volume historical novel *Mezi proudy* (Between the Streams, 1891).[2)]

Rabbi Abigdor Kara is the only medieval Prague rabbi of whom more is known than simply the name. He was the first personality of the ghetto to emerge from the anonymity of the medieval sources. There are several rabbis named in the Memorial Book of the Old-New Synagogue as having officiated there during the fifteenth century, but none of them seem to have left any writings. Rabbi Jizchak Mar-

וידבר

במדבר

יהוה אל־משה במדבר סיני באהל
מועד באחד לחדש השני בשנה
השנית לצאתם מארץ מצרים לאמר׃
שאו את־ראש כל־עדת בני־ישראל
למשפחתם לבית אבתם במספר
שמות כל־זכר לגלגלתם׃ מבן עשרים
שנה ומעלה כל־יצא צבא בישראל
תפקדו אתם לצבאתם אתה ואהרן׃
ואתכם יהיו איש איש למטה איש
ראש לבית־אבתיו הוא׃ ואלה שמות
האנשים אשר יעמדו אתכם לראובן
אליצור בן־שדיאור׃ לשמעון שלמיאל
בן־צורי־שדי׃ ליהודה נחשון בן־
עמינדב׃ ליששכר נתנאל בן־צוער׃ לזבולן אליאב
בן־חלן׃ לבני יוסף לאפרים אלישמע בן־עמיהוד
למנשה גמליאל בן־פדה־צור׃ לבנימן אבידן בן־
גדעני׃ לדן אחיעזר בן־עמישדי׃ לאשר פגעיאל בן־
עכרן׃ לגד אליסף בן־דעואל׃ לנפתלי אחירע בן־
עינן׃ אלה קריאי העדה נשיאי מטות אבותם ראשי
אלפי ישראל הם׃ ויקח משה ואהרן את

18

59/
Illustration in the Pentateuch published in Prague in 1530.

galit, who died in Prague in 1525 and was buried in the Old Jewish Cemetery, was the first recorded author, with his often quoted *Rules for divorce documents* and other collections of religious rulings frequently called upon by later writers.[3])

אלה

הדברים אשר דבר משה אל כל ישראל בעבר הירדן במדבר בערבה מול סוף בין פארן ובין תפל ולבן וחצרת ודי זהב: אחד עשר יום מחרב דרך הר שעיר עד קדש ברנע: ויהי בארבעים שנה בעשתי עשר חדש

Rabbi Jizchak Margalit lived at a time when the first Hebrew books were being printed in Prague. During the sixteenth century this printing press became a pillar of strength for the spiritual life of Jewish communities not only in Prague but throughout the Lands of the Czech Crown. It was also the direct cause of many confrontations with the spiritual and the secular authorities of the day, as we saw in the last chapter. The Prague Jewish community assumed great importance for the whole of Central Europe at the beginning of the new age, thanks to this, the first Hebrew press to be established north of the Alps, only forty years or so after the very first in Europe was set up in Rome in 1473. In Prague, the first texts to be printed were by Meir ben David, Shelomo ben Samuel the Levite, Mordechai bez Eliezer and Shemariah ben David, financed by two wealthy members of the congregation. Jeshaja ben Asher, ha-Levi Horowitz, and Jekutiel ben Isaac Dan, known as Zalman Bumsla, printed a book of prayers (1512), followed two years later by a volume of hymns of praise. That same year the press began issuing the Pentateuch with the commentary by Shelomo ben Isaac, known as Rashi. By this time the team of printers had changed; it now comprised Gershom ben Salomon ha-Cohen, Chayyim ben David Schwarz, and Jacob Epstein the Levite. In 1527 Ferdinand I gave Gershom ha-Cohen the monopoly of Hebrew printing, and he founded a long and famous line of Hebrew publishers. There can be no doubt that the Hebrew books printed by this press played a very important part in Jewish religious and cultural life, particularly at times when the Prague community suffered under edicts of expulsion (in 1541 and again in 1557). The successor to Rabbi Jizchak Margalit, Rabbi Abraham ben Abigdor, who died in 1542, was already able to see his commentary on the codex of Jacob ben Asher, and his books of prayers, in print.[4])

Between 1541 and 1564 the Jews of Prague

60/
Illustration in the Pentateuch published in Prague in 1530.

were twice forced to leave the city for temporary exile. This period of uncertainty was decidedly not favourable for printing Hebrew books, and no new titles are recorded. It was not until after 1568, four years after the return from the second exile, that the press became active again. During 1580—1600 there were several new titles issued each year. Hebrew books were still published after the fateful year 1618, the revolt of the Czech nobility, although diminished in numbers, and continued during the early years of the Thirty Years' War which the revolt unleashed, after the Hapsburgs triumphed at the Battle of the White Mountain. It was not until the 1630s that there came a longer pause in the work of the Hebrew press.[5]

The reign of Rudolph II favoured the press, which flourished during 1580—90 and during the first ten years of the next century. The Emperor encouraged Jewish learning, and at the same time the Prague community enjoyed for many years the efficient leadership of the wealthy and enlightened Mordechai Meisl. This was also a time when several outstanding European scholars were living and working in Prague, among them rabbis whose works were printed for the first time by the Prague Hebrew press.

It is indeed remarkable how cosmopolitan the Prague Jewish community was in the sixteenth century. Rabbi Eliezer Ashkenazi ben Elijah Rofe, who confirmed the statutes of the Burial Society recently established in the community (in Hebrew *Chevra kaddisha de gomle chassadim,* from Genesis 47, 29: Deal kindly and truly with me), came from Egypt, over Cyprus and Venice, serving as rabbi in Cremona and Poznan before coming to Prague, and went on to serve in Cracow, where he died in 1586. His book *The Work of God (Ma'ase ha Shem)* includes a commentary on the historical parts of the Pentateuch, and was printed in Venice. The chief rabbi in Prague in 1580—90 was Jizchak ben Abraham Chayyut, whose family came from Provence. Two of his works were printed in Prague: *A sermon for the first day of Pesach* and *A song for the eve of Pesach,* the first undated, the second published in 1587. In the early nineties Rabbi Jizchak ben Abraham

ויקרא

אל־משה וידבר יהוה אליו
מאהל מועד לאמר׃ דבר
אל־בני ישראל ואמרת
אלהם אדם כי־יקריב מכם
קרבן ליהוה מן־הבהמה מן
הבקר ומן־הצאן תקריבו
את־קרבנכם׃ אם־עלה
קרבנו מן־הבקר זכר תמים
יקריבנו אל־פתח אהל מ
מועד יקריב אתו לרצנו
לפני יהוה׃ וסמך ידו על
ראש העלה ונרצה לו לכפר
עליו׃ ושחט את־בן הבקר

61/
Illustration in the Pentateuch published in Prague 1530.

שפוך

חמתך על הגוים

אשר לא ידעוך ועל

הממלכות אשר

בשמך לא

קראו

שפוך עליהם זעמך וחרון

אפך ישיגם תרדוף באף

ותשמידם מתחת שמי ה'

62/
The title page of the *Haggadah* published in Prague in 1526. Woodcut. Facsimile in the State Jewish Museum, Prague.

Chayyut left for Poland, and his place was taken by Rabbi Mordechai ben Abraham Jafe, born in Prague but previously serving in Poland. Several parts of this rabbi's encyclopaedical work *Lebushim* (Raiment) were printed in Prague, but not until after his death around 1620.[6)]

Although his term of office was not the longest, the most famous Prague rabbi of those days was Jehuda Loew ben Bezalel, known in popular tradition as the Great Rabbi Loew and in Jewish religious writings as *MaHaRaL,* an abbreviation of his official title (*morenu ha-rab-rabbenu,* our rabbi and teacher) together with his surname Loew. For later generations Rabbi Loew became almost a fairy-tale figure, a remarkable magician whose profound knowledge of the Cabala (still believed by many people to be Jewish magic) enabled him to bring to life a clay figure, Golem, to be his servant. There are other legends, too, concerning Rabbi Loew and Rudolph II, the rabbi's battle with an angel, and many others. Some of these tales derive from the writings of one of his descendants who lived in the early eighteenth century, Moshe Meir Perls.[7)]

In reality Rabbi Loew was a Hebrew scholar in the true sense of the word, as well as being an outstanding representative of Jewish religious and cultural life not only in the Prague ghetto but throughout Central Europe. He was born about 1520 in a scholarly family. His grandfather, Rabbi Chayyim, came from Worms, and his eldest son Bezalel, the father of our Rabbi Loew, was also a rabbi, as in their turn were Rabbi Loew's three elder brothers. From 1553 to 1573 Rabbi Loew was regional rabbi in Mikulov in Moravia, before coming to the Talmudic school in Prague. When Rabbi Jizchak Meling died in 1583 it was expected that Rabbi Loew would become Prague's chief rabbi, but the choice fell on Rabbi Jizchak ben Abraham Chayyut, who was incidentally related to Rabbi Loew's wife. Rabbi Loew then left Prague for Poznan, but six years later, when Rabbi Chayyut quarrelled with the Prague elders and resigned his office, we find Rabbi Loew back in Prague, preaching on the 'High Sabbath' before Pesach, in 1589. This ceremony was usually entrusted to the Chief Rabbi, yet once again Rabbi Loew was not chosen. However, although the office fell to Mordechai ben Abraham Jafe, Rabbi Loew remained in Prague, teaching. He was considered a great authority, and in 1592 was received in audience by the emperor. That same year he was elected Chief Rabbi of Poznan and left Prague, only to return in 1597, at last in the office of Chief Rabbi. Here he died in 1609, the last years of his life being the most fruitful. As his epitaph tells us, he was the author of no less than fifteen works, most of which (nine books, three sermons and one memorial speech) appeared during his lifetime, several of them printed in Prague. Three other works he himself referred to were never printed and have not survived in manuscript.

Rabbi Loew was the most significant and most original of all the scholars of the Prague ghetto. His learning covered many fields, and besides Jewish religious philosophy and rabbinical wisdom, he wrote on ethical and educational questions. His work also differs from that of other scholars from the Prague ghetto in that he did not deal with halachist questions of Judaic law, but rather with religio-philosophical interpretation of the Haggadah, which comprises the narrative sections of the Talmud, and with other traditional Jewish literature.

His teachings reflect the Renaissance synthesis of traditional Judaism and the philosophy of the medieval Renaissance Jews, and he often employs philosophical terminology imbued with a religious content. There are traces of Jewish mysticism, cabalist thinking, although Rabbi Loew was not a true cabalist and did not use cabalist terminology.

He had a strong social conscience, seen not only in his ethics, but also in his conception of man in society. We could mention, for instance, his belief that all nations had a right to their own life, and his theory that society passed from the stage of all against all towards a harmonious social order.

Then too, Rabbi Loew was strongly influenced by the religious and ethical teachings of the original Hasidic movement (The Pious) which preceded the modern Hasidism of eighteenth century Eastern Europe. This later movement, not surprisingly, took over the religious and ethical ideas of Rabbi Loew and regarded him as its predecessor.

He made a considerable contribution to the history of education, elaborating a reform of Jewish education which in many ways points forward to the ideas of Jan Amos Komenský (Comenius; 1592—1670). Rabbi Loew rejected the formal scholasticism of Jewish schools in his day. His guiding principle was that teaching should move from the simpler to the more complex by a logical process, keeping in mind not only the matter to be taught but also the age and talents of the pupil. Among his modern educational ideas and observations, he stressed the importance of the pupil understanding what was learned. Besides the study of Talmudic texts he stressed the need to study the Bible itself (the Torah) and the Mishna.

The ideas put forward by Rabbi Loew can only really be traced for a time in the writings of his disciples, while his own works were forgotten until the 1790s, when they were revived by the popular movement of Hasidism in Eastern Europe. For his own contemporaries Rabbi Loew's ideas were beyond their comprehension, nor did they find an audience.[8)]

Rabbi Loew was followed in office by Ephraim Shelomo ben Ahron, brought from Łęczyca in 1604 to help the ageing rabbi. He was a popular and famous preacher, but although some of Rabbi Loew's ideas do appear in his sermons and an interpretation of the Pentateuch (printed during his lifetime), he did not attain the level of his teacher and predecessor in office.

Ephraim Shelomo died in 1619, and was followed as chief rabbi of Prague by Jomtob Lipman Heller of Wallerstein in Bavaria. He became famous for his commentary to the Mishna published in Prague in 1614—17. He was also the first Prague rabbi to write an autobiography. It was not published, however, until almost two centuries after his death, in 1836. His tenure of the Prague rabbinate was brought to an end by 'information laid' that he was involved in a treason plot being tried in Vienna, and only a great deal of money changing hands got him out of prison,

63/
L. Šaloun: Rabbi Loew. Statuary on the corner of the new Old Town Hall, Prague, 1908—11.

although there was certainly no truth in the allegations. He did not return to Prague, but died in Cracow in 1654. He is regarded as the most important disciple of Rabbi Loew, carrying on his teacher's line of thought. The latter encouraged him to write the commentary to the Mishna mentioned above, which became obligatory, in part or in full, in all editions of the Mishna. He also wrote a commentary to the Talmud compendium of Asher ben Jechiel, who died in Toledo, Spain, in 1327.

David Gans was a contemporary of Rabbi Loew, a disciple and an admirer, but his work took a different form. Born in Lipstadt, Westphalia, in 1541, he came to Prague at the age of twenty-three, and became the first Hebrew chronicler. His *Zemach David* (The Branch of David) was published in Prague in 1592. It comprises a chronicle of the world, and a chronicle of the Jewish people. The book is of inestimable value for the light it throws on life in the Prague ghetto, since it describes many events he experienced himself, and others based on reliable eye-witness reports. Gans was also interested in mathematics and astronomy. He paid several visits to Tycho de Brahe in his observatory in the imperial castle at Benátky on the river Jizera. De Brahe had been in Prague since 1599. Gans also knew Johannes Kepler. He published a short handbook on astronomy for the instruction of his sons. Entitled *Magen David* (The Shield of David), it was printed in Prague in 1612. A longer astronomical text was not published until 1754. Like Rabbi Loew, David Gans was typical of progressive Renaissance thought.[9)]

Rebecca (known as Rivka), the daughter of Meir Tikotin, was the first Jewish woman writer of Prague. She died at the beginning of the seventeenth century. She was the author of a short work on infant and child care, a handbook for midwives and young mothers, which was actually published twice (Prague 1609 and Cracow 1612). It is known only from quoted excerpts, as no copy has survived.[10)]

From the early seventeenth century the Jewish scholars of Prague tried to bring the mystic writings of the Cabala within reach of the ordinary people. Jissachar Ber ben Moshe Petachia published several studies of the basic cabalist work, the book of *Zohar,* as early as 1609—10. Later the works of important Palestinian scholars in that field were printed in Prague, particularly those of Isaac Ashkenazi Luria. Among local authors of books

דרוש נאה

ומשובח שדרש הגאון
האלוף בֿי במהרר יהודה בר
בצלאל זצל

בשבת תשובה בקק פראג בבית
הכנסת החדשה

נדפס פה קק פראג הבירה תחת ממשלת
אדונינו הקיסר רודולפוס ירה :

על ידי מרדכי בר גרשם הכהן זצל ומחוקק

64/
The title page of the 'Pleasant Sermon' of Rabbi Loew, *derush na'e,* 1583.

on the Cabala were two members of the well-known Horowitz family, Shabbatai ben Akiba and Jeshaja ben Abraham, whose *Two Tablets of the Covenant* was printed in several editions. Reuben Hoschke of Prague published two collections of excerpts from the entire cabalist literature, in 1660.[11)]

During the seventeenth century works in Yiddish were increasingly being published. Ordinary people, and women, rarely knew Hebrew, and there was a need for light reading, as well as works of devotion. Various translations and paraphrases of the Bible, often in verse, were published from the beginning of the century, as well as moral and religious reading: anthologies of excerpts from Talmudic and rabbinical literature, with explanatory notes. Among the lighter works printed in Prague or imported from elsewhere, travellers' tales of the journey to Palestine were very popular. One such book was the work of the Prague-born Gerson ben Eliezer Levi. Jewish ballads and songs were also printed. Some were of a religious nature, others dealt with historical events and catastrophes like the 'French' fire, which laid low the Old and Jewish Towns in 1689, persecutions, wars and plagues. Some songs were about the imperial family. Besides these serious ballads there were amusing songs like the *Three Obstinate Women* and there were chivalrous love stories. Historical works in prose were meant both for entertainment and instruction, like the story of the siege of Prague by the Swedes in 1648 written by Jehuda Loeb ben Isaac of Prague, or the Turkish siege of Vienna in 1683, by Meir Schmelka, who had kept a diary of the event. He, too, came from Prague. Stories about King Solomon were pure entertainment, as was the popular tale of a proselyte who married the Queen of the Demons in Western India. There were two Jewish women writers in seventeenth century Prague, Bella Horowitz and Rachel Raudnitz, who joined forces to write *The Story of the Time when there were no Jews in Prague,* published in 1701.[12)]

In the difficulties and uncertainties of Jewish life in Prague and throughout the Lands of the Czech Crown, the community needed people of business acumen, capable of acquiring some degree of influence in city and regional affairs. There were a number of such personalities in the ghetto from time to time, but we can only mention the best known and most important.

Among the wealthy and influential families in the Jewish Town in the sixteenth century was that of the Horowitz — their epitaphs speak of them in biblical words as 'a wall unto

65/
Haskara, the entry in the Memorial Book of the Old-New Synagogue, devoted to Rabbi Loew and his wife, Perl.

us, and they stood in the breach'. This referred to their success in protecting the whole community by the influence they achieved through their wealth. The name Horowitz comes from the Czech town of Hořovice, where the family originated. They were of the tribe of Levi, and the forerunners of many famous scholars and musicians. The father of the Prague branch of the family was probably Asher the Levite, son of Joseph. He was the Jewish mayor in 1481, and in Czech sources he was called Seligman or Žalman Hořovský (i.e. from Hořovice). His son Meir, buried in the Old Cemetery in 1520, inherited from his father-in-law Rabbi Jisrael Pinchas, what was one of the biggest houses in the ghetto at that time. Called 'U erbů' (At the coats of arms); the building housed a synagogue as early as 1492. Meir's brother Jeshaja was of more significance for the cultural life of the community, as a member of the consortium financing the first Hebrew printing press. On Jeshaja's death his duties in this respect were to be taken over by his eldest son Ahron Meshullam, but instead, in his proud arrogance, he quoted I Kings 12, 10—11: 'My little finger shall be thicker than my father's loins... my father hath chastised you with whips, but I will chastise you with scorpions.' Jeshaja's wife Rivka died in June 1515, and her gravestone is still in the Old Cemetery. He himself died either the same year or early in the next, as the *haskara,* the entry in the Memorial Book of the Old-New Synagogue testifies; it is dated 276, which unless the exact date is added, could be either 1515 or 1516. We do not know whether his gravestone has disappeared, or whether he was buried somewhere else, but stones of two of his sons are preserved in the Old Cemetery — that of the arrogant Ahron Meshullam and of the younger Shabbatai. The older son is frequently referred to in contemporary Czech and German sources, under the name Zalman Munka. He was without doubt not only the most influential but also the richest man in the community. The tax census for 1518—40 put his property at 15,000 Rhine guilders (largely in the form of property and securities). Ahron Meshullam was able to get exceptional privileges for himself and his family from King Louis Jagellon. Two members of the family were always to be among those elected to the Council of Elders, two were elected as members of the committee of the Jewish tax collectors, and the family were to have the right to choose one of the rabbis. The value of his property as listed was probably lower than in reality, for the Czech Chamber wrote to King Ferdinand in 1534 estimating its worth at 40,000 Rhine guilders. The king confirmed this privilege for Ahron's son Jisrael, in 1545. Already in his father's lifetime this uniquely privileged position of one man and one family had caused trouble in the community. The conflicts assumed such proportions that the rabbis of Poland and Germany decided that something would have to be done about the state of the ghetto in Prague. They called on Rabbi Joselmann, and together with the Chief Rabbi of Prague, Abraham ben Abigdor, he drew up a memorandum of twenty-three points aimed at settling the matter. Four hundred men were in agreement and willing to sign the memorandum, but the Horowitz party was so strong that they were willing to go to any lengths, even to assassinate Rabbi Joselmann. Three times he was forced to take refuge in Prague Castle. They then proceeded to accuse him of dishonesty, but failed because he had the support of influential rabbis in the surrounding countries, and in Austria and Italy. The Horowitz clan persisted in their accusations and the continuing conflict was one of the reasons for the expulsion of the Jews in 1541. The Czech Chamber had been wrongly informed about Joselmann's mission, and thought the Prague Jews had invited a foreign rabbi to their community without royal permission. It is a pity that the memorandum has not survived, so we cannot know what those twenty-three points were.

Since Ahron Meshullam was one of the Council of Elders, thanks to the privileges granted him, he was given a 'glejt' allowing him and his family to remain in Prague. Granted in 1542, this permission was renewed in 1544 and 1545. He figures frequently (as Ahron Meshullam or as Zalman Munka) in the Old Town books of contracts and debts in the first half of the sixteenth century, from 1507 until his death in 1545. Other Jews' names are far less frequent. Loans, purchases, sales and parcelling up of properties are recorded, while his many lawsuits are entered in the records of the Czech Chamber. From all we know of him, Ahron Meshullam must have been a very difficult man. In 1533 he was even accused of high treason, his home searched and his papers and property sealed. Yet only one year later Ferdinand confirmed all the special privileges granted to Ahron by Louis Jagellon. Ahron was at the root of many conflicts within the community itself, but his privileged position, and his connections with influential Czech noblemen, made him a powerful defender of his fellow Jews. He had special claim on the favour of Zdeněk of Rožmitál, the highest placed burgrave in the Czech kingdom, to whom he lent large sums of money up to the latter's death in 1535. Ahron is also remembered for building the Pinkas Synagogue in 1535. The memorial plaque he had placed there is still to be seen in the synagogue and is recorded in his epitaph.

Ahron Meshullam was not the only outstanding member of the Horowitz family. His younger brother Shabbatai, called Šeftl in Czech sources, while not such a wealthy man as his brother, is described in his epitaph as the head, the teacher, and the judge of the community. Although he is praised for his eloquence and his knowledge of the Scriptures, he is nowhere described as rabbi. His son Abraham Horowitz, the author of several books printed in Prague and in Poland at the turn of the sixteenth to seventeenth centuries, was a rabbi, while Shabbatai's grandson Jeshaja was Chief Rabbi of Prague from 1614 to 1621. He was the author of the famous *Shene luchot ha-berit* (The Two Tablets of the Covenant). Jochebed, the wife of Shabbatai Horowitz, died in 1551 and was buried in the Old Cemetery. She was the daughter of Rabbi Akiba of Budín, whom tradition called a great 'gaon' (great personality) and prince of the Exile. Rabbi Akiba held office in Prague, where he died in 1495 or 1496. We cannot say whether all that Moshe Meir Perls said of him in his *Megillat Juchasin* is true, but his daughter Jochebed was certainly married to Shabbatai Horowitz. Rabbi Akiba donated a lamp and a curtain to the Pinkas Synagogue

66/
Joseph Shelomo del Medigo. Etching by W. Delff in 1628, from a portrait by W. C. Duyster.

while he was still alive, that is to say some time before 1495.

Ahron Meshullam's heir was his eldest son Jisrael Horowitz, who died in 1572. He was not a scholar, but an important man in the community who served many times in the Council of Elders. His son Pinchas became a rabbi and went to Cracow, where he married the sister of the famous Cracow rabbi, Jisrael Isserles. There was another Pinchas Horowitz serving as rabbi in Prague at the beginning of the seventeenth century, but it is not known which branch of the family he belonged to. That he was one of the Prague Horowitz clan seems certain, since he was a Levite and also a member of the Pinkas Synagogue council, an office reserved for descendants of Ahron Meshullam, the founder. Pinchas Horowitz held office in Prague from 1610 to 1616, then in Fulda, whence he returned to Prague at some date unknown. He was a member of the rabbinical court, and was known both for his learning and for his work as a teacher. His wife Lipet was a granddaughter of Rabbi Loew.[13]

In the last third of the sixteenth century Mordechai Meisl played the same role in the Jewish community as Ahron Meshullam before him. Indeed he was far more commendable, for he was no bullying tyrant but a man of reason, kind and unselfish, given to acts of charity and mindful of the good of the community. He was a remarkably successful businessman whose enterprises never seemed to fail. He was a member of the Council of Elders from 1576, and later head of the Jewish community. Contemporary sources make it clear that he lent money at interest, even the imperial family itself being among his debtors. In 1581, for example, he lent the Empress Marie 2,000 thalers for 'kitchen supplies'. He also traded in various commodities, gold and silver (the Emperor Rudolph himself bought a valuable gold goblet from him), wool, unguents and so on, all wholesale. He also lent money on security, principally pawned jewels: the lady Marie of Pernštejn pawned jewels and gold plate with him in 1593, to the value of 2,541 thalers. When these valuables were redeemed four years later by Marie's sister-in-law, the lady Polyxena of Rožmberk, the interest on the loan amounted to 2238 thalers, little less than the value of the articles themselves. One thaler a week was the interest he demanded for a loan of sixty. Rudolph II was well-disposed towards Mordechai (Mark in the Czech sources) Meisl, and granted him many personal privileges. In 1591 Meisl received permission to build a synagogue. Since — in the words of the imperial decree — 'he gave us loyal service at any time, gladly', he was granted the extra privilege that neither he nor his heirs would have to pay taxes on this synagogue, and what was even more striking, to the end of Meisl's life no person would have the right to enter his house or his synagogue in order to check on him, nor the right to interfere in his commercial undertakings. Nor was this the only privilege the emperor granted him. In 1592 he was given special permission to lend money against bonds and register them officially with the supreme burgrave. Thus the ancient procedure abrogated at the beginning of the sixteenth century was renewed for Mordechai Meisl. A year later the emperor issued an edict taking Meisl, his wife and his property under royal protection in the case of complaints brought against him by Christians either in anger or for revenge. All these privileges were reconfirmed by Rudolph in 1598, with a paragraph specifying that Meisl, a financier who had served the empire well in the war against the Turks, could dispose of his wealth as he wished, and leave it to whomever he appointed. If he should die without an heir, the nearest relatives could inherit. This privilege was all the more valuable because both of Mordechai's marriages were childless.

All that Meisl did for the Jewish community is recorded in his epitaph, and again in great detail in the chronicle *Zemach David* (1592) by his contemporary, David Gans. The chronicler calls him a maecenas of learning, a hero of charitable works, a father to the poor and the tireless friend of his fellow Jews, and the head of the merchant estate. He himself paid for the building of the High Synagogue, donating many rolls of the Torah as well as gold and silver vessels to many synagogues in Prague, Poland, and Jerusalem. He had a *mikvah* for women built in Prague,

ספר אילם

המשלח מעיינים בנחלים לצר עילאה ימלל מילים ובו שתים עשרת
עינות מים ושבעים תמרים · כאהלים נטע ה׳ פוללים
שאלות נשגבות נוראות ממעונות אריות
מהררי נמרים ·
ישאול שאל הרב הכולל התורני ערינו העצני כמו״הר״ר זרח בר
נתן נר״ו מהרב השלם הפלוסוף הרופא האלוף כמו״הר״ר
יוסף שלמה דילמידגו נר״ו
איש קנדיאה ·
ועוד ניתוספו כתבי שאלות ותשובות מלאות חכמה כנשם
נרבות מהרב י׳ ש״ר הנ״ל ותלמידיו כלם למורים ברורים
נכוחים וישרים משמחי לב ·

נדפס פה העיר המהוללה אמשטרדם
בבית מנשה בן ישראל והוגה על ידו :
והיתה התחלתו בחדש אלול ·
שנת ומלאה הארץ דעה את יי לפרט קטן

67/
Joseph Shelomo del Medigo.
The title page of his book *Elim*,
Amsterdam, 1629.

as well as almshouses for the sick and the poor. He had the streets of the Jewish Town paved with stone, and last of all built the magnificent synagogue that bears his name, at a cost of over 10,000 thalers. He was also responsible for enlarging the Old Cemetery and for building nearby a 'meeting place for scholars', one of the three smaller buildings known as 'klaus', which stood on the site of the present Klaus Synagogue.

In accordance with the terms of the privilege granted him by imperial edict, Mordechai Meisl wrote his will on 1 March 1601, in the presence of the rabbis Jehuda Loew, Joachim Brandeis and Meir Epstein, and of Kaufmann Loewi, the official scribe of the community. The will sets out the arrangements to be made with the cities of Poznan and Cracow, both of them owing him considerable sums of money. The revenue accruing from his synagogue was to go to the poor, according to an earlier legacy referred to in his will. His banner was to become the property of the synagogue, and his brother's sons were to take care of the curtain, the mantle of the Torah, and other articles he had presented to the synagogue. His books were to be divided between his wife Frumet and his nephews. There were numerous other bequests of money to relatives and other individuals, totalling over 50,000 Rhine guilders. His two nephews were also to inherit his big house, as well as other buildings next to it with an entrance from the street. A codicil in the will referred to seats in the synagogue.

Not a week had passed since the signing of the will, and Mordechai was still alive, when the Emperor Rudolph II ordered that his decree allowing Meisl to write his testament freely, registered in the office of the supreme burgrave, should be crossed off the record and thus made invalid. Nor was that all: the emperor ordered his public prosecutors to examine the abrogated decree which he himself had issued. The report the prosecutors drew up covered all the stipulations of the imperial decree, although in reality only one was of importance for them: the right to write his testament freely. That right, in the view of these 'experts', could only be granted to noblemen and free gentlemen, and in exceptional cases to men of burgher status. The Jew Meisl, like all the Jews under the Czech crown, was in law the emperor's bondman, and indeed his prisoner, and did not belong to any of the relevant social categories. According to the laws of the kingdom, he had therefore no right to anything at all. In fact, the prosecutors were accusing the emperor of acting against the law, and they did not discuss the question of whether the emperor, as head of state, had the right to issue decrees running counter to the law. Nor indeed was Rudolph interested in the legal aspect of the matter. When Mordechai Meisl died, the em-

68/
The Prague physician Issachar Baer ben Jehuda Leb Teller. Portrait in his book *A Well of Live Water,* published in 1694.

peror's gratitude for services rendered died too, to be replaced by the conviction that the Jew's great wealth would be a useful addition to the imperial treasury, which suffered permanently from vast expenditure in excess of its limited revenue. Meisl died on 13 March 1601, and four days later bailiffs of the Czech Chamber confiscated his movable property, carrying away jewels, precious silverware, bonds, clothes and loose coins, said to be worth 45,000 Rhine guilders altogether. Nor was that all. Later tradition has it that the bailiffs came a second time and took away 471,250 guilders, but there is no confirmation of this in the contemporary sources. We do not know whether Mordechai was really so rich, but his wealth must have been considerable for it to be worth the emperor's while to go through the procedure of abrogating his own decree. To give some idea what the sums quoted meant at the time, the current expenses of the imperial court in the nineties of the sixteenth century amounted to between 400,000 and 550,000 Rhine guilders annually. The protests of Meisl's heirs and of the Jewish community were ineffectual, and two of the heirs, his nephews Shemuel Meisl and Moshe Kavka, were even sent to prison. After their release the authorities returned to them the two houses bequeathed them by their uncle, but with the explicit statement that this was 'not their right, but an act of clemency', and in part because Shemuel had paid debts owed by their uncle to butchers and to orphans. The Meisl inheritance was under constant scrutiny, and after the death of Rudolph a special commission was appointed to deal with the matter in 1614. It does not seem to have settled anything.[14)]

The last of these worthy men whose ability raised them above the average of their fellows in the ghetto and gave them access to the upper circles of Christian society where they could use their influence for the benefit of the community, was Jacob Bashevi. He came from Italy, and arrived in Bohemia with his brother Samuel in *c.* 1590. The name of Joseph Bashevi, Italian, is first found in the Old Town records of 1599; he may have been a member of the same family. We know practically nothing of what the brothers did after coming to Prague, but in 1599 the Emperor Rudolph was already according them privileges comparable to those enjoyed by Meisl. These privileges applied not only to the two brothers, but to their families and even to their servants. They were allowed to trade freely and to move about in all the lands of the Austrian crown and in the German states, without being obliged to wear the badge of Jewry. In addition, they had the right to be judged either by the emperor himself, or by a court appointed by him for the occasion. We do not know what they had done to deserve these privileges, but it can be assumed that in a short space of time they had shown themselves very capable merchants and financiers, willing to be of use to the imperial court. There is a record dating from 1610 of the purchase by Jacob Bashevi of a Christian-owned house on a corner in the parish of St Nicholas, at a price of 1,000 times three score of Czech groschen; the sum was to be paid by instalments. The following year King Matthias appointed him 'court Jew', directly subordinate to the supreme court marshal. At the same time the king confirmed all the privileges previously granted him by Rudolph. The culmination of Jacob Bashevi's career, however, came after the defeat of the Czech Estates' army in the Battle of the White Mountain. From 1621 onwards he bought up many houses in the vicinity of the ghetto, buying them from Protestants who refused to convert and sought religious freedom abroad. The Lord Lieutenant of Bohemia, Karl of Liechstenstein, officially transferred some houses to the ownership of Bashevi. The latter had been head of the Jewish community since 1616. In 1622 the Emperor Ferdinand II elevated him to the peerage — the first Jew ever to receive that honour — with the title of Treuenberg. At home in 'high' politics, Bashevi co-operated both with Liechtenstein and with Albrecht of Waldstein (Wallenstein). He was the tax collector and is also said to have had a share in the minting of the debased 'long' coins of the period. He used his influence to protect his fellow Jews in the Czech lands from the mercenaries of the emperor, who were no better than those of the enemy. He gave the Jewish town yet another synagogue, called the Great Court (Velkodvorská), dating from 1627 and built in Late Renaissance style.

Unlike Mordechai Meisl, Bashevi did not die peaceful and rich. His enterprises were often very risky, and were probably the cause of his fall. Early in 1631 he was arrested and imprisoned on what was certainly a trumped-up charge, and although he was later freed, he never regained his privileged position. He took refuge in Jičín under the powerful protection of his former patron, Albrecht of Waldstein. The fall of Albrecht, and his assassination at Cheb in February 1634, meant the end for Jacob Bashevi. What property he had was confiscated, and he died the same year, impoverished, at Mladá Boleslav, where he is buried.[15)]

In the seventeenth century, during and after the Thirty Years' War, none of the rabbis in Prague reached the importance and fame of Rabbi Loew and some of his disciples. Reuben, the son of Rabbi Hoschke and son-in-law of Rabbi Shelomo Ephraim Luntshitz, drew up an Index to cabalist literature and an Index to the Torah; he died in 1665. Ahron Simon Spira-Wedeles (the Pious) was Chief Rabbi from 1640 to 1679, but although he was revered as a holy man right up to the end of the nineteenth century for his ascetic life and his piety, he left no significant writings. On his death the office of Chief Rabbi should have passed to his son Benjamin, but the Prague community refused to accept him because 'he did not study but spent his time with low market people and idling in inns.' Instead they proposed two names, Gabriel of Eltsch in Poland and Abraham Brod of Roudnice. The choice dragged on for several years until the Archbishop of Prague, Jan Bedřich of Waldstein, was asked to settle the matter. He had no objections to the Polish rabbi, on condition he brought no Polish Jews to Prague with him. Rabbi Gabriel did indeed come to Prague and take office, but neither Abraham Broda nor Benjamin Wolf Spira-Wedeles came off too badly, since they shared the office of regional rabbi. Benjamin's son Elijah, who died young in 1712, is buried in the Old Jewish Cemetery. His epitaph praises his learning, and he did in fact leave a small but important body of work. He wrote a commentary to one of the parts the *Lebushim* of Mordechai Abraham Jafe for the new edition of that work published in 1689 and 1701, and also wrote a commentary on the *Shulhan aruch,* as well as notes on six tracts in the Talmud. These two works did not appear until well after his death, in 1757 and 1768 respectively.[16)]

An important Jewish scholar who spent the last years of his life in Prague during the second half of the seventeenth century was Joseph Shelomo del Medigo. Well learned in Jewish religious literature, he devoted himself primarily to astronomy. Born in 1592 at Candia in Crete, in a rabbinical family of Venetian origin, he learned Latin, Greek, Italian and Spanish from childhood, and besides the traditional Hebrew religious literature studied Greek and Roman philosophy, physics and astronomy. At the age of fifteen he went to Italy, and studied medicine (among other subjects) at the University of Padua. He was a pupil of Galileo. After seven years in Italy he returned to his native Candia, leaving in 1619 for Egypt. After some time in Cairo he moved to Constantinople, where he added the Cabala to his studies, and found it failed to catch his enthusiasm. He then travelled north through Moldavia to Lublin and Vilna. In eastern Europe he earned his living as a doctor, and for some time was personal physician to the Polish Prince Radzivill. Leaving eastern Europe for the west, he became a rabbi in Hamburg, moving successively to Glückstadt, Amsterdam, Frankfurt-am-Main, and finally Prague. Settling here towards the end of the Thirty Years' War, he died in Prague in 1655.

Although he wrote much, only three of his works were printed: *Elim,* published in Amsterdam in 1629, is a scientific work; the next is cabalist (Basel 1629—31); and the third, a letter to Rabbi Zerach ben Nathan of Troki not published until 1840, is part of a scientific discussion of his *Elim.* Del Medigo's principal work, *Bosmath bath Salomo* (Bosmath, daughter of Solomon) is known only from references to it in his own writings and those of his disciples. It was an encyclopaedic work covering all the branches of knowledge then studied, including philosophy and ethics as

69/
The Chief Rabbi of Prague, David ben Abraham Oppenheim. Portrait of 1718—36. From F. M. Pelzel's *Effigies virorum eruditorum.* Copperplate engraving by J. T. Kleinhardt and J. Baltzer.

well as the natural sciences. The manuscript has not survived, nor have we any description of the work, for Del Medigo would not allow any of his followers to study it. His *Elim* includes tracts on mathematical subjects, geometry and astronomy. It was very progressive for its time, and drew not only on Del Medigo's vast knowledge of ancient and contemporary writings, but on his own critical and highly original mind.[17)]

Two events of the second half of the seventeenth century had a considerable influence on life in the Prague ghetto. First, the rising against the nobility in the Ukraine, led by Bohdan Chmelnicki, in 1648, brought on bitter persecution of the Jews there. Jewish migration changed direction, and although it was regarded as most undesirable by the authorities, a great influx of Jews from Poland, Lithuania and the Ukraine came to swell the population of the ghettos in the Czech Lands. The second event was the emergence of Sabbatai Zewi (or Sewi), who was recognized as the Messiah by many Jews in the diaspora. The persecution he suffered brought him a large following in Jerusalem, Palestine, Syria and Smyrna. The movement then spread to Central Europe, and in the crowded ghetto of Prague conflicts between the orthodox and the followers of the new movement (which was soon pronounced heretical) became acute. Rabbi Jonathan Eybenschitz, who preached for a time in Prague, was one of those accused of the new heresy. He died as rabbi of Altona in 1764. Thanks to his good relations with the ecclesiastical authorities, he published several tracts on the Talmud; they are among the poorest printed in Prague (1728—39).[18)]

David Oppenheim, born in Worms, was regional rabbi of Moravia from 1689, officiating in Mikulov; in 1702 he was elected Chief Rabbi of Prague. His own writings were few, but he was well known for his remarkable collection of Hebrew books and manuscripts. He could afford to indulge his collecting hobby, having inherited a considerable fortune from his uncle Samuel Oppenheim the financier, who lent large sums to the Emperor Leopold to finance the war against the Turks. Oppenheim's library comprised about six thousand printed works and a thousand manuscript, the nucleus being a collection of books given to his uncle Samuel by Prince Eugene of Savoy. Oppenheim could not keep his library in Prague, where Hebrew books were subject to church censorship, and housed it with his kinsman in Hanover. The library remained in the family after its owner's death, and was later transferred to Hamburg, whence it was acquired complete by the Bodleian Library in Oxford. Oppenheim's own writings remained in the tradition of Talmudic rabbinical learning, but he also worked on a geographical and historical dictionary dealing with the topography of the Talmud.[19)] This was never published, and it is assumed that he did not complete it.

The last important rabbi of the eighteenth century was Ezechiel Landau, an authority on halachist questions whose word was accepted throughout Europe. He was born in 1713 in Opatów in Poland, and received the traditional rabbinical education in Vladimir, Volhynia, and Brody in Galicia. From 1746 a rabbi in Yampole on the upper Dniester, he was appointed Chief Rabbi of Prague and head of the *yeshiva* (Talmudic school) in 1755. A very learned scholar with an unusually acute mind, he was also extremely conservative in his views and clung to the orthodox traditions. He opposed all new ideas, particularly those of the Age of Enlightenment, which were having no little influence on eighteenth century Jewish life. His writings are made up mostly of traditional responses and interpretations of the Talmud. He was followed in office by his disciple Eleazar Fleckeles (1754—1828) who was equally orthodox, so that he rejected the Sabbatians and their later fraction the Frankists, as well as modernists who accepted the ideas of the Enlightenment. He wrote three volumes of responses. There were two more writers in the rabbinical tradition during the nineteenth century, Simon Lasch who died in 1868, and Shemuel Freund, a prolific halachist writer, who died in 1881.[20]

By the end of the eighteenth century the ideas of the Enlightenment had penetrated into the Prague ghetto, leading to efforts for the emancipation of the Jews, to put them on an equal footing with the other peoples of the Austro-Hungarian monarchy. The Jewish movement began in Berlin, where the philosopher Moses Mendelsohn (1729—86) and like-thinking workers for Jewish emancipation began publishing Hebrew language periodicals propagating enlightened ideas. Soon similar journals were being printed in Vienna. This development caused sharp conflicts between the followers of orthodox Judaism and the modernists, especially in the eastern parts of the Empire. In northern Italy, where assimilation of the Jews was much more advanced, these incidents were unknown. The orthodox position gradually lost ground in Bohemia and Moravia, but much still needed

70/
The Chief Rabbi Ezechiel Landau. Lithograph by F. Šír, *c.* 1830, from an earlier portrait.

to be done by way of training and education. One of the strategies chosen by the assimilation movement was the translation into Hebrew of great works of world literature, and particularly the German classics. Schiller was very popular, but Lessing, Herder and Goethe were also published in Hebrew. Gradually a 'modern Jewish literature' began to emerge, short pieces which found a place in almanacs and magazines. There were different trends within the emancipation movement in Prague. The more conservative wanted to free people's minds from superstition and fanaticism, while preserving the foundations of Judaism intact. The less orthodox worked for greater assimilation to Christian society. All were agreed, however, on the need to work first for Jewish emancipation.

Among the Jews in the Enlightenment movement in Prague, Herz Homberg of Libeň called for Jewish elementary schools to be set up in the spirit of the educational reforms instituted by the Emperor Joseph II. Others were Peter Beer, headmaster of the Jewish Normal School and himself a writer of historical and didactic works in the modern spirit. The brothers Baruch and Juda Jaiteles belonged to the more orthodox trend. The grandson of Chief Rabbi Ezechiel Landau, Moses Landau, greatly forwarded the movement in Prague. As owner of a prosperous printing works and head of the community, he also wrote short pieces for various magazines.[21)]

The nineteenth century also saw the birth of Jewish studies in the modern sense. The founders of this branch of learning were Leopold Zunz in Berlin, Samuel David Luzzatto of Trieste in Padua and Shelomo Jehuda Rapoport of Lvov. The last named was Chief Rabbi of Prague from 1844. After completing an edition of the Talmud, Rapoport applied the new methods of historical biblical criticism to forgotten periods of Jewish history which had never been researched. His major work was a series of biographies of old rabbinical authorities. He also planned a voluminous encyclopaedia of Talmudic life and institutions, of which only the first part, the letter Aleph, was completed. As a young man he wrote poetry, and adapted Racine's *Esther* as a religious

71/
Samuel Landau, head of the Jewish religious court in Prague. Lithograph by F. Šír, *c.* 1830.

performance for the feast of Purim. He wrote only in Hebrew, and besides his contributions to Viennese magazines he wrote introductions to the works of other authors. He corresponded with Luzzatto, who also contributed. Rapoport wrote the introduction to K. Lieben's collection of epitaphs from the Old Jewish Cemetery, *Gal-Ed,* published in 1856. He died in Prague in 1867.[22)]

The last important scholar linked to the Prague ghetto by his office was Rabbi Jindřich (Heinrich) Brody, as the ghetto itself was gradually disappearing. Born in Užhorod in 1862, he was trained in Talmudic schools in Carpathian Ruthenia and at the rabbinical seminary in Berlin. Chief Rabbi of Prague from 1913 to 1930, he died in Jerusalem in 1942. He was renowned for his knowledge of medieval Hebrew poetry, and published numerous critical editions.[23)]

72/
Unknown artist: Portrait of Eleazar Fleckeles, head of the Jewish religious court in Prague. Oil on canvas, mid-nineteenth century.

73/
A. Machek: Portrait of the Chief Rabbi of Prague, Shelomo Jehuda Rapoport. Oil on canvas, *c.* 1840.

/IV/ THE SYNAGOGUES OF PRAGUE

The synagogues and the Jewish Town Hall are the only historic buildings to have survived the slum clearance scheme which swept the Prague ghetto off the map. Not all the synagogues of the day survived, nor have all those still standing preserved their original appearance. Two late Renaissance synagogues, Cikán and Great Court (Velkodvorská), restored in early Baroque style after the fire of 1689, were not considered of architectural interest and fell victim to pick and spade. The same fate befell the Wechsler Synagogue which stood at the eastern end of Široká Street. Even before the clearance took place, the Old Shul in Dušní Steet, after several earlier changes, was destroyed and replaced by the pompous Temple. The eclectic architectural style of this building combined Renaissance proportions with Moorish decorative elements, which being of Oriental origin were thought appropriate to a Jewish house of prayer. The Old Shul disappeared without a trace, and nobody thought to investigate whether the building was not largely of medieval masonry. The loss of the Cikán and Great Court Synagogues is particularly sad, because they certainly represented pure Renaissance architecture even if we assume that their original appearance was probably hidden under repairs carried out after the 1689 fire.

Historically, the synagogue (in Hebrew *bet ha-kneset*) is a relatively late institution which came into being after the destruction of the Temple in Jerusalem in 586 B.C. The Temple, where sacrifices were offered, was the centre of religious life for the whole of Israel. Yet the religious traditions of the Jewish people had to be preserved, and so 'assembly houses' (in Greek *synagogé*) were built. This was where the people gathered to worship and pray. Burnt offerings and other sacrifices were no longer part of these gatherings, for they could only take place in the Jerusalem Temple. There were prayers, reading and interpretation of the Torah, sermons and discussions. Even when the Temple was rebuilt under the Maccabees (135—63 B.C.), these 'assembly houses' continued in use in Palestine until the fifth century A.D. when Theodosius II came to the throne. The situation of the Jews became unbearable. The Jerusalem patriarchate and the *sanhedrin* (Jewish Council — from the Greek *synedrion*) were abolished and most of the Jews scattered over Europe and parts of Asia and Africa. This was the diaspora (scattering) called *galut* in Hebrew, i.e. exile. Then the synagogues became the centre not only of religious life for the Jews, but a place where public affairs were administered. They also served as schools. Only gradually, and only in larger communities, were town halls built to accommodate the administration, and schools *(bet ha-midrash)* which might also be used for prayer. The Town Hall and a separate school were not built in Prague until 1560. From the beginning of the seventeenth century, however, it can be said that the synagogues of Prague were used only for worship.

Although the idea of the synagogue was brought with them from the Jewish home in Palestine, the architecture was influenced

74/
Inside the Old Shul. Etching dating from the 1860s. From the book by B. Foges and D. Podiebrad, *Altertümer der Prager Josefstadt,* Prague 1870.

both by the time and the place where synagogues were built. The earliest influence was that of the Roman basilica, as it was for the early Christian churches. In medieval Spain, Moorish architecture played an important role, as can be seen particularly in the two Toledo synagogues, La Blanca and El Transito, and that of Cordoba. All three were transformed into Christian churches after the Jews had been driven out of Spain. In the Romanesque and Gothic periods, synagogues built in Central and Western Europe were both single nave and double nave structures. Although the three-nave design was already usual for Christian churches, it is interesting that Jewish builders did not adopt it. There is no need to look for models for the single nave synagogue. It was the simplest way of building — so long as the space concerned was not too wide. It would be given either a ceiling resting on beams, or a barrel vault or groined vaulting over not too great a space. In view of the technical possibilities of the time, a wider building called for different treatment. This was where the double nave became useful. It was already used in the Christian world both for secular buildings such as the great halls of Romanesque palaces and large houses, several of which have survived in Prague, and for ecclesiastical architecture. Monasteries were frequently built in this way, especially the chapter-house. The Romanesque synagogue of Worms, for example, which was destroyed by the Nazis in 1938 and then completely razed to the ground in 1942, had a double nave with a six-partite groined vault resting on two piers along the main axis. The Jews of Regensburg also built a two-nave synagogue, known only from an engraving by Albrecht Altdorfer in 1519, when the Jews were expelled from the city and their synagogue destroyed. Although still Romanesque in style, the Regensburg synagogue was larger than the one in Worms, and vaulted with an eight-part groined vault resting on three piers placed along the main axis.

Contemporary Christian architecture was not the only influence on the form medieval synagogues took. As we have seen, the Palestinian tradition was formed by the specific character of the religious service, reflected primarily in the simple style of the interior. In the Ashkenazi synagogues of Western and Central Europe, the Ark of the Torah (in Hebrew the *aron ha-kodesh*) is placed on the east wall, the wall that faces Jerusalem. The synagogue has the same orientation as the Christian church, where the altar is also placed at the east end.

The fundamental part of synagogue worship is reading from the Torah. The Torah — the five books of Moses — is of the highest significance in the Jewish religion, and enjoys the utmost reverence, comparable to the Host in a Catholic church. It is written in Hebrew characters on a scroll of parchment, according to certain rules. The text must contain no mistake, and the scroll must be without blemish. A damaged scroll, or one with a mistake by the scribe, cannot be used. The scrolls of the Torah must be carefully preserved, and the reverence felt towards then is shown by the beauty of the ornament. A linen band, often beautifully embroidered, keeps the scrolls from unrolling. Then the Torah is wrapped in a special cloak, often of rare cloth such as brocade or velvet, and adorned with embroidery. A silver tip is added to the wooden rollers which hold the scroll, and there is a silver shield, a silver pointer *(yad)* shaped like a hand, and sometimes a silver or gilt crown. Thus adorned the Torah is laid in the Ark. In medieval synagogues this was a niche in the wall, fitted with a door, and sometimes, as in the Old-New Synagogue, with architectonic frame. In later centuries the *aron ha-kodesh* became more like a Christian altar. The visitor to the synagogue cannot as a rule see the elaborately ornamented door of the Ark, because in front of it hangs a curtain of rich cloth, often embroidered.

Besides the reading of the Torah, there are prayers to be sung or said, and sometimes a sermon will be given as in Christian churches. Most of the service, and particularly the readings from the Torah to which individual men are called, do not take place in front of the Ark, but in the centre of the synagogue, where there is a raised platform, often large, surrounded by an elegantly worked metal screen. This is the *almemor* (in Hebrew *bimah*), and in older synagogues the seats were placed around the almemor rather than turned towards the Ark.

Since only men could directly take part in the services, and women were not allowed in the main hall, what came to be known as women's galleries were built on, originally called the women's bay. These were not directly connected with the central nave, but built with open arches. 'Winter' synagogues were also built, where it was possible to provide heating in winter for those who came to pray.

There is no tower and no bell. Any suggestion of a tower or spire on the façade of a modern synagogue is purely decorative. The faithful were never called to prayer by bells, but by a synagogue employee known as the *shammes* (in Hebrew *shammash*), or in German *Schulklopfer,* a word derived from the word 'shul' used for the synagogue. The shammes went round the houses of those who regularly came to the synagogue, knocking on the door to announce that it was time for the service to begin. It was and still is a condition for the service to take place that there must be at least ten adult men — *minyan* — in the synagogue. If there is no minyan, there is no service, and each must pray on his own.

As in Catholic churches, a lamp burns perpetually in the synagogue, the *ner tamid.* In the vestibule there is a basin and a water tank, for the ritual washing of hands.

Since even the smallest Jewish society will meet regularly for prayers, we can assume that wherever there were a few Jewish families, there will have been at least one room set aside for prayers. Thus we are justified in thinking that the first Prague synagogue was contemporaneous with the first Jewish settlement. The first mention of a synagogue dates from 1124, in the outer bailey of Prague Castle. It can be assumed that it was built earlier, perhaps in the course of the tenth century. We do know that it was burned down when Conrad of Znojmo besieged Prague in 1142, and that it was never rebuilt.[1)]

The next synagogue was built on the other bank of the river Vltava, within the Old Town and close to the Church of the Holy Spirit (which was of course built later). This was the Old Shul, the religious centre for a small

75/
The east façade of the Old-New Synagogue. Langweil's model of Prague.

Jewish settlement which may have arisen after the Little Quarter synagogue was destroyed in 1142, but could have been even older. The written sources tell us nothing until 1315, and then again it is mentioned in 1389, when it was devastated during the great pogrom. According to ghetto tradition, nevertheless, it was 'the first and oldest shul, built many centuries ago', as we read when the community was pleading for its preservation after the fire of 1689. It is said there that after the pogrom it was not restored for about a hundred years, when at the end of the fifteenth century it was re-opened for Jews who had been expelled from Spain and Portugal. Some of the old prayers used in services at the Old Shul suggest that the congregation were *Sephardim.* Today we are not in a position to decide whether this was due to *Sephardim* arriving in the fifteenth century, or whether the original founders of the synagogue in the early Middle Ages were not Jews of oriental origin. Between the sixteenth and eighteenth centuries the synagogue is said to have been rebuilt several times, but it is more likely that repairs and alternations of varying degree are meant. We have detailed information about some of these. The shul was 'miraculously spared' during the fire of 1689, because — according to a report by the community in 1690 — it was built of stone, vaulted, and with a tiled roof. In 1693 Johann Baptista Allio was sent to inspect the shul, because the authorities had been informed that although the Jews were not allowed to restore it because it was to be demolished, they had repaired it. He found that a 'corner of the women's gallery' on the garden side, which had been damaged by fire, had indeed been rebuilt. However, this was a lean-to, and not the main building. Two sections of the roof had also been repaired, doubtless at the same corner. The gallery may have had a shingle roof. A new gate had also been made. Negotiations for the preservation of the Old Shul dragged on into 1704, and permission was only given after the Jews had paid the Emperor Leopold 20,000 Rhine guilders. The Archbishop of Prague then set certain conditions, because the Church of the Holy Spirit was very close: two windows were to be bricked up, the entrance moved to the other side, away from the church, and the wall surrounding the synagogue was to be made higher.[2)]

Unfortunately we do not know how much damage was done to the Old Shul by the fire of 1754. J. F. Shor drew a plan of the ghetto with a group of buildings which included the shul. The plan had no individual sites marked. The site was designated by the number 1, which should mean that all the buildings had burned down. Since the synagogue had walls and vaulting of stone, however, we can assume that only the wooden parts of the building suffered, and perhaps the roof beams, which could have caught fire under the tiled roof.[3)]

That the building retained its medieval appearance can be seen from Langweil's model of Prague, which shows it as an oblong structure with a span roof. The shorter sides ended in triangular gables. The longer south side was strengthened by simple buttresses between the five arched windows at irregular intervals — at the corner, and beyond the second and fourth window from the eastern end there are no buttresses. On the north and south sides there were low lean-to additions which probably served as a vestibule to the south and women's gallery to the north. There are two pointed windows in the east wall, and set higher up between them a third small window. On the side towards the Church of the Holy Spirit the shul yard is separated from the street by a high wall. A contemporary engraving shows that the single nave was vaulted, it would seem in Gothic lierne style. This would confirm the reconstruction said to have been carried out at the end of the fifteenth century. There is a gallery on the west wall which seems to be a later addition. The *aron ha-kodesh* takes the form of a Gothic altar, but it is difficult to say whether the engraving shows the original stone architecture, or a Neo-Gothic reconstruction, or a combination of the two. There is no almemor in the middle, but it is possible that the original almemor was removed in 1837, when the Old Shul became the first synagogue in Prague to introduce the reformed rite. There are two rows of pews arranged as in Christian churches. Leopold Zunz officiated in the Old Shul until 1845. He was an Oriental and Hebrew scholar, and one of the founders of biblical criticism. Later he moved to Berlin. The reformed rite allowed for the use of music, and so an organ was installed in the Old Shul, and the Czech composer František Škroup was put in charge of

76/
The Old-New Synagogue from the south-east. Photographed *c.* 1890.

the synagogue music. He was the author of both the first Czech opera and the Czech national anthem. He spent the time from 1836 to 1845 at the Old Shul.

Between 1840 and 1850 the interior of the Old Shul was given a Neo-Gothic look, the first synagogue in the ghetto to be changed in this way. Most of the congregation were wealthy Jews who were no longer satisfied with the Temple. In 1867 it was completely demolished, even its foundations, leaving no documentation that would have helped us to date the building.[4)]

It was replaced by the Spanish Synagogue, in a style that seemed imposing enough. Designed by Ignác Ullmann and Josef Niklas, it is an ecletic combination of Renaissance and Moorish elements both on the exterior of the

77/
The west façade of the Old-New Synagogue.

78/
The Old-New Synagogue from the north-east.

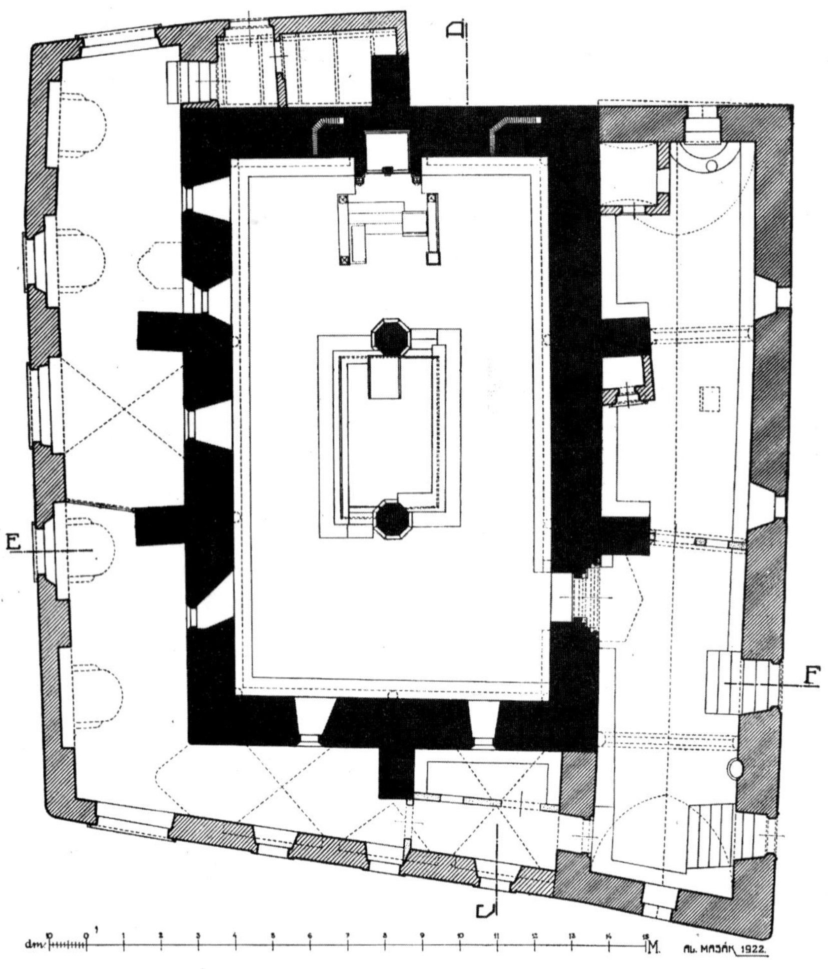

79/
The lay-out of the Old-New Synagogue on ground floor level.

building and inside. The main building work was completed in 1868, while the interior decoration took up to 1880. The Spanish Synagogue was the last to be built in the ghetto.

The second oldest synagogue in the ghetto, and today the oldest surviving building, is the Old-New Synagogue, originally known as the Big or New Shul. When the family synagogue of the Wechslers and the Duscheneses was built in Široká Street during the sixteenth century, also called the New Shul, it became necessary to find a distinguishing name for the older building. It was then called Alte neue Schule, in German, later shortened to Altneuschul — Old-New Shul or synagogue. The synagogue was built in the thirteenth century, at a time when the Old Town of Prague was being fortified, with much building going on there.

Today the Old-New Synagogue is the only example left of the double nave synagogue, as we have seen in the introduction to this chapter. It cannot be assumed that the influence of the double nave pillared halls of rich Prague houses on the design of the synagogue was a direct one. At that time the Jews moved about a great deal, in frequent contact with the Jews of neighbouring countries. It seems more logical that the Romanesque Worms synagogue, or the somewhat later one at Regensburg, dating from the first half of the thirteenth century, provided the model for the Prague building. The double nave plan, however, was carried out in the architectural forms of early Gothic. Yet it would seem that in Prague this basic scheme was enriched with some new symbolical features.

The outwardly simple oblong building of the Old-New Synagogue terminates at the east and west end in a tall stepped brick gable in the late Gothic style. As seen today, they bear marks of the purist restoration of the building by Josef Mocker, the architect, in 1883. The outer walls of the synagogue are strengthened by relatively low, solid buttresses, oblique towards the top, which are higher than the roofs of the low annexes built to the north, south and west sides of the building. There is one pier in each of the end walls, and two on either side wall. The double nave is roofed with six five-partite vaults resting on the octagonal piers. Why the five-partite form was chosen is a question often discussed. We believe that it sprang from the desire to employ the numerical symbolism so dear to Jewish mystics and cabalist thought. The Old-New Synagogue has twelve windows, five on each of the north and south sides, and two in the west wall. In order to keep the number of the tribes of Israel, twelve, the bays on the west wall are blind. The round windows in the east wall were not pierced until later. Originally there was only one small window above the Ark of the Torah. The round bosses of the vaulting have been given a similar leaf ornament to that on the corbels below the shafts of the ribs.

The Ark of the Torah — *aron ha-kodesh* — in stone, shows at least two stages. The pilasters on either side of the niche have a relief ornament of grapes and acanthus leaves, and terminate in chalice-shaped capitals repeating the acanthus motif and ending in pairs of spirals. The plinths are shaped like volute corbels resting on diamond bosses. The pilasters bear a cornice with bead moulding; the centre section is sunk. This is Renaissance work, but behind the cornice the original Gothic triangular tympanon rises, with a high relief ornament, a vine with leaves and bunches of grapes. The simple moulding framing the tympanon carries a design of crabs. It appears from the records of repairs carried out in the synagogue in the 1880s that the right pilaster was then in a very bad state, and had to be strengthened with metal bands. In 1920 the whole of the Ark was radically repaired. Both pilasters were taken to pieces and restored. Today the niche has a bronze door with beaten ornament, dating from the first half of the last century. Stone steps lead up to the Ark; on the left is a simple stone lectern for the cantor (*chazzan*). A sandstone balustrade on each side of the steps shows plate tracery; each ends in a column bearing the same motif in relief. They are topped by an obelisk, certainly also dating from the Renaissance. On the southern side the obelisk has been replaced by a moulded plinth bearing a flat stone on which the seven-branched candlestick stood. The stone benches along the south and north walls, now panelled in wood, have survived since the Middle Ages. In the centre, between the two pillars, stands the almemor, surrounded by a high wrought iron grille on

80/
Length-wise section of the Old-New Synagogue.

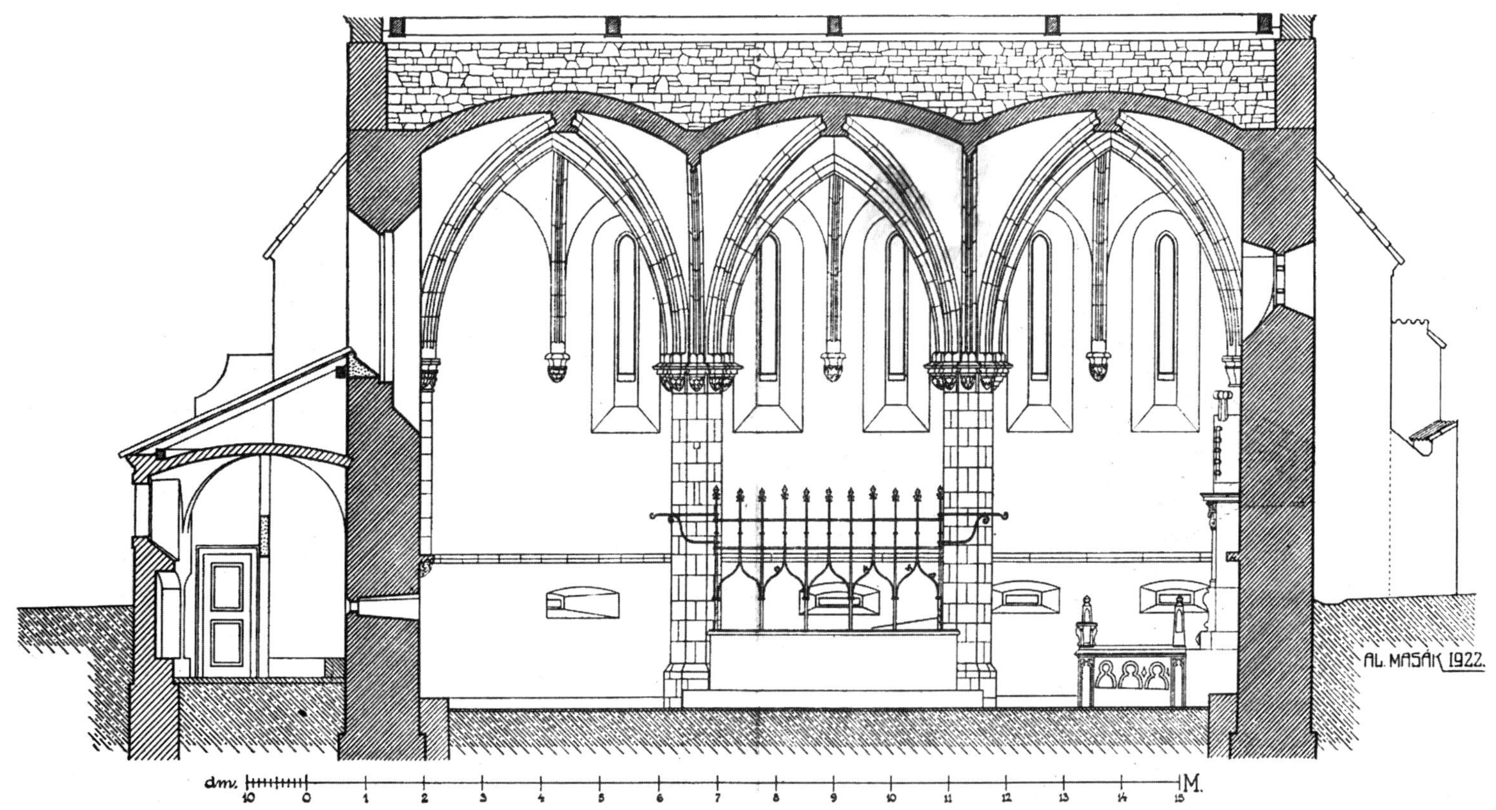

which late Gothic ogee arches are already combined with early Renaissance elements.

The only ornament on the outer walls of the synagogue, surrounded on three sides by low annexes, is the arched portal giving access to the main temple from the southern vestibule. The tympanum, over a plain lintel, is filled with a leaf and grape design, the spirally twisted branches growing from a vine with twelve roots, a clear symbol of the twelve tribes of Israel. The stiff character of the relief carving suggests a later stage of early Gothic. Earlier writers dated the synagogue as 1260, but a somewhat later date is now suggested, in the last quarter of the thirteenth century.

We have seen that the south, west and north walls of the synagogue are surrounded by low annexes, of which the south wall is the most interesting. At one time the archaic features of this vestibule were thought an argument for putting the date of the synagogue back in time, but there are several interesting points to be noted in the relationship between the vestibule and the main hall, hitherto ignored, which suggest that the vestibule may be the older building. The question can only be decided by investigation in depth, to determine whether this annexe originally stood on its own, in which case it could have served as a synagogue; or whether it was part of a build-

81/
South vestibule of the Old-New Synagogue, looking eastward.

women's gallery. This suggests that there had been an earlier annexe here, probably not vaulted, before the Renaissance rebuilding. The year 1732 on a plaque with the Hebrew inscription, over the last window in the western annexe, relates to the single-axis northern bay, which dates, like the whole of the northern women's gallery, from 1731—32.

In the south vestibule there are two small, independent structures, one in the north east corner and the other by the west side of the east buttress. They still bear Renaissance features, and served as money-boxes for the taxes paid by the Jews.[5]

Unlike most of the other synagogues, the

82/
The Gothic portal of the Old-New Synagogue leading from the south vestibule.

83/
South vestibule of the Old-New Synagogue, looking west.

ing whose masonry was incorporated in the synagogue built in the last quarter of the thirteenth century. We cannot exclude the possibility that the builders started work on the vestibule and the main hall simultaneously, some time in the first half of the thirteenth century (this would explain the type of vaulting and the ribs in the vestibule) and that the latter was finished first. It could then have served for prayer. It was certainly used for this purpose later, as the stone pillar of the cantor's lectern on the east wall testifies. The building of the present synagogue could then have been completed half a century later. The Old-New Synagogue was decidedly not the only medieval building to grow slowly and by stages, with intervals in between which would account for changes in style.

At the western end of the north wall of the vestibule is a late Gothic portal leading to the

Old-New was not built round. The open space around it served as an inner marketplace for the ghetto. Thanks to this open space, and the solidity with which it was built, it escaped devastation by fire.

From the time the Old-New Synagogue was completed no more were built until the second half of the fifteenth century, which does not mean that private prayer rooms did not exist in homes. It was not until 1482 that the New Jewish Shul was built for the new Jewish settlement in V jámě in the New Town (today's Školská Street). Both the settlement and the synagogue were short-lived, as we saw in Chapter I. After 1490 nothing was left of either, and we have no idea what the synagogue looked like.

Of far greater importance for Prague Jewry was the Pinkas Synagogue built at the end of the fifteenth century, on the south-west edge of the Jewish Town. It stands to this day, and forms part of the State Jewish Museum. It was built as a private prayer house in the precincts of the house At the Coats of Arms, which belonged to Jisrael Pinchas. We first find it mentioned in contemporary sources in 1492, but it is not clear from the document whether the synagogue was founded by Rabbi Pinchas, or by his son-in-law Meir Horowitz. The synagogue was mentioned in a contract between members of the family. We do not know, either, how long at that time the house remained in Jewish hands.[6)]

The Pinkas Synagogue is the only building surviving from the lost ghetto to be studied by archaeologists. This happened twice, in the early 1950s and 1970s. During the first excavation remnants of the walls of a roughly square building were found under the western end of the main nave. The leader of the team believed this to represent the remains of a Romanesque synagogue dating from the eleventh or twelfth century. The second excavation revealed hitherto unsuspected cellar space beneath the synagogue as it stands. A water tank in the cellar is believed to be a ritual bath dating from the thirteenth century. We cannot say with any certainty, of course, whether the water tank, similar to many in other Prague houses, was used for ritual purposes only after the house passed into the hands of the Horowitz family. The hypothesis that a Romanesque synagogue existed here is based on the theory that Jews had been settled around Široká Street since long back.[7] One thing at least is clear: the earliest history of the Pinkas Synagogue is still full of unanswered questions today, and will long remain so.

There is absolutely reliable evidence for the building of the existing synagogue, however. It is enshrined in a marble memorial plaque inscribed in Hebrew characters, stating that Ahron Meshullam Horowitz had it built. This plaque, originally on the west façade, has now been placed in the west vestibule. The year 1535 given there refers to the year building work began; we do not know when it was finished. The author of the monograph on the subject considers that the main building rose in two stages.[8] In the first, which she places around 1520, the three eastern bays, including the almemor, were built. Shortly afterwards the synagogue was extended westwards with a further two bays, and a vestibule of two bays built on to the south. Since this second stage was not too extensive, it could have been completed (in essential) by the year of inauguration. If indeed there was an older family synagogue under the western part of the present synagogue, this would have been the logical way to proceed. Christian churches were built along the same lines, the old one serving until part of the new building was standing, either east or west.

The new synagogue was built as a single nave chamber, with a reticulate groined vault resting on diminished columns which are late Gothic in character. These columns are polygonal and fluted, showing the influence of the early Renaissance, as do the rosettes in the square bays of the vault, and the smaller rosettes where the ribs meet. The subtly designed nave had a stone Ark of the Torah, fragments of which were found in the 1950s in a hollow beneath a later Ark, in the east wall. These stone fragments are still late Gothic in style. The remains of the original almemor were also found. It stood more or less in the centre of the eastern part of the nave, and was an oblong with south-east and north-west corners bevelled. These fragments, together with the Renaissance columns and late Gothic ogee arches, show that the stone-work of the almemor, like the whole building, belonged to the transitional period between Gothic and Renaissance. The portal which was reconstructed in situ from fragments that were found, is already purely early Renaissance in style. The sloping fluted pilasters on either side bear a finely moulded lintel. The frieze shows historicizing motifs and Hebrew lettering, the Star of David and the pitcher which is the symbol of the tribe of the Levites to which the Horowitz family belonged. The cornice which finished off the portal is relatively massive.

This was the appearance of the synagogue while it formed part of the Horowitz home, up

84/
The interior of the Old-New Synagogue with the *aron ha-kodesh* in the background.

85/
The almemor, the Old-New Synagogue.

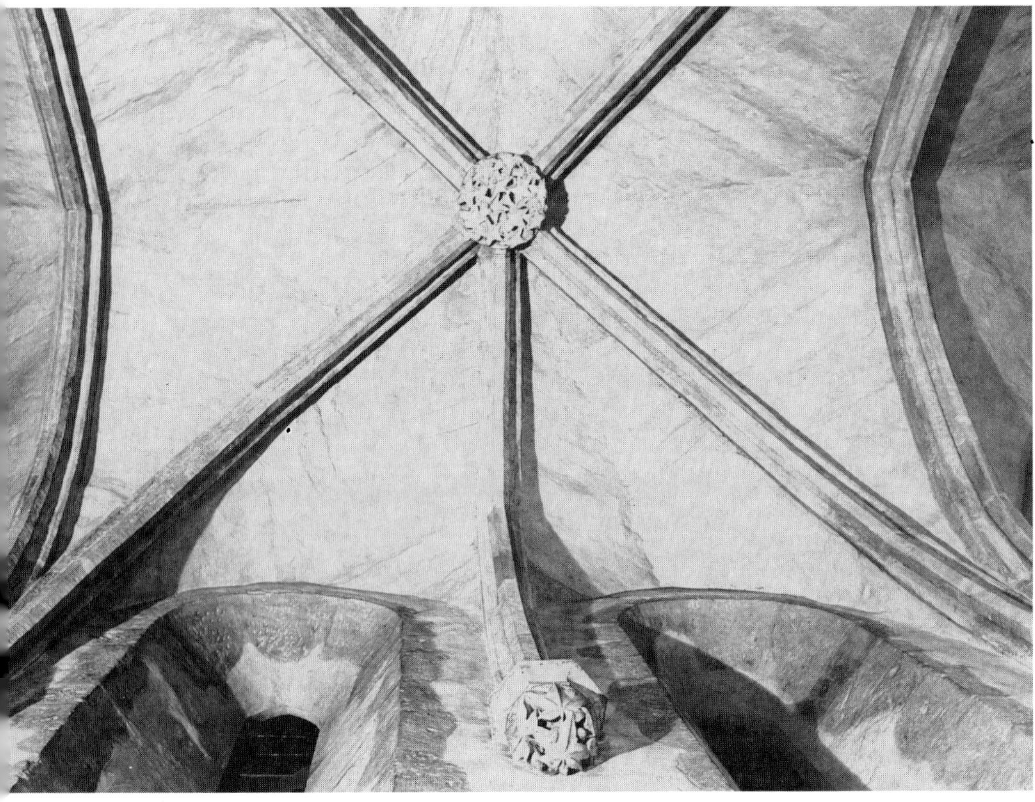

86/
Spandrel of the five-partite vaulting in the Old-New Synagogue.

87/
A keystone on the vaulting of the Old-New Synagogue.

to the beginning of the seventeenth century. The house passed from one generation to another either by inheritance or by bequest, recorded in the contract book of the Old Town, and later in the Jewish White Books *(Libri albi Judaeorum)* while the owner was still alive. In these documents the house is still called 'At the Coats of Arms' at the beginning of the seventeenth century, while the synagogue, when relevant, is not named. The first mention of the synagogue as such is in an entry of 1566: 'the house "At the Coats of Arms" lies by the Munk shul'. In 1601 Šťastný Hořovský bequeathed 'one quarter of the house At the Coats of Arms and one quarter of the seats in the shul to his son Pinkas Izák...'. It is not until 1609 that an entry recording the purchase of a house in the immediate vicinity reads: 'behind the Horowitz house leading to the Pinkas Shul'.[9)] It can be assumed, then, that the name 'Pinkas shul' or synagogue is of later date, and it is difficult to determine which of the Pinchas Horowitz gave his name to it. During the sixteenth century the name Pinkas occurs frequently in the family, until it could almost be taken as a synonym for Horowitz.

In the early seventeenth century there was serious litigation among the heirs to the synagogue, concluded in 1607 by an involved compromise according to which the synagogue was to be managed by representatives chosen from several branches of the Horowitz family. This agreement was confirmed by a rabbinical court consisting of the rabbis Shelomo Ephraim Luntshitz, Jehuda Loew ben Bezalel and Jeshaja ben Abraham ha-Levi Horowitz. Soon after this dispute was settled the Pinkas Synagogue was rebuilt in late Renaissance style. This would date to the end of the first or beginning of the second decade of the seventeenth century, and definitely before the rebellion of the Czech Estates in 1618. The builder was Juda Coref (Goldsmith) de Herz, who also shared in the building of the Meisl Synagogue. He died in 1625, and credit for building both synagogues is accorded him in his epitaph. The changes ascribed to him include the rebuilding of the south vestibule and its vaulting, the ground floor of the women's gallery and a new gallery over it which gives on to the main chamber through semi-circular arcades with a stone balustrade on flat pilasters. No doubt the west façade of the south wing and the windows facing into the courtyard are also his work. The south vestibule gives access to the entrance hall of the synagogue, situated at a lower level, over a broad staircase.

The repairs carried out after the Jews returned from exile, in 1744—48, probably only concerned technical matters. Accounts preserved in the archives of the State Jewish Museum refer to repairs to the roof and drainpipes, with perhaps some changes in the east wall, round the Ark of the Torah. However, these have been overlaid by later work.

After the flood of 1771 seriously damaged the interior, it was completely repainted by K. Happe. The almemor then acquired its present appearance. The relief carving of the stone was chiselled off and the balustrade covered with painted stucco. The colour-scheme of the interior was rosy violet, painted to resemble the veining of marble. The rich Rococo wrought-iron grille of the almemor was donated by the nobleman Joachim of Popper, probably in 1739.

In the second quarter of the eighteenth century the synagogue was extended by the purchase of surrounding houses, and by the early nineteenth century the complete group of buildings numbered 20 to 29 belonged to it. These were small buildings to the south and east, which were later built up to form larger houses, of one or two additional storeys; on the east side of the synagogue, in particular, the houses were then of three storeys. The houses on the southern side kept their original character at least up to the 1830s. On Langweil's model these houses still have twin Renaissance windows, or early Baroque.

88/
A capital, the Old-New Synagogue.

89/
A capital, the Old-New Synagogue.

90/
A keystone, the Old-New Synagogue.

the ground floor and the first floor were deformed. During this 'modernization' of the synagogue both the original almemor and the Renaissance portal were removed. Fortunately, on orders from the rabbinate, all the parts of the Ark of the Torah, the almemor and other original furnishings were buried, so that they could not be used for any other purpose. Thus the original furnishings of the Pinkas Synagogue were saved because the rabbinate acted in accordance with sixteenth century religious rules.

A few decades later the area around the synagogue was changed out of all recognition by the slum clearance scheme. The building itself, which had been part of a group of small houses, now stood alone. It now stood very low, compared to the raised level of what was Josefovská Street, corresponding to the upper floor of the synagogue. There were doubts at the time whether the synagogue itself should be preserved, but the regional conservator Luboš Jeřábek intervened and persuaded the

91/
A console, the Old-New Synagogue.

A new pewter door to the Ark of the Torah was made in the years 1838—41; this still survives. In the forties new seats were commissioned, modelled on those in the Old Shul.

In 1860 the conservative administration of the synagogue was made more democratic; it was run by an elected committee of two supervisors and three assistants. In that year — as in every other — floods damaged the synagogue building, and the new committee decided to modernize it radically. According to the accounts, work began in 1862. The floor of the nave was raised to the level of the women's gallery to prevent greater damage by flooding. The lower women's gallery gave onto the nave through half-oval arches. To gain more space, a wooden loft was added forming a gallery. The height proportions of the nave were of course spoiled by the raising of the floor level. The decorations were designed by Josef Leizner and the painter Nácovský carried out both the painting and the stucco work. In the 1870s the staircase was widened and as a result the vestibules on

92/
A console on the west pillar, the Old-New Synagogue.

Central Commission in Vienna to insist that the synagogue be preserved.

In 1923 it was suggested that the building might be used as a museum, and examination of the property was entrusted to Hugo Richter. In the banked up earth along the east wall of the nave, dating from the 1860s, he found fragments of Gothic stone-work, parts of the original decoration of the synagogue. The investigations were not completed and the idea of using the building as a museum was dropped. It served its original religious purpose until the Nazis occupied Prague in 1939. Surprising as it might seem, the Pinkas Synagogue was restored during the Nazi occupation, but the work was irresponsibly carried out, and not even completed. After World War II the Pinkas Synagogue was deserted and unused, a useless piece of property belonging to the Jewish community. It became more and more dilapidated. In 1950 the Jewish Museum became a state institution, and among other things it acquired the Pinkas Synagogue. Investigation and restoration of

93/
The shaft of the lectern in the south vestibule, the Old-New Synagogue.

94/
Western end of the women's gallery, the Old-New Synagogue.

the building continued from 1951 to 1959, when the Pinkas Synagogue became the 'Memorial to the victims of Nazi persecution of the Jews of Bohemia and Moravia', those who had perished in concentration camps and on death marches. The names of 77,297 dead were inscribed on the walls of the nave, which had been restored (as far as was possible) to its original state. The designers, Jiří John and Václav Boštík, painted these minute inscriptions covering the walls from top to bottom.[10)]

Unfortunately this restoration of the building had not included sufficient insulation from damp, and ground water soaking into the walls damaged the interior and especially the names inscribed on the walls. The museum had to be closed. Work then proceeded on improved insulation, and revealed vaulted cellars below ground, with a ritual bath — *mikvah*. These have also been restored so that when everything is ready, they will be included in visitors' tours of the synagogue.[11)]

During the Renaissance several other synagogues were built in the Jewish Town, the oldest being certainly the Vysoká (High) Syn-

95/
Northern end of the women's gallery, the Old-New Synagogue.

agogue, so called because instead of being on the ground floor of the building, it was on the upper floor connected with the Town Hall next door. The synagogue most probably served for prayers when the elders of the community and clerks employed at the Town Hall required it. There was a smaller chamber which was probably used for less important religious services. Today the synagogue is shut off from the Town Hall, but this chamber belongs to the latter. The chronicle of David Gans tells us that Mordechai Meisl, later the primas (head) of the Jewish ghetto, had the High Synagogue built in 1568. The builder was Pancratius Roder, who came from northern Italy. It is not clear from the chronicle whether this was a completely new building, or the adaptation of an older shul. It is true that the reign of Ferdinand I, and especially the years from 1541 to his death in 1564, were not favourable to expansion of the ghetto. This was the time of repeated exile and uncertainty, when it would be unlikely that the Jews would consider making notable additions to their Town Hall. We therefore assume that Pancratius Roder built the synagogue next to the Town Hall from the foundations up.

The High Synagogue is slightly oblong in ground plan, vaulted in typical Renaissance style, with lunettes in the corners. This was the usual treatment in wealthy houses and palaces at the time. There is an opening on the south wall, leading to the women's gallery next to the staircase. This is modern, with two columns supporting a straight lintel. Above it, at the level of the lunettes in the main ceiling, there are two closed windows which gave on to the upper storey of the women's gallery. There are three windows in the north wall, rebated in semi-circular moulding, dating from the early nineteenth century. The *aron ha-kodesh* dates from 1691, when the synagogue was repaired. It seems to have been damaged during the 1689 fire, although the vaulting remained intact. The Ark is executed in the style of early Baroque altars, with typical features and details. Perhaps part of the Renaissance Ark was incorporated in it.

When the synagogue was last restored in 1977—79, it was revealed that the pilasters which break up the line of the walls were added subsequently. The original decoration of the walls runs unbroken behind them. They were probably added at the time of the early Baroque decoration of the interior. In 1982 the original polychrome on the Ark of the Torah was uncovered and restored.

Today the first floor of the High Synagogue is connected with the ground floor, where the rooms all have Renaissance vaulting. They were not connected until 1883 and until then it was possible to enter the synagogue only from the Town Hall next door. In the second half of the nineteenth century the passage in the northern part of the ground floor was walled up. The present entrance in Červená (Red) Lane was not made until 1935.[12])

The most imposing late Renaissance building in the whole of the Jewish Town was the Meisl Synagogue. The wealthy head of the Jewish community decided at the age of sixty-two to buy a piece of land and build his own synagogue. For two hundred times threescore Czech groschen he bought land from his brother-in-law. The same year he probably began building, the Jewish architects Juda Coref de Herz and Josef Wahl drawing up the plans and supervising the work. Permission to build was given by Rudolph II in August of the following year, when the new synagogue was already half-built and several thousand Rhine guilders had already been invested in the project. It was completed in 1592 on the festival of *Simchat Torah* (Joy of the Torah), and the first services were held there. According to the chronicler David Gans over 10,000 thalers had been spent on the synagogue. It was not only spacious but also beautiful. The principal nave, with women's galleries, had twenty columns of hewn stone. Meisl donated a magnificent temple curtain, and a Torah with its cloak. He also gave the synagogue the banner of King David, which the synagogue was allowed to use under a privilege granted in 1598. (All these precious objects are preserved in the collections of the State Jewish Museum.)

We know little about the subsequent history of the synagogue. In the documents concerning the confiscation of Mordechai Meisl's property, dragging on until the last quarter of the seventeenth century, we read that 'after

96/
North façade of the Pinkas Synagogue.

the death of Meisl the Jews rented the synagogue out' — but to whom and for what purpose is not stated. The whole thing may have been a misunderstanding, the renting of seats in the synagogue being taken to mean the renting of the whole building. It is said that the Meisl Synagogue was burned down in the 'French' fire of 1689. This does not agree with the report sent to the Czech Chamber by the Jewish community in 1694, which lists the Old-New, Meisl, Pinkas and High synagogues as having been spared. According to the report on the state of the synagogues in the ghetto, drawn up the following year, the Meisl Shul was 'completely in order', which does not mean 'restored to complete order', for the same words are used to describe the synagogues which had not been damaged. Nevertheless, the Meisl Synagogue was sealed, apparently for unspecified debts. It is of interest that the community made no special effort to have this synagogue reopened, while an obstinate struggle to preserve and reopen the Old Shul went on for many years. However, it was not only after the 1689 fire that the Meisl Shul was closed. It is noted as 'closed' in a list drawn up in 1670. There may be some connection here between the closing of the Shul and a report on the state of the ghetto drawn up for the Czech Chamber after the fire of 1689, which states that the Chamber owed the Jews 50,000 Rhine guilders for the synagogue, but had only paid 15,000. This may have referred to a settlement concerning the estate of Meisl, of which the synagogue was a part.

It is clear from all this that the synagogue was not rebuilt after the 1689 fire. It is of course probable that it was damaged by the 1754 fire, and later repaired or rebuilt. Unfortunately we do not know the extent of building work done. One thing is certain: both the original Renaissance synagogue and any later changes all disappeared beneath the Neo-Gothic restoration of 1894, when a vestibule designed by the architect Králíček was added. Without detailed investigation we cannot say whether the groined vault over the principal nave is Neo-Gothic, or only restored in that style. All the interior decoration, including the Ark of the Torah, is in the Neo-Gothic style. The main façade of the synagogue, in Maislova Street, was also restored in this style. All that remained untouched was the southern façade and the two side aisles with women's galleries on both floors. It is not

97/
Gothic cellars with the *mikvah* (ritual bath) in the Pinkas Synagogue.

98/
The interior of the Pinkas Synagogue in the 1960s, before the present restoration work.

99/
The memorial plaque Ahron Meshullam Horowitz had carved to commemorate the building of the Pinkas Synagogue in 1535.

100/ ▷
The Renaissance reticulate vaulting and the women's gallery in the Pinkas Synagogue.

103/
The High Synagogue, showing the early Baroque *aron ha-kodesh* and part of the Renaissance vaulting.

101/
The north façade of the High Synagogue.

102/
The staircase of the High Synagogue showing part of the Renaissance vaulting above the ground floor.

תורה צוה
לנו משה מורשה
קהלת יעקב
כתר
תורה

impossible that the ceilings of the galleries are still the originals put in by Meisl, and that they have only been subject to later repair. Today we may still consider the Meisl Synagogue an example of the late Renaissance in architecture, in spite of the Neo-Gothic exterior and details of the interior decoration.[13)]

The last of the historic synagogues of the ghetto to be preserved is the Klaus (Klausová) Synagogue. It is also the only early Baroque synagogue, although its origins go back to the Renaissance. Towards the end of the sixteenth century Mordechai Meisl bought from Christian owners some gardens lying outside the area of the ghetto. Some of the ground was used to extend the Jewish cemetery. On one part Meisl built three smaller houses known as 'klaus'. Tradition has it that in one of the 'klaus' the famous 'Great Rabbi Loew', Jehuda Loew ben Bezalel, taught. One of the others was a prayer house and the third a ritual bath-house. The list of Prague synagogues drawn up in 1670 states that one 'klaus' was used by students while another was given over to preaching. The 1695 list describes them as the 'lower, upper and front klaus'. They were all burned down in 1689 and replaced by a new shul, beautifully built (according to the list), and called the New Klaus.

104/
The east façade of the Meisl Synagogue before Neo-Gothic restoration. Langweil's model.

The building of the Klaus Synagogue was completed in 1694. Judging from Langweil's model dating 1826—37, the main building had two-storeyed annexes on the north and west sides, which were lower than the main nave. The women's gallery will certainly have been in the west annexe, while the vestibule and more room for the women will have been housed in the north annexe. The architectonic appearance of these annexes, and particularly the arrangement of the windows, still gives the impression of early Baroque, so that we can assume that they were either contemporary with the main body of the synagogue, or only very little later. The ceiling of the lower storey of the northern annexe may date from late Baroque. In 1883—84 the western women's gallery was raised to the height of the principal nave, and given a similar ceiling separated by a band; a spacious balcony was added. At the same time the gallery in the north annexe seems to have been renovated. The plans were drawn up by Bedřich Münzberger, who also redesigned the exterior façade. The interior decoration was the work of Antonín Baum. The eclectic character, and the similar style of the stucco work on the ceiling of the nave and the balcony, lead us to conclude that except perhaps for a few basic details, this is all part of the 1883 renovation.

105/
The present east façade of the Meisl Synagogue.

106/
The west façade of the Meisl Synagogue after Neo-Gothic restoration.

107/
The interior of the Meisl Synagogue, looking east.

The *aron ha-kodesh* takes the form of an early Baroque altar; it was executed in 1696 at the expense of the wealthy Samuel Oppenheim, uncle of the Chief Rabbi of Prague, David Oppenheim. The lower part of the Ark is of stone, faced with imitation brownish-red marble; the upper part is of wood, with a dedicatory inscription in a carved cartouche.

The Ark was restored to its original appearance during the late restoration work in 1979—84, and the synagogue now houses an exhibition of old Hebrew manuscripts and incunabula. Originally there was an almemor more or less in the centre of the Klaus Synagogue, and the seats were arranged round the walls, as they still are in the Old-New Synagogue.[14)]

Now we must turn to those synagogues in the Jewish Town of Prague which have not survived. Some were lost after the 'French' fire of 1689, while others fell victim to the slum clearance campaign at the turn of our own century.

The most important was the New Synagogue inaugurated at the end of the sixteenth century by Rabbi Wechsler, on the first floor of the house bearing the number 113, at the east end of Široká Street. There were four semi-circular chamfered windows. The Ark of the Torah resembled a Baroque altar and the ceiling had a stucco ornament. The synagogue was burned down in the fire of 1689, but even before, in lists drawn up in 1666 and 1670, it cannot be identified with certainty. At the time it was known either as the New or as Wechsler Synagogue. The first reference to it is in 1699, as Wechsler's shul which was not in the list of six to be renovated in the ghetto after the fire. Whether it was renovated then, we do not know, but probably during the first half of the seventeenth century. It was burned down again in 1754, and renovated in late Baroque style with Rococo ornament on the façade. We can see what the outside looked like, from Langweil's model. There were ritual baths in the next house, but both buildings were demolished in 1897.[15)]

The Cikán Synagogue, built by Salomon Salkid Cikán in 1613, was late Renaissance in origin. It stood inside the group of buildings between Rabínská and Cikánská Streets to

108/
The east façade of the Klaus Synagogue.

109/
The interior of the Klaus Synagogue, looking east.

the south of the Old-New Synagogue. It was damaged in the 1689 fire, and by the time the 1695 list was drawn up, had been partially restored. It was one of the six synagogues whose restoration was permitted, and we can assume that work was completed during the next few years. Isachar Bumsla was responsible for the reconstruction of 1701. Langweil's model and contemporary photographs show it to have been an oblong building with three windows in the west façade. There were four windows in each of the long sides, corresponding to four pairs of triangular bays. Between the windows were pilasters supporting sections of a richly moulded cornice. The Ark of the Torah, in the usual Baroque altar form with a high, two-stage superstructure, stood in a niche in the east wall of the single nave. There were low annexes on the west and north sides of the synagogue, one serving as a vestibule and the other as the women's gallery. The synagogue was certainly not as seriously damaged in the 1754 fire as Schor's plan implies, with the number 3 meaning 'burned to the ground'. The walls and the vaulting certainly survived, while the wooden timbers will have burned along with the interior furnishings, which were mainly of wood. In 1883 the reformed rite was introduced in this synagogue, and a choir trained. At the time of the slum clearance scheme the Cikán Synagogue was not considered of sufficient historical importance to be preserved and it was demolished in 1906.[16)]

110/
The Cikán and Great Court Synagogues, dating from the late Renaissance and later demolished. Langweil's model.

The third synagogue which was not spared was the early Baroque Velkodvorská (Great Court), also known as the Bashevi Shul. It stood in the north-west corner of the same group of buildings as the site of the Cikán Synagogue. In 1627 Jacob Bashevi bought a plot of land with several houses on it, and had a new synagogue built there, we do not know by whom. It may have been designed by one of the architects working for Albrecht of Waldstein, with whom Bashevi was on very good terms. In the 1670 list it is described as the 'Synagogue of the Great Court'. It burned down in 1689, but was among those listed for renovating. From the 1695 list it appears to have been completely restored. It was again damaged in the fire of 1754. It was a tall building, with the exterior showing two storeys. There were five windows in the longer side walls, and three in the west wall, with arches in the Moorish style, the result of nineteenth century adaptation. Langweil's model shows the synagogue without external ornamental features. An early photograph of the north side shows two windows, with the entrance between them. The building had a hipped roof. There were two windows lower in the east wall, and a round window higher up between them, over the Ark of the Torah. The Ark had been renovated in Neo-Renaissance style. In a surviving photograph of the interior of the synagogue, the Ark ends in a segmented tympanon with two columns above, and a central conch. The Ark seems to be largely the result of nineteenth-century renovations, carried out when the women's gallery was built in the western part of the building. The almemor in the centre was not disturbed, although the benches stood in rows, and not round the walls. This unusually interesting synagogue, documenting the transition from the late Renaissance to early Baroque, was demolished as lacking in architectural interest.[17)]

We must mention briefly the prayer rooms, synagogues or shuls which were always springing up and disappearing again in the ghetto. Most of them came to an end after Leopold I issued a decree, following the fire of 1689, that there should be no more than six syn-

111/
Houses between the former Rabínská and Cikánská Streets, with the Cikán and Great Court Synagogues, demolished in 1906. Langweil's model.

112/
J. Minařík: The Cikán Synagogue. Oil on canvas.

agogues in the community. From records and official lists dating from before and after the 1689 fire, however, we know that there were twelve synagogues there at the time. The 1666 list even gives fourteen, because it enters the three 'klaus' as separate prayer rooms. The list also gives the synagogue belonging to Benjamin Lippmann, the Kauders shul, a synagogue in the yard of Chajim Shames, and the Bashevi and the Great Court synagogues as separate buildings. The 1670 list gives twelve synagogues, grouping the three 'klaus' together. The shul in the yard of Chajim Shames may be identical with that in the house of the Jewish mayor, Fanta. There was another in a private house close to the cemetery, but the owner's name is illegible. There was a shul in the Saxenhaus' private house, on the corner above the house 'At the Three Wells'. The twelfth synagogue listed is that of Josef Ginspurger, in the house 'At the White Rose'. However, there is also a list of unofficial shul, dated 1695. At that time there were fourteen, of which seven were sealed off. They were all in private houses. The first in the home of 'sergeant Eckh', the second in the Town Hall (besides the High Synagogue there seems to have been another, perhaps the smaller room mentioned earlier), the third in the home of Josef Anschel Racheles, the fourth in the Passau house (this may refer to the Bashevi house), the fifth in that of Jacob Grünhütl, the sixth in that of the widow Sachsl, the seventh in the house of Salomon Töper. All these had been sealed. The eighth was in the house of Mark Cordule, the ninth in that of Jacob Brandeis, the tenth in that of Majer the doctor, the eleventh in the home of Abraham Budmann, the twelfth in that of Lazar Gander; the thirteenth was Jacob Enschel's, and the fourteenth 'in the rabbi's house' — probably the house of the Chief Rabbi.

In spite of prohibitions private shuls were constantly re-appearing. In a declaration by Václav Vražda of Kunvald in November 1725 it was again decided to close all these illegal meeting places. Only one was to be left, for the sick, presumably attached to the Jewish hospital. The shul belonging to Benet Náchod, permitted in 1702 for study purposes, was also used for prayers, which was forbidden. It was to be closed down, like the 'study shul' in the house of Anshel Günzburg, which opened without permission. At the same time negotiations were going on for a shul to be opened (or perhaps already open) by David Karpeles and Moshe Glaser. It was to serve the elderly who could not attend services in any of the public synagogues. This synagogue may have been identical to the Popper Synagogue, formerly Lippmann's, near to the Old Jewish Cemetery, where the hospital also stood.[18)]

The later years of the eighteenth century, as we have seen, were by no means favourable to the Jews. The emperor's permit was required before a private prayer room could be set up. Not until the last quarter of the century, under Joseph II, did the situation ease. In 1782 a private synagogue was set up in the home of the respected Mosheles family, and it was probably not the only one of its kind. It disappeared in the clearance scheme, along with the house itself, which was of historic interest.[19)]

The attempts to achieve assimilation and equal rights for the Jews, the emancipation campaigns of the early nineteenth century, did not offer good conditions for building new synagogues in the ghetto. Indeed it would have been hard to find room for such buildings in the overcrowded streets. It was not until the second half of the century, when Jews could live where they wished in Prague, that new synagogues of historic styles were erected in Prague suburbs, e.g. in Smíchov in 1863. The original appearance of the Smích-

113/
The Wechsler Synagogue in Široká Street, later demolished. Langweil's model.

ov synagogue disappeared when the architect L. Ehrmann adapted the building in functionalist style. In 1861 another synagogue was built in the Karlín suburb, combining Moorish with Neo-Romanesque forms. The biggest Prague synagogue, built in the Vinohrady suburb in 1896—98 by Wilhelm Stiassny was destroyed in an air-raid in 1945.

The last Prague synagogue, designed in pseudo-Moorish style, known as the Jubilee or the Jerusalem Synagogue, was erected in 1904—06 in Jcruzalémská Street in the New Town of Prague (arch. W. Stiassny and A. Richter). In our days it is used for the Jewish divine service as the second Prague synagogue beside the Old-New one. The old synagogue in Libeň (now also in a suburb of the capital) had been damaged by successive floods, and was replaced in 1946—57 by a Neo-Romanesque building on a higher ground.[20)]

The last of the historical buildings of the ghetto to survive is the Town Hall. It is first mentioned in documents dated 1541, and it can be assumed to have been standing for some time. We have no idea what the building looked like, but it was very probably pure Gothic. It most likely stood where the present Town Hall has stood since 1564, the earliest period at which it could have been rebuilt in Renaissance style, during the reign of Maximilian II. The rebuilding may have taken place in two stages. It was damaged by the fire of 1689, and repairs entrusted to Pavel Ignác Bayer, according to contemporary records. After the second great fire in the ghetto in 1754, the whole building was rebuilt in the spirit of late Baroque, from plans by Josef Schlesinger of Wroclaw. Even before the 1689 fire the Town Hall boasted a spire with a clock. This was restored in 1701. The spire

114/
The Temple, built in the 1860s to replace the Old Shul. Designed by I. Ullmann and J. Niklas.

115/
The interior of the Temple in Dušní Street, looking east.

116/
The Jewish Town Hall, rebuilt in late Baroque style after the fire of 1754, designed by Josef Schlesinger and completed in 1763.

117/
The late Baroque vestibule of the Jewish Town Hall.

was again restored when the building was adapted in 1763. A new clock was installed, and a small bell hung in the spire. The memorial for that year mentions a loan of 20,000 Rhine guilders which made it possible to rebuild the ghetto and its public buildings. Besides the Town Hall this included the treasury, the hospital, the home of the Chief Rabbi, a well and a big gate.[21)] The Town Hall retained its late Baroque character, that of a small palace with a wealth of decoration on the front and side façades, its mansard roof with elegant little gables, and rising above, the picturesque spire perched on the north-west corner of the building. The clock face in the northern gable is a Hebrew one.

118/
The clock tower of the Jewish Town Hall with the Hebrew clock-face in the north gable.

/V/ THE OLD JEWISH CEMETERY

The Old Jewish Cemetery, the 'field of the dead', is today the only locality of the former ghetto of any size which still remains intact. During the clearance carried out at the turn of the nineteenth to twentieth century, the more recent part of the cemetery was razed. This was the northern tip of the cemetery, the nearest to the river bank, the ground on which the Museum of Decorative Arts now stands. Little remains of that northern plot, while a small area near the Pinkas Synagogue also fell victim to the clearance scheme. However, the Old Cemetery is still the largest Jewish cemetery in Europe, and the only one to be in a good state of conservation. The two older European cemeteries, that of Worms which was in use as early as the eleventh century, and the one in Frankfurt-am-Main, used for burials from the thirteenth century, were both destroyed by the Nazis.

Burials probably began in the Prague Old Cemetery around 1430. As we know, it was not the oldest Jewish cemetery in Prague, having been preceded by the Jewish Garden in the New Town, which was done away with by King Vladislav Jagellon at the end of the fifteenth century. From about 1440 there were two Jewish cemeteries in use, which may explain why there are only thirteen gravestones in the Old Jewish Cemetery which date from the fifteenth century. The oldest of all, that of Rabbi Abigdor Kara, dates from 1439. The first reference to the purchase by the 'elders and the whole Jewish community' of a house with a building lot, facing the brothel and the next to 'the Jewish garden where the dead are now buried', dates from 1440. It is thus clear that part of the cemetery was already the property of the Jewish community, although we do not know when it was acquired. It was extended several times at later periods, by the purchase of land lying towards the river bank. On the plan drawn for the Knights of Malta shortly after the middle of the seventeenth century, the Old Cemetery covered the same area as it did shortly before the clearance scheme was put into effect. Before the north-west corner and the area south of the Museum of Decorative Arts were then cleared, the bones of the dead, and the gravestones, were transferred to the remaining ground of the cemetery. The bones were buried on the 'nefele' mound next to the Klaus Synagogue, while the gravestones were placed mostly in the north-west corner. Fortunately there were no more changes in the cemetery. In 1911 the diminished cemetery grounds were enclosed by a wall designed by the architect Bohumil Hypšman.[1)]

Burials took place in the Old Jewish Cemetery up to the year 1787, when interment within the city was forbidden under Joseph II. It is interesting that there are no features of late Gothic style even on the oldest gravestones, which date from that period. Beginning with that of Rabbi Abigdor Kara virtually the same type of gravestones persists through the fifteenth and sixteenth centuries. It is an oblong stele, planted vertically, with a narrow projecting frame, rectangular in cross-section. The surface with the inscription is thus as it were sunk. The horizontal top of this frame usually bears the superscription giving the name and perhaps the titles of the deceased. All the fifteenth century and most of the sixteenth gravestones are of fine sandstone, which has blackened with the course of time. The lettering is deeply incised. This simple type of stone was already in use earlier. The fragments of gravestones brought to the

Old Jewish Cemetery from the New Town Jewish Garden, and embedded in the revetment of the 'nefele' mound behind the Klaus Synagogue are of the same type. The closest analogy to this Prague type of stone can be seen on the few existing illustrations of the Worms cemetery produced before the Nazis came to power, and depicting gravestones of the late thirteenth and early fourteenth century. These oblong steles in the Prague cemetery are essentially functional in type. Attention is directed solely to the surface bearing the inscription, which was somewhat protected from the trickle of raindrops by the protruding stone frame.

In the middle of the sixteenth century we find the first modification of the traditional type of stone. The rectangular shape persists, but the inscription is sometimes executed in relief. Besides fine sandstone, marble from Slivenec near Prague is sometimes used. Over the centuries it lost its original deep reddish-brown colour and faded to pale pink under the influence of air, sun and rain, but unlike sandstone it does not blacken. During the second half of the sixteenth century more ornament in relief and some attempt at composition can be seen. The inscribed surface may end in a semicircular arch above, forming a shallow alcove. Where there are two inscriptions, the design is repeated twice. On the simpler stones the raised stone frame shows typical Renaissance moulding. The cartouche is now used, usually in a simple form, and a few emblems such as the Star of David or a bunch of grapes appear. The segment of the stone between the rectangular frame and the curved line over the inscription is filled with a typical Renaissance motif of three leaves in relief. The lintel is sometimes shaped like a low tympanon, either triangular or segmental in form. These newer forms are, however, not general. Side by side with stones of a later style we still find the traditional gravestones, carved at the same time. Symbols do not appear more frequently until the 1580s. A favourite is the pitcher motif on gravestones of men of the Levi tribe — the first example is on Asher the Levite's stone, 1581. A little later we find the emblem of hands raised in blessing, the symbol of the tribe of the priestly Cohens; Levi Cohen, son of Alexander, 1585, was the first. More advanced Renaissance forms became common in the 1580s. The stele often ends in a triangular tympanon or a cusp spiralling upwards, or alternatively with a boss in the centre, variously shaped and enriched with bent wings. Slender half-columns or pilasters, often only very slightly raised in relief, may frame the inscription. It was not until the end of the sixteenth century that contemporary ornamental motifs became frequent; the treatment is sometimes rich. Pinnacles, festoons of fruit, medallions and cartouches appear to ornament the broken pediments, while the architectonic design of the gravestone is stressed by the half-columns in relief at the sides. More emblems are now carved in relief, no longer symbolizing the tribe to which the deceased belonged — the Levites or the Cohens — but referring to his name and — less frequently — to his profession. The figure of a bear is found on many gravestones, symbolizing the name Beer; a lion marks the resting place of those called Loew or Levi; a stag for the Hirsch family, a fish for the Karpeles.

Imposing tombs in the shape of a sarcophagus begin to appear in the early seventeenth century, formed by a stele at each end, two longer side slabs, and two more to form a span roof. Such tombs were the privilege of important people in the ghetto who had done much for the community, like Mordechai Meisl for whom the first tomb was built in 1601, or those who were famed for their learning and were spiritual leaders of the ghetto — famous rabbis. The best known of these is the tomb of Rabbi Loew of 1609. The physician, astronomer and mathematician Joseph del Medigo was also given a magnificent tomb in 1655, although he had lived and worked in Prague only for a short time. The tomb of Hendl Bashevi, with its rich ornament, is an exception. She was the wife of Jacob Bashevi of Treuenberg, the well-known financier and the first Czech Jew to be raised to the nobility. It was certainly he who had the tomb set up, and who, as head of the community, could take the liberty of using this style, normally reserved only for outstanding men. In the eighteenth century the use of con-

119/
The north-west section of the Old Jewish Cemetery, partly demolished during the clearance scheme to make way for Sanytrová Street (now the 17th November Street), showing the Klaus Synagogue. Langweil's model.

120/
The Old Jewish Cemetery, panoramic view with the Klaus Synagogue in the background.

temporary motifs continued, and the ornament on gravestones was often very rich, and even eclectic. Contemporary documents show that the stones were carved by Christian masons who used the same motifs as in their own work. The wishes of the customer also had to be taken into account. In the eighteenth century marble was used almost without exception for gravestones.[2)]

It is of interest to note that in the Old Jewish

Cemetery the most usual form of Jewish gravestone, with a semi-circular top, makes only sporadic appearance.

Of primary significance for Jewish gravestones, however, is not their shape, however much that may interest us, but the inscription on them. For the general visitor today these stones are not interesting, for there are few who can read Hebrew. Even for Jews with a basic knowledge of the language it is difficult

121/
Fragments of tombstones from the 'Jewish Garden' in the New Town, built into the revetment of the *nefele* mound behind the Klaus Synagogue.

to read these texts inscribed without punctuation marks. We shall therefore deal with the inscriptions on the gravestones in the Old Jewish Cemetery in greater detail.

In the Middle Ages, the Renaissance and the Baroque period, Jewish epitaphs usually included the name of the deceased, the name of his father, and where relevant, that he belonged to the priestly tribe (*cohen, cohanim*) or to the tribe of the Levites (*levi, leviim*). This was on men's graves; that a woman was of either tribe was not stated. Then followed the titles of the deceased, and perhaps of his (her) father: Master, Rabbi, scholar, honourable, etc. The next part of the text comprises words of praise, and adjectives describing the good qualities of the deceased. An important man would by given a list of offices held in the community, and other ways in which he had served his fellows. The books written by scholars and famous rabbis would be listed. The inscription usually ends with blessings and wishes for the dead person's life in the after-world.

An important item in the inscription, which may refer to the time of death or to when the gravestone was installed, is the date. In older epitaphs it comes at the end, but from the middle of the sixteenth century it began to appear in the first line, a habit which became general from the early seventeenth century.

These are the basic elements of the epitaph, usually enriched with similes and metaphors taken from the Bible or Jewish religious writings. Jewish eitaphs become a kind of occasional Hebrew poetry.

The dating of a gravestone is important for its chronological classification. The date is made up of the year, the month, the day of the month and the day of the week. It is not always easy to transpose the Hebrew year to the Christian calendar. Prague epitaphs give the year in the usual way, 'from the creation of the world', but very often the full figure is not used. This would give the year 5199 as the date of the first burials in the cemetery. Using the 'small count', the figure for the millennium is omitted and only the century is given. Hebrew has no special sign for numerals, and uses the letters of the alphabet. To calculate the date it is necessary to be acquainted with the Jewish calendar. The Jewish year is a lunar one, differing from our solar year by roughly eleven days. It has twelve months of 29 or 30 days. Since however the Jewish festivals take place according to the seasons, so that *Pesach,* for example, must come in spring and *Succoth* in autumn, something had to be done to level out the difference between the solar and the lunar year. This was achieved by instituting a leap year of thirteen months instead of twelve. There are seven Leap Years in every nineteen-year cycle. The Jewish calendar year has two beginnings, one in spring and one in autumn. The months are counted from the spring New Year, while the synagogal year begins in autumn, with the seventh month, and the year dates from then. The synagogal New Year is movable with respect to the Christian year, so that the first month, *Tishri,* of thirty days, may begin anywhere between 4 September and 5 October. The succeeding months all begin accordingly. The thirteenth month of a Leap Year is placed after the month of *Adar* and is called the *Second Adar (adar shei* or *ve adar).* It can only fall in March, and has always 29 days. Adar is followed by the first month of spring, *Nisan,* which begins in March or April.

The synagogal year also sets it out that certain festivals may not fall on certain days in the week. The Day of Atonement, for instance, *Yom Kippur,* must not fall on a Friday or a Sunday, so that there will not be two holy days in succession on which burials may not take place. Similarly the 'Great Hoshanah', the seventh day of the Festival of Booths *(Succoth),* must not fall on a Saturday. The calendar therefore has to be arranged to prevent this. The two autumn months of *Chesvan* and *Kislev* can have 29 or 30 days as required. This allows seven possible calendars for normal years and another seven for Leap Years. When calculating the year given in an epitaph it is important to consider which day of the week is mentioned, along with the current day of the month. The days of the week are denoted by numbers, the first being Sunday and the seventh Saturday, usually called the 'Holy Sabbath'. A complete date might read: the fourth day of the week (Wednesday), the second day of Nisan, in the year 303

122/
The tombstone of Menachem, son of Moshe, 1529. At the base, probably for the first time in Europe, the Star of David is carved.

123/
The tombstone of Ahron Meshullam, son of Jeshaja Horowitz the Levite, known as Zalman Munka, 1545.

by small count. In many cases we find discrepancies which can be explained as the stonecutter's error, or that of the author of the inscription, committed as he counted back. In principle, the dead were buried the day they died, except when that was a Friday evening, so the funeral could not be held before the arrival of the Sabbath, or Saturday. Burial could not be carried out on the Sabbath, and had to wait until Sunday.

We must make special mention of those epitaphs where the year is not given in Hebrew letters as such, but in a chronogram, the letters forming part of one or more words. This is similar to the use of Roman numerals to give the date in some Latin inscriptions. The practical reason for giving the name of the deceased and the date of his death was that it was then clear when prayers were to be offered for him. The way the name was written, with the tribe to which he belonged, was important in the days before registers were kept. Exact details were necessary when drawing up marriage contracts and divorce documents.

The way the name of the deceased was presented in epitaphs underwent certain changes in the course of time, as it did in the case of Christian epitaphs. At first only the given name was recorded, sometimes defined by the father's name: for example, Josef, son of Jechiel, on a gravestone dated 1539. A woman's given name was usually followed by that of her husband, while her father's name might be given in the text of the inscription. The reverse might occur, but it is rare. Later both names are usually given in the superscription, as in this inscription on a gravestone of 1540: 'Rechlein, daughter of Jacob Cohen, wife of Zalman Meisl.' Some inscriptions gibe the deceased's family name as well as his own. These are usually old families like the Kara, Margalit or Epstein families. Besides old family names, we find those derived from the place the family came from or lived in. Very many Jewish family names come under this heading, like Horowitz, given in Czech sources as Hořovský, i.e. coming from Hořovice; Brandeis, from Brandýs; Tausk, from Taus (in Czech Domažlice). These names are sometimes distorted, as in Bumsla or Bunzla, from Boleslav, which was Bunzlau in German. That such names were long considered as denoting the place of origin can be seen from the fact that in many inscriptions they do not follow directly after the given name, but are separated from it by the word 'a man', e.g. Ahron Meshullam, son of Jeshaja the Levite, a man (from) Horowitz. There can be no doubt about the original meaning: a man from Horowitz, from Brandýs, and so on. Besides Czech place names there are of course others, particularly German and Polish.

In Prague inscriptions we can also find surnames formed from the genitive of the name of the ancestor, like Abraham Shlojmls, i.e. son of Shlojml, originally Shelomo; Jeshaja Paltiels, i.e. son of Paltiel. In some cases the genitive of a mother's or wife's name may be used: Perls, the son or husband of a woman called Perla.

Biblical and Old Hebrew given names are often found in Prague inscriptions followed by currently used names: Jehoshua known as Heshil, Jekutiel known as Kaufmann, Menachem called Mendl. The common name is sometimes added directly: Ahron Meshullam, with the equivalent Zalman. Sometimes the common name is given in the superscription while the text gives the Hebrew name: Lippmann above, und Uri in the text. Some of these common names correspond to more than one Hebrew name: Zalman was used both for Meshullam and for Shelomo; Gumprech for Ephraim, Jacob and Mordechai; Mordechai was also rendered by Mark or Markus. Sometimes the common names are so far from the original Hebrew that the connection can no longer be traced, as in Kecil, one of the equivalents for Moshe, or Karpl, widely used for Nathan.

Family names were not as a rule derived from a man's profession: *chazan* (cantor), *shammash* (sexton), *shochet* (kosher slaughterer), *rofe* (doctor or bath attendant), *kaccab* (butcher). Gradually, however, the profession appeared in Czech or German surnames: Goldschmied (side by side with the Hebrew Coref), Schnirdreher (rope-maker), Švec (shoemaker).

Jewish surnames formed from abbreviations form a distinct and unique class. The

124/
The tombstone of Shabbatai, the son of Jeshaja Horowitz the Levite, 1554 or 1555.

125/
The Old Jewish Cemetery in spring, looking south-east.

well known name Recha, for example, written *R"J"CH* in Hebrew, is an abbreviation of the words Rabbi Jizchak Chazzan; Remad is short for Rabbi Moshe Dayyan. Such names became frequent in the eighteenth century.

Given names for women, like those for men, were biblical or Old Hebrew names: Sarah, Rivka, Leah, Esther, Dinah, Hannah, Havvah, Jochabed, Judith. In Prague inscriptions, however, we find many folk names im-

plying good qualities, or beauty, like Ejdl (noble), Gutl or the Czech Dobrish (good), Liba (lovely, charming — perhaps the equivalent of the name Libuše), Slavva (famous), Shejndl (beautiful), Cart (gentle), Krasl (probably beautiful), Braundl (dark-skinned). Names derived from Nature were popular: Bliml (flower), Rouzl, Rézl or Roza (rose), Hendl (little hen), Feigla (little bird), Pavva (peahen) and also Peiarl (pearl). The

126/
The tombstone of the martyred Rabbi Chayyim, son of Rabbi Jizchak Cohen, 1576. The inscription is carved in relief and surrounded by cartouche motifs.

name Kreindl (little crown) may also have come from a biblical simile. The etymology of names like Tuna, Yentl, Lipet, Kauna and Masha is not clear, Michla may be a feminine form of Michael, while Jutl and Jitl are perhaps diminutives of Judith. Rikl is the diminutive of Rivka, Rechlein of Rachel.

The words *ha-Cohen* and *ha-Levi* originally had nothing to do with family names, but simply showed that the person in question belonged to one or other of these tribes. The abbreviations *k"c* (*kac,* meaning 'Cohen cedek', priest of justice), and *sg"l* or *s"l* *(segal, sal,* for 'Segan levijjim', prince of the Levites), were originally only used for out standing individuals. The abbreviation *sg"l* occurs for the first time in Worms in 1427, *k"c* in Frankfurt as late as 1580. The first use of *sg"l* in Prague was in 1522, on the gravestone of Rabbi Simon Stang, referring to his father.

Other Levites are simply described as *ha-Levi.* The next reliably dated use of the abbreviation *sg"l* comes from 1582, and refers to Asher, the father of the deceased Alexander. This gravestone also provides the first example of the pitcher symbol, denoting the tribe of the Levites. On the other hand, the abbreviation *k"c* is much more frequent. The 'priest of justice' was not so important an epithet as 'prince of the Levites'. It is first found on a gravestone of 1532, commemorating one David, son of Judah.

Besides the names by which Jews were known in the ghetto, in the sixteenth century other names were given them in official Prague documents. It is frequently impossible to identify these names (used for example in the 1546 *Description of the Jews in Prague*) because they seem to have no connection with those inscribed on our gravestones. Names like Tausk, Dilka, Anav, Hankls or Epstein are the simplest. Some identifications have also been confirmed, like Munka for Horowitz, Vokatý for Cohen, Kalamář for Meisl; Kokeš sometimes means Paltiels, Hošek is identical with Jehoshula or Hešil. In many cases, however, these are mere hypotheses and there remain very many names where even hypotheses cannot as yet be put forward.

The title of the deceased, particularly in the

case of men, plays an important role in gravestones inscriptions. As in the Christian world, earlier centuries were more modest and sober than later ages, when the true meaning of titles and their original significance were lost and they gradually became purely formal. Nevertheless titles reveal social stratification, and an understanding of how they developed is essential for appreciation of funerary inscriptions.

The most frequently used title is that of Rabbi, often given only in the abbreviation *r.* The original significance of the title, 'teacher, master', had been lost long before the time of the first gravestone on the Old Jewish Cemetery. By that time the title was given to any man with a certain level of rabbinical training. Even later, the title came to mean no more than 'Mr.'. The title of rabbi is also hidden in the word *bar,* the Aramaic for 'son', often used in Prague inscriptions instead of the Hebrew word *ben,* because *bar* can also be read as the abbreviation of *ben rabbi,* the rabbi's son, when it is followed by the name of the deceased's father.

Since the title rabbi had lost its original solemnity by the fourteenth and fifteenth centuries, another way of denoting those to whom it should by right be given had to be devised. Thus arose the title *h"r"r,* meaning *ha-rab rabbi,* teacher rabbi, or the teacher, our rabbi. The highest title was that expressed by the abbreviation *m"h"r"r (morenu ha-rab rabbi),* our master, our teacher the rabbi. At the time the first Prague inscriptions were drawn up, this title was given only to men who actually occupied the office of Rabbi or *Dayyan,* i.e. member of the rabbinical court.

Another title which came into use later, *k"h"r"r (kebod ha-rab rabbenu),* honourable rabbi, our rabbi, was one of lesser importance, having lost its original force as had the title *h"r"r.* Both were used for people with any level of rabbinical learning. Even less dignity went with the title *k"m"r (kebod ma'alat rabbi),* honourable rabbi. It became the least of the titles employed, and was given even to men with no education, meaning no more than 'Mr.'. Men in rabbinical office were later given the title *m"c"h (morenu ha-rab),* our rabbi and teacher.

127/
The tombstone of Sheindl, wife of Gabriel, 1583. This typical Renaissance style was long thought to date from the year 979. This deliberately wrong date was intended to prove that the cemetery was older than it actually was.

128/
The tombstone of Levi Cohen, son of Alexander, 1585. This is the earliest example in the cemetery of a carving representing the hands raised in benediction, the symbol of the priestly tribe of Cohen.

A true rabbi, later called Chief Rabbi, was entitled 'father of the rabbinical court', in Hebrew *ab bet-din.* He was in fact the chairman of the court of rabbinical judges, or *dayyanim.* In the case of a few rabbis there is another special title, the very honoured title *gaon.* Originally standing for the rector of the ancient Talmudic schools of Babylon, it was later the title given to outstanding rabbinical scholars. Another word used to denote a scholar was *chaber.* In the Talmud this word meant one who strictly observed the rabbinical rules regarding ritual purity, as distinct from ordinary people, called *am ha-arets.* Later the latter word became the contrary of *chaber,* an educated man, and thus an ignorant person. The term *chaber* is rare in Prague inscriptions, and is translated as 'scholar'. Later, this epithet could only be applied, as a special honour, by the rabbi in office, who issued special confirmation of the title.

The titles *aluf* and *katsin,* on the other hand, were given to important men who were not particularly noted for their learning; the literal meaning of both is 'prince'.

There were also titles referring to public office in the administration of the ghetto. *Gabbaj,* or head, was used in Prague inscriptions to denote the head of the charity funds. *Rosh* meant head, in the sense of leading representative of the community, while a title of high honour was *parnas,* one who took care for the well-being of the community.

The lowest but by no means unimportant office in the community was that of *shammash,* verger or sexton. The *shammash* was the factotum and confidant of those who frequented the synagogue, and also fulfilled certain official duties. He was present, for instance, at negotiations between Jews concerning the transfer of landed property, along with the elders.

Besides the *shammashim* whose duties lay in and around the synagogue, there were *shammashim* at the rabbinical courts. From the seventeenth century onwards there were several such courts in Prague, at various levels of competence. Later the Chief Rabbi had his personal *shammash.*

The *shammashim* of the Burial Society,

newly organized in 1564, had a special standing. They were members of the Society, elected to the office of *shammash* for a period of three years. They were often called upon to handle considerable sums of money and valuables, especially when the mourners had not the ready money to pay for the grave and burial, and were forced to give valuables in pledge. This was either redeemed, or if not, auctioned and the proceeds given to the Society's funds. There are records of such transactions in the old account books of the Society between 1701 and 1713. The Society *shammashim* were also entrusted with the effects and property of the dead, particularly when there were no direct heirs. In some cases, of course, such property was taken to the Town Hall for safety.

Finally there is the term *kadosh,* saint, found in some Prague inscriptions. Originally this was a title of honour, given to martyrs who laid down their lives 'to sanctify the name of the Lord'. It appears to have come into use in the second half of the fourteenth century. Later the word lost its original force and was used for anyone who did not die a natural death; unnatural death was regarded as a form of atonement. It is decisive, however, if it is combined with the words 'May the Lord avenge his blood', used only for those who died a martyr's death.

There was only one title given to women, *marat* (lady). The Aramaic form is still used as a given name today: Marta, Martha. The only exception is the title *rabbanit,* 'the rabbi's wife', given to the wife or widow of a rabbi or a *dayyan*; it could perhaps also be used for the daughter of a rabbi, even if her husband did not hold the office of rabbi.

An indispensable part of Hebrew epitaphs was the eulogy. The commonest phrase is 'of blessed memory'; the words of the Book of Proverbs 10,7 are more rarely used: 'The memory of the just is blessed'. The former is expressed by the abbreviation *z"l,* the initial letters of *zikrono li-beraka;* the latter by *zc"l: zekor tsaddik le-chayye ha-olam haba.* It is not until 1490 that these two texts begin to appear in Old Cemetery epitaphs.

Besides these simple eulogies, some epitaphs present more extensive formulas, like

129/
The tombstone of Moshe, son of Rabbi Jacob, and his wife Kresl, 1585. One of the many 'double' tombstones.

'his memorial for life in the world to come', expressed by the abbreviation *z"ts"l"h"h,* the initial letters of the Hebrew words *zeker tsaddik le-chayye ha-olam ha-ba,* or 'May the memory of the righteous be a blessing for life in the world to come', in Hebrew *zeker tsaddik li-beraka le-chayye ha-olam ha-ba,* written as the abbreviation *z"ts"l"l"h"h.*

Epitaphs sometimes include eulogies on those still alive, like 'may his rock protect him', where the 'rock' — as often in the Bible — is the Lord; the abbreviation *y"ts* stands for the Hebrew words *yishmerehu tsuro.* There are many such eulogies on the living, more frequent in later epitaphs.

Eulogies which include pleas touching on life after death are different, and it is they which are most characteristic for Jewish epitaphs. They are rarely found except in this context. The most usual formula used in Prague epitaphs is: 'May his (her) soul be bound in the bundle of life' (I Samuel 25, 29), expressed in the abbreviation *t"n"ts"b"h* — the initial letters of the Hebrew *tehe nafsho (a) tserura bi-tseror ha-chayyim.* This abbreviation is still used in Jewish epitaphs today, even when the rest of the inscription is in Czech and not in Hebrew. It is usually placed at the end of the epitaph, together with the date. It was rare for the whole quotation to be given in full. In earlier times it was accompanied by the words *amen* or *sela,* repeated once or twice. There is an extended form of this eulogy, too, which is occasionally found; for instance, 'May his soul be bound in the bundle of life, with all the other righteous souls', or 'May his soul be bound in the bundle of life with the Lord, Ruler of the Heavens, until the day of return'; or 'May his soul be granted eternal life'; 'May his soul be remembered in the world to come'.

In epitaphs of outstanding men or those well known for their piety, broader phrases were also used, such as: 'May his death redeem all Israel', or: 'May his death wash away all the sins of the people'.

All these eulogies reveal a firm belief in the after-life. Expressions of sorrow and despair are much rarer, like 'Woe to them that are lost and cannot be found on the earth', or 'Woe to that day when he died too soon'. Even here,

130/
The tombstone of Mordechai Meisl, 1601 — the first tomb in the shape of a sarcophagus to be placed in the Old Jewish Cemetery.

131/
The tombstone of the first Jewish woman writer in Prague, Rivka, daughter of the rabbi Meir Tikotin, 1605.

132/
The tombstone of David Gans, chronicler and astronomist, 1613.

133/
The tombstone of Jehuda Loew, son of Bezalel, and his wife Perl, 1609. This is the most famous stone in the cemetery.

however, the emotion expressed is not one of pessimism as regards the life to come, but sorrow for an earthly loss.

Martyrs' epitaphs often include a call for vengeance: 'May the Lord avenge his blood', or 'May the Lord of vengeance vent it upon them'.

Naturally phrases referring to death and burial also occur in epitaphs. The desire for euphemism led to a great many synonymical expressions. The biblical words for death, *mat* and *gava,* occur rather rarely. The most frequent euphemism is *niftar,* 'he has gone, departed', usually followed by 'to his world'. Another frequent phrase is 'he was taken' or 'was gathered to his people', in the biblical phrase; we also find 'he was gathered in holiness', or 'in purity'. Such phrases as 'he was taken from the earth', or 'he was taken away from me' are very rare. In a frequent metaphor, death is seen as the departure of the soul: 'his (her) soul departed', sometimes with the additional words 'in holiness and purity'. Some epitaphs are more poetic, and we read that 'her soul rose to the heights of Heaven', 'his soul returned home', or 'his soul returned unto the Lord'. Very rarely we find such phrases as 'she became a living soul', 'his soul bowed down unto the dust', or 'he gave his soul into the hands of the Lord'.

Many of the euphemisms employed stress that the after-life is something higher than life on earth: 'he ascended to the heights of the mighty', 'he passed on high to intercede for his people', 'in holiness he entered the world to come', 'he went into the dwelling of peace', 'he was gathered unto his rest'. This category also includes phrases referring to God as 'the Judge who has put out this candle', 'He who dwelleth in His habitations hath taken him', 'the King of Peace hath taken him to Himself'.

Special phrases were sometimes used on the epitaphs of scholars, to show the respect in which they were held by the people: 'he has been taken to the schools on high'.

The words of Jeremiah, 'for death is come up unto our windows' (Jer. 9,20) became popular at a later period. Another special group of euphemistic phrases includes such words as: 'the Lord took him unto Himself and left life to us and the rest of Israel', 'she

left life behind for the sons of her people', 'to Israel he left joy and gladness and rejoicing'. 'His glory and splendour have passed away', or 'Fallen is the diadem, fallen the crown', give a grimmer view of departure from this world.

There are far fewer expressions used to denote burial and the grave itself. The biblical words for funeral, grave and to bury are used, as well as euphemistically nuanced words like 'lay' and 'hide'. The biblical 'Let this stone and this pillar be a witness to us' is not frequently used.

It is rare to find the inscription 'this monument was put at the head', which is characteristic of many Frankfurt epitaphs. Generally speaking, compared to Frankfurt and Worms cemeteries, the Prague Old Jewish Cemetery offers a much greater variety of texts on the surviving gravestones.

The greater part of the epitaph, in Prague, is given over to praise of the good qualities and praiseworthy deeds of the deceased. The laudatory words and phrases used to describe men, however, differ fundamentally from those chosen to praise women. The qualities most praised in men were loyalty, uprightness, reliability, honesty particularly in business, a just mind, simplicity and modesty. Besides these traits of character, men were particularly praised for intellectual qualities — good sense, wisdom, circumspection, and eloquence.

A man's attitude towards his fellows was praised in such expressions as 'a man of peace', 'he hated lies and injustice', 'there was no place in his heart for sin and hate', 'where he ruled neither oppression nor strife were heard', 'he loved the upright'.

Besides the right attitude towards others, charitable deeds were often praised: 'a man of pity and charity', 'full of mercy', 'he performed deeds of mercy for the living and the dead', 'generous and charitable, he did good in Israel', 'he did not shame the poor man by turning him away', 'he willingly lent to the poor', 'he was a pillar of strength to the poor', 'he welcomed travellers hospitably', 'the door of his house was open wide', 'he gave his bread to the needy', and so forth.

Charity was not considered an expression of a good heart, but primarily the fulfilling of a biblical commandment, and thus part of religious life. The sphere is described most often in terms of 'God-fearing' and 'piety'. These qualities are praised, for instance, in such phrases as 'prepared to serve Him', 'together with the strong he delivered the Lord's justice', 'in all his deeds his thoughts were on Heaven', 'all his longing, his mind and his hopes were turned towards the Lord', 'he devoted his soul to the service of the Lord', 'he was ready to carry out all His commands', 'he walked in the paths of honour and righteousness', 'from his wealth he gave his tithe to the Lord'. Many epitaphs praise the fervency and ardour of the deceased in prayer, and his zeal in frequent attendance at the synagogue.

Although this main part of the epitaph is also concerned with how his fellows regarded him, their attitude is rarely explicitly recorded. 'He was respected by the people', 'beloved of God and men', 'loved by great and small', are a few of the phrases. There are also biblical references such as 'his name was seen on the gates (of Heaven)', 'he gained a good name', 'who can count his virtues'. This can be negative: 'it is praise to keep silent about him'.

Occasionally the wealth of the deceased is mentioned: 'his days were filled with wealth'. Later on, the origin of the family becomes the subject of praise: 'of a very famous family'. It is very rare indeed, however, to find any reference to the way the deceased earned his living. There is only one epitaph which tells us that 'he lived by the work of his hands'.

The greatest praise expressed in epitaphs is reserved for learned men. On the one hand, the scholar is said to have spent his time studying the Torah, 'he set the time for the Lord's learning' or 'he studied incessantly and never loitered'. On the other hand, his real knowledge of the Scriptures and rabbinical writings is stressed: 'he was at home in learned books', 'he was at home in all books of wisdom and in the books of the Scriptures', 'he knew all the writings', 'well learned in all six sedarim', 'he was a father of learning and a father to hand it on', 'he delved into the learning of Israel and longed for the wisdom of the Cabala and sought it out'. It was stressed as

134/ *(Page 163)*
The Old Jewish Cemetery in summer. View of the cemetery around the grave of Mordechai Meisl.

particularly praiseworthy that the deceased spread learning by 'setting up disciples', or in more general words, 'he spread the Torah in Israel'. Here we find reflected the belief that it was especially praiseworthy to support scholars, as in: 'his house was open to all who spent their time in study'. During the Baroque period all these formulas were inflated often to hybrid freakishness, as can be seen on some epitaphs of the seventeenth and eighteenth centuries.

It is rare indeed to find any reference to the appearance of the deceased, such as 'his face was like that of a king', 'a handsome man, and tall', or 'his voice was pleasant and his appearance cordial'.

In the vicissitudes of Jewish life, the fickleness of their standing in the eyes of the Czech authorities, the Jews needed men capable of acquiring influence with the secular authorities. Such men were known as *shtadlan*, 'intercessors'. We find such individuals praised in their epitaphs for their readiness to help others, or the community as a whole, standing up for them without fear. They are described in biblical terms: 'he stood in the breach and built a wall for now and forever', or: 'he was a wall unto us, and stood in the breach'; sometimes 'he stood guard at the breach'. These are metaphors from military tactics, to be taken figuratively.

Adjectives describing personal qualities are more frequent in women's epitaphs than in men's. The most usual are 'valiant', 'virtuous', 'good', 'unspoiled', 'upright', 'respected', 'perfect', 'irreproachable', 'noble', 'simple', 'loyal', 'straightforward', 'true', 'prudent', 'rare', 'pure', 'just', 'pleasant'. Praise for a woman's appearance is also more frequent than in the epitaphs of men: 'charming', 'lovely'; the epitaphs are sometimes linked to the woman's name, as in 'Dobřiš [i.e. good] in name and deed', or 'Sheindl [i.e. beautiful] in name, and praised for it'. On the other hand, it is extremely rare for any mention to be made of intellectual qualities: a woman 'of clear mind', 'wise heart'.

There are special sayings to describe women, like 'her husband's crown', 'as bright as the sun', 'she was a light in the people of Judah', or 'a priestess of the Highest'.

135/
The tombstone of Hendl, wife of Jacob Bashevi, 1628. Hendl was the only woman to be honoured with a richly decorated sarcophagus, as she was the wife of a very well-known man.

136/
The tombstone of the Chief Rabbi of Prague, Simon Wolf Auerbach, 1632.

In their relations with other people women are praised primarily for their honesty and straightforwardness: 'all her deeds were honest', 'honest in all she did'; as with men this frequently referred to the woman's commercial activities.

Of course charity is a constant theme: 'she performed her acts of charity in secret', or 'she gave alms in secret'.

In religious life, like men, women were praised for their piety, for being God-fearing, fervent in prayer and zealous in attendance at the synagogue. It is extremely rare, however, that a woman is praised for devoting herself to study. We read in one epitaph that the dead woman 'preached to other women'; another 'explained the prayers for holy days to other women'.

The epitaphs in the Old Jewish Cemetery of Prague have their specific style which can be defined. We must of course bear in mind that the surviving material is not complete. Nevertheless the number of gravestones still preserved, almost 12,000, is no mean proportion of all those ever laid in place here. During the last century many of the inscriptions became badly weathered and are illegible. Some were copied, not always accurately, and since they can no longer be identified, or are sunk too deeply into the ground, it is no longer possible to check how correct these copies are. Today they are preserved in the State Jewish Museum.

Unlike the epitaphs in the Worms and Frankfurt cemeteries, those in the Prague Jewish cemetery are remarkable for their variety. It is strange that the language of these epitaphs has not yet been subjected to lexicographical analysis, although it offers much of linguistic interest. There are many phrases and expressions not attested elsewhere, which could serve a study of vernacular Hebrew over four centuries. There are many biblical parallels used in the texts, showing the authors' desire to keep as closely as possible to the language of the Bible. On the other hand, a lack of feeling for the language often draws the author closer to everyday speech. The desire to make full use of biblical and other parallels is the hallmark of the musive style which flourished, as we shall see, in the seventeenth and eighteenth centuries. It was the aim of these authors to incorporate the greatest possible number of biblical quotations and echoes, drawing also on old religious writings. Sometimes the quotations are used in their original sense, but far more often they acquire a new meaning, either by a slight change, or by setting them in a new context.

Another characteristic of these epitaphs is the attempt to co-ordinate the subject matter by the use of rhyme. Although our material is far from being true poetry, nevertheless this formal element is reminiscent of Spanish and Italian Hebrew poetry known as *makama* (from the Arabic), where a chain of incidents is described in rhythmical, rhymed prose, with metrical lyrics inserted at intervals. Our Prague epitaphs do not rise above the level of folk rhymes, often crude, which influenced the choice of adjectives and often resulted in faulty grammar. Only in a few epitaphs, particularly those of important men in the ghetto in the seventeenth and eighteenth centuries, is there any attempt at literary style.

The first to take an interest in the epitaphs in the Old Cemetery was Moshe Wolf Jeiteles, the registrar of the Burial Society. In the first half of the nineteenth century he copied a number of the older and more important epitaphs. This formed the basis for the publication of *Gal-Ed* ('this mound bears witness') by his successor in office, his son-in-law Koppelmann Lieben, in 1856. *Gal Ed* includes copies of 170 epitaphs dating from 1439 to 1787, an introduction by the Chief Rabbi of Prague Shelomo Jehuda Rapoport, and notes on individual epitaphs by a private scholar, Simon Hock of Prague. Soon after this the Burial Society began a systematic record of all the epitaphs in the cemetery, the most active part being taken by David Podiebrad of the Society. To facilitate the task, the cemetery was divided into thirteen sections marked A — N. Copying continued on the initiative of the later Chairman of the Burial Society M. A. Wahl, carried out from 1876 by Leopold Popper. Stones which had sunk into the ground were dug up, so that the complete text could be copied.

The original notebooks have been preserved in the archives of the Society, and are now

137/
The tombstone of the rabbi Nehemiah, called Feiwl Duschenes, son of Abraham the Levite, 1648.

in the State Jewish Museum. They have not been published in full, but were used by Simon Hock for his book *Die Familien Prags,* published after the author's death by David Kaufmann, in Bratislava, 1892. The book gives 7,833 brief references to the content of the epitaph texts, drawn from the copies made of 11,653 epitaphs. The most recent and fully annotated text of the oldest 170 epitaphs is that edited by the outstanding scholar of medieval Hebrew, Dr Otto Muneles, who supplied both a translation and a commentary on the texts. Later, he extended this work to include important seventeenth and eighteenth century epitaphs, but this has unfortunately not been published.

We have selected a number of these epitaphs, both for the interest of the person they refer to, and for the text itself. Our epitaphs are arranged chronologically, and include both simple and more elaborate texts. The long inscriptions on seventeenth and eighteenth century tombs are given in short extracts — usually the introductory passages.

1

m'h'r'r Abigdor Kara
Here lies buried a man who understood the beauty of songs,
Who taught the Torah to many and singly,
Well versed in learning,
In all the books of wisdom and the Scriptures,
Our master and teacher, Rabbi Abigdor Kara,
Son of the martyr Rabbi Jizchak Kara;
He was respected by his people,
He passed away and into his own world,
On the Sabbath, the ninth day of the month of Ijjar,
And was buried on Sunday the tenth of Ijjar 199 in the small count. (25. 4. 1439)
May the Lord justify him in judgement,
For he has passed into His house;
May his soul be remembered in the world to come,
And be bound in the bundle of life.
Amen amen amen sela sela sela

We have spoken of Rabbi Abigdor Kara in Chapter III. His gravestone is displayed in the Klaus Synagogue, State Jewish Museum, Prague. The inscription is no longer legible, and has been translated from a copy made in the nineteenth century.

2

m'h'r'r Pinchas, may the memory of the just be blessed.
His goal was earnest,
He spread learning;
Here he rests,
A wise teacher;
And I lament
For the wisdom of him
Who gave us shade is silent;
M'H'R'P (inchas) may his memory be blessed,
The first day on the eve of the Day of Atonement 256 (27. 9. 1495) mourned by the great and by the elect,
May his soul be bound with all pure souls in the bundle of life.

We have talked of Rabbi Pinchas (Pinkas) in connection with the Pinkas Synagogue.

3

R i v k a, daughter of Rabbi J o m t o b, of blessed memory, pious and virtuous, wife of the noble J e s h a j a H o r o w i t z of blessed memory; her soul departed the seventh day of the nineteenth month (Siva) 275.

This is a lament, mourn, ye angelic messengers and powers,

Over the death of a mother in Israel

Who lies hidden in this mound of earth,

May her good works help all the sons of the Covenant from generation to generation,

For all her deeds and intentions were directed towards Him who created the mountains,

Peaceable were her words and goodly her speech,

138/
The Old Jewish Cemetery in autumn, looking towards the Pinkas Synagogue.

139/
The tombstone of the Chief Rabbi of Prague, Ahron Simon Spira, 1679.

Her lips moved in prayer and supplication,
Her mouth spoke the noble thoughts of her heart.
She was laid here on the first day, the twentieth of Sivan, in the year 275 (3. 6. 1515) amid weeping and lamentation.
May her soul be bound in the bundle of life.

Rivka was the wife of Jeshaja Horowitz, an important person in the Prague ghetto in the early sixteenth century (see Chapter III). The epitaph of 1515 speaks of him as dead, but according to contemporary sources he was still alive in that year. The stonecutter may have incised H (5) instead of Ch (8), so that the correct date may be 1518.

4

m'h'r'r Jizchak Margalit, may the memory of the just be blessed.
And as Jizchak grew old, his eyes grew dim,
Head and father of the rabbinical court, wise and modest,
He walked in justice and his deeds were just,
And he died and was buried by Moshe and Jacob, his sons,
With great honour, and fragrant was his oil,
And when he died men saw that the pillar of his cloud departed
And the people wept that his days had not been fulfilled,
And Moshe did not know that his countenance glowed,
I lift my voice for our master and teacher, Rabbi Jizchak,
And let all who hear lament with me,
He died on the twenty-fifth of Adar 285 in the small count (20. 3. 1525).
May his soul be bound in the bundle of life.

The text of this epitaph carries many biblical parallels. The dead man belonged to the Margalit family, which was widely influential in the fifteenth and sixteenth centuries, particularly in Germany. Rabbi Jizchak was the author of the *Rules for Divorce Documents,* but otherwise little is known of his work. His gravestone is one of the best preserved early Renaissance stones in the Prague cemetery.

5

M e n a c h e m, son of Rabbi M o s h e, may the memory of the just be blessed.
From the fountain of mine eye the tears run down,
Menachem is far, and goeth into oblivion,
He studied the Torah without loitering,
A wise leader in learning
And in wealth and good deeds on this earth,
Those who wrought wisdom ate at his table,
He paid his tithes unto the Lord from his wealth,
At a ripe old age he joined the sons of the highest.
On the day of the Holy Sabbath, the twenty-fifth of Elul 289 by the 'count' (30. 8. 1525).
May his soul be bound in the bundle of life.

We have reproduced this gravestone because it is the first in Europe to bear the sign of the five-pointed Star of David; this is not likely to be a question of ornament alone. The name Menachem, 'the Comforter', belongs to the 'son of David'. Menachem was the father of Nechama, the second wife of Ahron Meshullam Horowitz, which may explain why Ahron Meshullam was buried close to Menachem. Otherwise little is known of him.

6

A z r i e l, son of J i s r a e l of blessed memory. Eye after eye is washed with tears,
For fallen is the crown that could not endure,
The righteous perished and was buried in the earth.
Valiant he was, and stood in the breach;
Head and leader in the congregation,
His wisdom supported all the sons of the land;
And his face was that of a king,
So just and upright was nowhere else in the world;
And filled with the fragrance of learning, and teaching,
All his desires and thoughts and hopes were turned towards the Lord;
And he was gathered unto his people with a good name on Friday, the third day of Tébét, in the year 291 by the small count (23. 12. 1530).
May his soul be bound in the bundle of the living.

140/
The tombstone of the son of Rabbi Spira, the regional rabbi Benjamin Wolf Simon Spira, 1715.

That the deceased was an important man in the community can be seen from the words 'he stood in the breach', used for those who could use their influence with the secular (Czech) powers. This aspect is further stressed by the words: 'his wisdom supported all the sons of the land'. Nevertheless, we know practically nothing of his life from contemporary sources.

7

Rachel, daughter of Rabbi Kalonymos of Venice,
Lamentation and sorrowful tears fill my voice
As I mourn the young and
courageous woman, her husband's crown;
Her mind was clear and her soul like the sun
Rachel, lovely to see and admire
Daughter of Rabbi Kalonymos of the great city of Venice;
Her deeds were always directed by the Law and the words of the scholars
And now she has been taken from us for the sins of her generation.
She died the twentieth day of Elul in the year 291 by the small count (2. 9. 1531).
May her soul be bound in the bundle of the living.

This is an example of an epitaph to a young woman, a foreigner, praised not only for her good deeds, but also for her beauty. It is interesting that the name of the husband of the beautiful Rachel is not given in the epitaph.

8

m'h'r'r Abraham, son of m'h'r'r Abigdor, may his memory live on in the world to come, and may his soul be bound in the bundle of life.
Father of wisdom
Exalted in her secrets
Great eagle of many colours;
M'H'R'R A(braham),
May his memory be blessed,
Master and son of a master,
He gathered the wisdom of the Lord for more than twenty years
As father of the rabbinical court, the Talmudic school,
The Torah was always his pleasure,
And he was versed in the Scriptures and all the books of wisdom
And his soul departed in the year 303
On the twenty-seventh day of Tishri (7. 10. 1542)
And there was weeping and wailing
And may his soul be bound in the bundle of the living
With the Lord, the Master of the Heavens.

We have spoken of Rabbi Abraham in Chapter III. There is an additional inscription on this gravestone, a short epitaph to the ritual butcher Jacob the Levite, who died a year before Rabbi Abigdor. We do not know whether there was a family relationship to explain this additional epitaph.

9

Shelomo, son of Gershom, may the memory of the just be blessed.
He who is buried here was a man of peace,
Where he ruled there was neither oppression nor conflict,
He watched at the gates of the house of prayer
Morning and evening, yesterday and the day before;
Shelomo was his name, son of Gershom,
He printed books in all purity,
And was a priest of the Lord on High.
307 by the small count (1546-47).

The deceased was the son of Gershom ha-Cohen, founder of the first printers of Hebrew books; their work is discussed in Chapter III.

10

Ahron Meshullam, son of Rabbi Jeshaja the Levite,
Blessed be his memory, from Horowitz.
Here lies a lord of the land,
Who built a wall and stood in breach.
Call forth all who mourn, for one of the pious is dead;
He never wavered to intercede, even where great danger threatened,
And he built a wonderful house of prayer to the glory of the Lord, praise to Him,
For from Him comes wisdom,
The poor were his beloved,
May his good works stand us in good stead, we

who remain here,
Look, here lies the just, on earth perfect and noble k'm'r
Ahron Meshullam, son of Jeshaja the Levite, of blessed memory, HOROWITZ.
And he was buried on Sunday the fifth of Elul 310 by the small count (17. 8. 1545).

We have said much about the difficult character of Ahron Meshullam Horowitz, in his day the most important member of the Prague Jewish congregation; his epitaph gives only words of praise, recalling his positive contribution to society.

11

Shabbatai, son of Jeshaja the Levite,
a man of Horowitz.
Here is laid a man of faith,
A rocky summit,
Who spoke justly and declared what is true;
The head, leader and judge of the community,
He led his people and judged them justly;
A man of eloquence, an intercessor, a scholar,
Son of an intercessor and son-in-law of Akiba, Prince of Exile;
May He grant thee a high place in Heaven and may He send a Redeemer for all His people.
In the year 315 according to the small count (1554—55),
May it so happen, that eye to eye we shall see 'the Lord returneth to Zion'.
May his soul be bound in the bundle of life.

We have spoken of Shabbatai, brother of Ahron Meshullam, in earlier chapters. The date is given twice on his gravestone, once in the normal manner and once as a chronogram 'The Lord returneth to Zion' (Isaiah 52,8).

12

Here lie the ashes of the martyrs Rabbi Jisrael, son of Jeshaja Horowitz, and his son-in-law Rabbi Moshe, son of Joel,
Who delivered up their souls to the flames
And declared the name of the Lord before the people,
For their bodies were pure, without guilt,
And both called 'Shema Jisrael' out loud
And breathed their last with the words 'He is One!'

141/
The tombstone of the Chief Rabbi of Prague, David Oppenheim (often written as Oppenheimer), 1736. This tomb is similar to that of Benjamin Wolf Simon Spira, dated 1715.

142/
The tombstone of Simon, son of Jehuda Lejb Kuh the Levite, who was one of those who did a great deal for the ghetto and its inhabitants. One of Kuh's benefactions was the foundation of a scholarship for poor rabbinical students. He died in 1773, and his tombstone has a marked late Baroque character.

And their death caused great commotion,
For there was nought in the teachings of Moses
Which could be brought against them;
And the glory of Jisrael passed into the reign of darkness,
And Moses came down in the dark shadows around.
The sixth day, the 27th Kislev 329 by the small count (17. 12. 1568).
May their souls be bound in the bundle of life.

Nothing is known of the reason why these two rabbis were executed, nor do we know what their relationship was to the Prague Horowitz family. Both names are recorded in the Memorial Book of the Old-New Synagogue, but without noting who had this *haskara* entered.

13

Abraham Moshe, son of Rabbi Jechiel Winternitz of blessed memory,
Bitterly I raise my voice in lament
For a just and pious man who left this world
Before he reached the age of thirty years,
Head of the congregation and leader of the land in justice;
Moshe was his name,
And he did not desert the people;
But interceded with kings and princes,
His name was written on the gates;
For he interceded often for the rich and for the poor,
For one and for all in the congregation,
As for those who are no longer here on earth,
He stood at the head of the faithful;
And with his companions he regained our privileges
And prevented our expulsion, as all know well;
Therefore lament over such a man;
And may his merits intercede with God for us.
He died on the sixth day, the eighteenth of Nisan by the small count (1. 4. 1572) and was buried in the presence of all
And left behind to Israel joy and rejoicing and gladness.
Amen! May God's will be done!
May his soul be bound in the bundle of life.

In the third quarter of the sixteenth century it was Abraham Moshe Winternitz who took the place of Ahron Meshullam Horowitz. He held the office of Jewish mayor several times between 1548 and 1571, and was a founding member of the Burial Society, whose charter was issued in 1564.

14

h'r'r Jisrael, son of Zalman Jeshaya Horowitz the Levite, may his memory be blessed in the world to come, may his soul be bound in the bundle of the living.
My father, my father, the chariots of Israel,
Shepherd and rock of Israel,
His righteousness is as strong as the mountains,
And his judgment in Israel, the chain of the generations of Israel,
The tens of thousands of the people of Israel,
His father, of blessed memory, built a temple to the Lord,
And gave his soul for his people Israel,
And fixed the times to study the Torah of the Lord,
He was generous to the poor for the Lord's sake,
And his son, h'r'r' Jisrael, followed in his father's footsteps,
On the fourteenth of Tishri 333 (21. 9. 1572) the glory of Israel departed,
And was given the privilege to be laid to rest by the side of the House of the Lord.
May his just deeds intercede for the house of Israel.

Jisrael was the eldest son of Ahron Meshullam Horowitz, and his epitaph is also a hymn of praise to the father's good deeds. Each line is taken from one of the books of the Old Testament, and the frequent repetition of the name Israel is certainly a reminiscence of the name of the deceased. In its style this epitaph already foresees the musive style we have discussed at the beginning of this chapter.

15

Rivka Nechama, daughter of m'h'r'r Joseph, the head of the Levites, Minz, blessed be his memory.
Oh that my head might be of water
And my eyes run with tears,
For our hearts are faint,
Death hath come up unto our windows;
Her children are stricken and cannot be comforted,
My dove, my undefiled, bright as the sun;
A mother rejoicing in her children,
The only child of her own mother,
The King of Peace hath taken her unto Himself.
She departed in the eve of the New Year 334 (28. 8. 1573) by the small count.

The name Minz, originally Meinz, is derived from Mainz. The deceased Rivka may have come of a family which moved to Prague around the middle of the sixteenth century, when the Jews were expelled from Mainz. Her epitaph is composed of textual parallels to Old Testament quotations, but they have been chosen so as to express the personal and even the intimate feelings of the bereaved.

16

Sheindl, wife of m'h'r'r Gabriel, in the year 740.
Here is laid a virtuous and pious woman,
Who took care that her dealings were honest,
Her daughters rise up and call her blessed,
Her name is praised at the gates,
Her soul departed and thus the perfect woman, daughter of Rabbi Jehoshua, departed from us,
May the memory of the just be blessed,
Pleasant, she left for her world on Thursday, the day of the new moon in the month of Kislev 740 (!) by the small count (the correct date would be 344, i.e. 16. 11. 1583).

The text of Sheindl's epitaph is common enough, and we have given it here because at some point the date had been changed in order to show the great age of the cemetery; the year 740 would correspond to A.D. 979 in the Christian calendar. In the middle of the last century S. R. Rapoport already cast doubts on this date, in his introduction to the edition of epitaphs from the Old Jewish Cemetery. A similar change was made in the date of the grave of Jehoshua, the son of Jehuda, 1583, which was then given as 702, or A.D. 941. The gravestone of Sheindl, itself, is one of the good examples of a late Renaissance style, with carefully cut lettering and an arcade motif with grapes in relief, and three fishes in a round medallion on each side.

17

The dear Marath Liba, wife of Abraham Perls, the second day, the twenty-fifth of the month of Tammuz, 347 by the small count (3. 8. 1587).
Beneath the weeping oak lies a virtuous and honourable woman;
As is her name, Liba, of the priestly tribe of God on high,
Linked with learning, her crown is of alabaster, marble, of pearls and precious stones,
She performed works of charity for the living and the dead,
Early in the morning she hastened to prayer and song;
Her hand went out to help the needy,
And therefore our hearts grieve,
May her merits intercede for us.

The epitaph to Liba is a typical example of a text for a woman's grave, but the interesting point is the woman's name, Líba, which is certainly the equivalent of the Czech Libuše.

18

The noble and generous k'm'r Mordechai, son of Shemuel Meisl
in the year of the 'princes' of the Lord (361) by the small count, woe unto us for the crown is fallen from our head and 'the perfume of our cheeks' (361) by the small count (13. 3. 1601).

The head and leader of all the sons of exile, k'm'r Mordechai, son of Shemuel Meisl, we had thought we would live in his shadow, for his love for us was great.

He was charitable to all men; he built a synagogue for divine service in a most magnificent building, hospitals and baths, and had the streets of the Jewish town paved with stone; he purchased a garden to enlarge the cemetery and established a house where the wise could gather, and showed his charity to thousands learned in the Torah...

The epitaph on the tomb of Mordechai Meisl, the oldest in the Prague cemetery, dates from the beginning of the seventeenth century. The first lines, quoted above, are inscribed on the head stone, while the list of good deeds continues on the end stone; here it is stressed that 'he stood in the breach for all the sons of his time with all his strength, all his heart and all his soul'. The upper side panels of the tomb bear inscriptions of a later date, stating that the tomb was repaired in 1725, after the 'return from exile' in 1759, and again in 1850.

19

Rivka, the daughter of m'h'r'r Meir Tikotin, departed the twenty-fifth of the month of Nisan, by the count 'Rivka this rock', may her soul be bound in the bundle of life (13. 4. 1605).

Many daughters have been valiant, but you surpassed them all; our hearts trusted her as Abigail, that her good deeds would protect us while she lived; she was given as a burnt offering, as a lamb for atonement; day and night she preached to the women in the city of the faithful; tears were shed by all who came and went as she was buried and hidden in the earth.

We have spoken of Rivka, the first woman Jewish writer in Prague, in Chapter III. Her gravestone was originally wrongly dated 1550, and the mistake rectified only after the epitaphs were studied again in 1955.

20

Thursday the eighteenth of Elul 369 (17. 9. 1609) Rabbi Jehuda, son of Bezalel.
The Lion, a great gaon in Israel, powerful with the 'higher' and the 'lower' / he entered everywhere with or without permission / passed through every garden of paradise untouched / he was wiser than any who learns and teaches the Law / nothing escaped his notice / he gathered together and united both great and small / he wrote endless works / and the yield of his labours was over fifteen books / a comely string of pearls to frame his cheeks / the written teachings and their interpretation were one in the folds of his gown / his hand was raised in all fields of knowledge / he of-

fered the bread of the noble to all the children of his time / his answers to questions were victorious and apt / in opening new learning in the six orders of the Talmud / in explanations of Rashi and the Tosafots was his strength / in rare and penetrating wisdom / for those who encourage knowledge of God and man / he made clear the vision of the Hebrew / and not only was his wisdom great among the powerful / but he taught his knowledge earnestly and wisely / and by wise study he drew up many rules / to protect the biblical and rabbinical commands /
his wise words were as tent pegs / and he ordered the siege of the city for future generations / woe to the pious! woe to the humble! they called upon each other //

This, the first part of the long epitaph, covers half the head-stone and the lower stone along the north side of the tomb; the other half of the headstone is inscribed with the epitaph to his wife Perl, who died a year later:

Wednesday, the twelfth of Ijjar 370 by the small count (5. 5. 1610).
The righteous woman he chose, Perl, daughter of Rabbi Shemuel / a goodly woman, her husband's crown, his heart trusted her in repose and in bond / her deeds were as comely as incense / blessed was she among the women in the tents / the sky was covered in cloud for her / as for Sarah and Rivka, the dough she prepared was blessed / from Sabbath to Sabbath her light burned bright / like Leah and Rachel she was the root of the house / in the service and labouring for Him who reads the Heavens //...

Both epitaphs continue side by side on the end-stone, again with introductory phrases and the date of death. This is followed by a section devoted to Rabbi Loew and then one devoted to both together; this spreads on to the lower stone along the south side of the tomb. Record of repairs to the tomb in 1752 and 1815 has been cut into both upper stones of the tomb.

21

Thursday the eighth of Elul 373 by the small count (22. 8. 1613).
Here lies buried m'h'r'r David Gans, the author of Zemach David, the son of m'h'r'r Shelomo Gans, of blessed memory.
May his soul be bound in the bundle of life.

The famous historian, mathematician and astronomer whom we discussed in Chapter III, unlike his contemporaries, was given a modest epitaph, but his principal work was not forgotten.

22

He died on Thursday the seventh of Adar 379 by the small count (21. 2. 1619).
Here lies buried a man of God, a great prince in Israel, the head of the school and father of the rabbinical court and leader of the scholars of the sacred congregation of Prague, m'h'r'r Shelomo Ephraim, may the memory of the just be blessed.
It was he who wrote six books in his wisdom, and made clear the vision of Israel, and they were: City of Heroes, Ephraim's Gleanings, The Road of Life, Precious Instruments, Lips of Knowledge, Pillar of Marble. He has bent his steps towards the scholars gathered on high, may he rest in peace with Him, His name be praised, for ever with the souls of the pure and undefiled and may his soul be bound in that bundle.
Raise a great and bitter lament / over a just man who was an intercessor / he entered the City of Heroes with his wisdom / and he spread our learning among the strong / and taught many, many disciples / may his good deeds intercede for generations to come / may the yoke of eternal peace lie on the summits of the mountains / may his life be bound in the bundle of life / may he walk upright before the face of the great King / in the year 'send me' the Redeemer who will lead us to glory //...

The epitaph of Shelomo Ephraim Luntshitz continues on the other slabs of the tomb, in phrases which are variations of those in the introductory section. The upper slab on the north side of the tomb bears the date of repairs to the tomb, after the 'exile', in 1752. We have discussed Rabbi Ephraim's term of office in Prague, in Chapter III; he was a disciple and the successor to Rabbi Loew. In his epitaph sentences of sober fact alternate with exaggerated flowery phrases, many of which are well known from earlier epitaphs.

23

Wednesday, the fourth of Tammuz 328 by the small count (4. 7. 1628).
The gracious Hendl, daughter of Ebrl Gerorim, may the memory of the just be blessed, wife of the head and noble leader of his generation, k'm'r Jacob, son of k'm'r Abrahamb(at)' Sche(eba), may the memory of the just be blessed.

And Jacob set up this memorial in sorrow / and all the people cried and lamented / over this noble lady, our leader / buried and hidden here / gone is her glory, gone her magnificence / as the voice of the crowds in the city of the faithful / we all follow her paths / Alas! for the pious, the model of humility / virtue, chastity and purity / she left this world as pure as when she entered it / hastening to fulfil the commandments, the lesser and the greater / and ever stood in the front rank / hastening morning and evening to prayers / and her heart was turned towards God in faith / in awe, in pious modesty, with clear speech / in the order and according to the commands of Rabbi Hemenun / commandments for a light and learning for a torch / her hand stretched out, her right hand grasping firmly //...

The epitaph continues on the side slabs on the north side of the tomb; the end-stone repeats the superscription with the date of death, followed by phrases of praise for the deceased, which continue on the south side slab. There is no mention of any damage to the tomb, or any repairs. We have mentioned the dead woman's husband, Jacob Bashevi of Treuenberg, in the first chapters of this book.

24

The wolf was torn apart early in the morning on Wednesday the seventeenth of Marcheshvan 392 (12. 11. 1631).

The head of the house of learning and father of the rabbinical court for the Czech Lands, the pious great gaon m'h'r'r Simon Wolf Auerbach, son of Rabbi David Tebel, may his memory be blessed.

Daylight be cursed with bitterness / the constellations have disappeared / the heavens covered in cloud / for ever must we weep for the father of the rabbinical court, buried in the earth / the seventeenth day of the month when the moon wanes / he was a bastion unto us / calming anger and strife / when he died the sun grew dark / as when the wise die / and the stars could be seen in daylight / and blood flowed in the gutters / hailstones fell from heaven / pillars collapsed / pictures were washed out / statues demolished / trees and the cedar torn up by the roots / Alas! Oh Lord! the learned and the untaught bewail him / the men of the city, the women and the children //...

Rabbi Simon Wolf Auerbach officiated only very shortly in Prague, but was given a pretentious tomb. He could hardly have made much of an impact during the year or two he spent in the city. We quote his epitaph here because of the unusually gloomy and almost apocalyptic images employed throughout the text. There is an inscription on the lower slab on the south side, to the effect that the tomb was repaired in 1752.

25

Tuesday the twenty-first of Kislev 415 by the small count (1. 12. 1654).
Here lies buried the aged widow Rachel, wife of the great gaon m'h'r'r Lipman Heller the Levite, the author of the 'Tosafot Jomtob', may the memory of the just be blessed. Memorial on the tomb of Rachel 'until this day' (i.e. 415) by the small count.

A rabbi's wife who made it possible for her husband to learn and to teach both old and young / her wealth made his fame, so that he could write innumerable works / pious in all her being, her good deeds were comely in justice / she was exceptionally pious like Obadiah (the servant of God) / day by day she carried out charitable works in secret / we shall not find her equal in the days to come, nor for generation unto generation / may her soul be bound in the bundle of life //

We have mentioned Rachel, and her husband Rabbi Jomtob Lipman Heller of Wallerstein, in Chapter III. He was one of the greatest authorities of the seventeenth century, and was often called after the title of his best-known work, *Tosafot Jomtob.* Naturally the epitaph to Rachel contains much that praises her famous husband. Rabbi Jomtob Lipman Heller died the same year (1654), on the ninth of August, in Cracow. His widow came from a wealthy Prague family, the Teomins, descendants of the Horowitz, and after his death she seems to have returned to Prague.

26

Cry: oh, desolation! on the Feast of Succoth 416 by the small count (16. 10. 1655).

Our remarkable rabbi, universal scholar, divine philosopher, great among physicians, m'h'r'r Joseph, physician from Candia, who was father of the rabbinical court in Hamburg and around Amsterdam, son of the honourable h'r'r Elijah Del Medigo, may the memory of the just be blessed.

143/
The Old Jewish Cemetery in winter, looking south-east, towards Široká Street.

Lift up your voice in lament, in sorrowful complaint and mourning / may your voices be raised in sorrow / with the bitterness of wormwood / for a prince who was strong in the siege has fallen / he who was the crown of the wise in interpretation of the stars / gone is his wisdom, lost is his judgment / there is none like him left in the world / west, east, south or north / the Spirit of the Lord breathed in him / his fame was spread abroad / his soul is hidden by the wings of the great God //

The text of Del Medigo's epitaph continues over the other slabs of his tomb, but is no longer legible today; it mentions his works of astrology as well as his knowledge of the Mishna and the Talmud. The gravestone was brought here before the clearance scheme was put into effect, from an area which was demolished. We have discussed the personality of Joseph del Medigo in Chapter III.

27

On Saturday, in the night before Sunday, the twenty-ninth of Kislev 'the dead' from the time of the Creation of the world (5440, i.e. 3. 12. 1679) / glory passed away and the magnificent tower fell, the instruments of the shrine, the diadem and the crown / the anointed of the Lord, the perfume of our cheeks, the prince of the Lord, the ruler of the Torah / the great and famous gaon / pious and humble, the rabbi of the whole of Israel, the father of the rabbinical court and the head of all the assembled scholars, m'v'h'r'r Ahron Simon Spira, may the memory of the just be blessed, gone is the glory and the grandeur //

Simon, the Just, taught and officiated as rabbi in Prague for forty years / he covered Frankfurt, Lvov, Lublin, Cracow and Vienna with his net / In the fast that came after the other he had none of the pleasures of this world, not the slightest / in winter nights he would refrain from sleep to study the Tanaite writings, the Law and the orders of the Mishna, which he knew by heart / who would count up all his writings, rousing respect / for one who has plunged to the depths to bring up rare and forgotten judgments and send them to the ends of the earth //

The epitaph continues on the other slabs of the tomb, in the same spirit. There is no mention of any restoration of the grave later. We have discussed Simon Spira Wedeles in the third chapter of this book.

28

Friday, the eighth of Tebet 448 by the small count (12. 12. 1687).

Here lies buried one of the holy congregation of those who show their charity (Chevra kaddisha, the Jewish Burial Society), the revered k'h'r'r Baer, a great and experienced doctor, son of k'h'r'r Leib Braun.

He taught the art of curing sicknesses and other great secrets / at all times ready to help the poor and needy / he was the shepherd of all physicians, and those who went astray he led back to the true path / may his soul be bound in the bundle of life //

The dead man, whose name is symbolized by the bear carved on his gravestone, was the author of the Yiddish book of medicine published in Prague, entitled *Studnice živé vody* (A Well of Living Water), but undated.

29

Great was he in Sheshach (i.e. Babylon in the Talmudic sense) and great was his reputation in Rekat (i.e. Tiberias, or the Jerusalem Talmud) / the fourth day was his light extinguished / 5497 counting the generations (12. 9. 1736) / cursed be the day / for the light of the Torah was hidden / the great candle was put out / the great light which should have shone by day / he who held the power over the Babylonian and the Jerusalem Talmud and the supplements to the Tosafot / David explained these texts / the father of the rabbinical court, our lord and rabbi / who could express his praise? / David, our shepherd and father for fifty years / m'v'h'r'r David, son of Rabbi Abraham Oppenheim, blessed be his memory.

He trained many disciples, and wrote innumerable works, interpretations of the Talmud and commentaries to the whole of the Torah / innumerable correct decisions and legal inspiration, who else could promulgate such decisions / only he who carried within

יום הששי ויכלו השמים

והארץ וכל צבאם ויכל אלהים ביום
השביעי מלאכתו אשר עשה וישבת
ביום השביעי מכל מלאכתו אשר
עשה ויברך אלהים את יום השביעי

ברוך אתה יי אלהינו מלך העולם
שהחיינו וקימנו והגיענו לזמן הזה

ברוך אתה יי אלהינו מלך
העולם בורא פרי הגפן
ברוך אתה יי אלהינו מלך
העולם אשר בחר בנו

himself the fulness of the Scriptures / his knowledge of legal works cannot be measured / his sharp insight and wise judgment plunged deep into the waters of the controversy between the supporters of Abbaj and those of Rabb (two Talmudic authorities) / an old man sat in the house of learning / but David came with the right answer / since our rabbi died, fear of sin and humility has vanished, before this he was father of the rabbinical court in Brest, in Mikulov and the region of Moravia / and then he was named rabbi and leader of the community in Bohemia, the community of Jeshurum / David honoured in the synedrion / his light shone as far as Hebron in the east / and the rose of Sharon in the Holy Land / it was a sad day for Israel / may he gaze upon eternal beauty and linger in the halls of the Lord / Amen //

This text is an excellent example of the musive style; it continues in the same spirit over the other slabs of the tomb of Rabbi Oppenheim, spoken of in our third chapter. Facts are interspersed with exaggerated phrases and similes, and with references to Talmudic authorities. At the end of the epitaph his generosity towards the community is praised; he paid double tithes. There is no reference to any repairs carried out on the tomb.

30

The night of the holy Sabbath, the seventeenth of Kislev 530 by the small count (14. 12. 1769).

And the people lamented: what is going to happen to us? and it was right to lament and weep over our misfortune / for the crown was

144/
Celebrating the festival. An illustration in the liturgical book *Seder zemirot u-birkat ha-mazon,* printed in Prague, 1514.

145/
Hunting the hare. A mnemotechnical device, illustrated in the Prague 1514 edition of the *Seder zemirot u-birkat ha-mazon.*

146/
The tombstone of Joseph Shelomo del Medigo. An engraving by Václav Popelík, *c.* 1860 (B. Foges — D. Podiebrad, *Altertümer der Prager Josefstadt,* Prague 1870).

torn from our heads, the prince of the Torah / our rabbi, our great and famous light, the gaon known throughout the world, the joy of his contemporaries / who is like him, a scholar of justice, one of the pillars of the world, the head of the rabbinical court in our great community / our learned master and rabbi m'h'r'r Meir, son of the Great Rabbi Fischl Bumsla / may the memory of the just be blessed for ever.

The child was blessed while his mother lived, the house was filled with light / he studied earnestly, drove sleep from his eyes, the night was as bright to him as the day / he supported the house of learning, increased the knowledge of all who entered into his gates / for over forty years he trained many disciples, and led them to stand on their own / so that many became rabbis capable of making religious decisions / he was given problems to decide by rabbis of his generation, which he dealt with wisely / who could measure up to him, who could describe his magnificent attributes, for none can replace him //

His voice was heard whenever he entered the holy place with explanations, with lectures or with terrifying exhortations to turn sinners to the right path / alas! oh, Lord, alas! how great was he! Let all congregations of the dispersed lament over this great son of our leader / his mother-in-law, his father-in-law m'v'h Moshe Ginzburg, may the name of the just be blessed, the dayyan of our court, who died on his journey to the Holy Land and was buried in the parish of Zidon, bearing his crown / may his good deeds intercede for us / and may his soul be bound in the bundle of life //

The continuation of this epitaph mingles facts with flowery phrases — for instance, that his library was destroyed in the ghetto fire of 1754, while the conventional phrases repeat what we have read in the introduction to the epitaph. It is difficult to say whether the deceased really merited all this praise, since none of his written works have survived.

31

Tuesday the twelfth of Sivan 547 by the small count (29. 5. 1787).

Here is buried a just and upright man, one of the holy brotherhood who carry out the service of charity (Chevra kaddisha) / he was the last to be buried here, according to royal decree / may His Majesty be elevated / the noble, the respected k'h Moshe, member of the administration, the son of k'h'r'r Lipman Bek, may his memory be blessed, early in the morning and in the evening he joined in the prayers / and in commerce and other affairs he behaved uprightly / may his soul be bound in the bundle of life //

This is the last gravestone to have been erected in the Old Cemetery; it is short, simple and to the point. The deceased was no rabbi, no scholar, and the age of flowery musive epitaphs was past. This epitaph serves for the thousands of unremarkable styles in the cemetery. The deceased were not known for great services, or else they simply could not afford a gravestone with a long epitaph. Their memory is no less sacred.

147/
The tombstone of the Chief Rabbi of Prague, David Oppenheim. An engraving by Václav Popelík, *c.* 1860.

/VI/ ART IN THE PRAGUE GHETTO

This chapter gives a brief survey of synagogue art, and in this context we must talk about festivals and the articles reserved for use on these special days, in Jewish households. We shall also touch briefly on other *objets d'art* which either emerged from the ghetto, or were inspired by it, in artists of Jewish and non-Jewish origin. There are the woodcuts which illustrate the Hebrew books printed in Prague, the drawings and (later) painted portraits of important Jews and members of their families, and finally the drawings and paintings of picturesque nooks and corners of the ghetto. Also included are the works of artists from the first half of the nineteenth century onwards, which show what the ghetto looked like right up to the time of its destruction.

Talking of synagogue art, we must remember that this is an art sui generis. It developed in two distinct spheres, the first being that of the synagogue itself. It had a broader significance than purely religious, since the synagogue was not only the setting for religious observance, but the centre of civic life and the centre of education. The art of the synagogues, where it is bound up with religion, shares many features with the religious art of Christianity, at least in so far as the latter served liturgical ends. In the synagogue, as in the church, we find curtains and frontals, often richly embroidered, as well as cult vessels usually made of precious metals. Their purpose may have been different, but in both cases the essential themes are set by tradition.

Here we come up against a fundamental difference, however. Christian art does not exclude the portrayal of the human form on any liturgical object, while it is absolutely forbidden in Jewish religious art. Synagogue art thus lacks the whole sphere of monumental painting and sculpture. There was and is no place there for this type of art. The art of the synagogues is essentially one of ornament, of symbols, and of the written word, without which scarcely any article used in religious observance can be found.

The second sphere of Jewish religious art is that of the religious life of the family. Every festival required its special accoutrements and vessels, as strictly ordered by tradition as those used in the synagogue. In the sphere of the home, however, there was greater iconographical freedom, so that portrayal of the human figure was not absolutely excluded. Outwardly, the difference between the religious life of a Jewish and a Christian household was that in the former certain cult articles were prescribed, while in the latter it was a question of choice. To give a practical example: in an orthodox Jewish household a *mezuzah* — a small box containing a strip of parchment inscribed with a Hebrew prayer — is necessarily fixed to the right doorpost. In a religious Catholic household there may be a

148/
K. Würbs — S. Langer: The Old-New Synagogue. An engraving dating from the second quarter of the nineteenth century.

149/
The Renaissance *aron ha-kodesh* in the Old-New Synagogue with the curtain drawn back; originally the early Gothic aron from the thirteenth century.

holy water stoup by the door, but it is not prescribed.

To return to art in the synagogue: the most important immovable article is the Ark of the Torah — *aron ha-kodesh* — while in older synagogues there is also the raised platform from which the Torah was read, and where the rabbi addressed the congregation. Both the Ark of the Torah and this platform (the *almemor,* from the Arabic *al-minbar,* or the *bimah*), are architectonic works and follow the dictates of contemporary style.

The decoration of the Ark of the Torah employs practically all two- and three-dimensional motifs accepted by the style of the day. Gothic and Neo-Gothic designs present crabs, violets, while Baroque prefers Corinthian columns, finials, obelisks, vases and spirals in relief, festoons of leaves and fruit, conch shells in niches, and so forth. There are of course several symbols that are distinctive for the Jewish religion, such as the two tablets of the Law, the hexagram or Star of David, the *menorah* (seven-branched candlestick), the

150/
The early Baroque *aron ha-kodesh* in the High Synagogue; dating from the end of the seventeenth century.

crown, the Ark of the Covenant, a sacrificial altar, a table with sacrificial bread, and the wings of the cherubim. It does not seem to have been laid down which particular symbols should be employed. A cartouche with an inscription was often used, most frequently in the lower part of the plinth of the Ark.

The ornamentation of the Ark of the Torah differs very much from that of a Catholic altar. The niche itself is closed by a double door, not a single panel, and is much bigger. The mensa, or altar top, is lacking. The worshipper in the synagogue does not see the door enclosing the Torah. Usually a work of art in its own right, the door is hidden from the common gaze by a curtain, the *perochet.* This is a symbolical representation of the curtain which divided the most sacred part of the Temple in Jerusalem from the main, accessible part. This curtain is attested in the Gospels, for it was rent at the moment Christ died. The synagogue curtain is usually oblong in shape, and of a size suited to the Ark of the Torah for which it was intended. It hangs from a horizontal bar, and is drawn to one side. It never hangs in folds, but quite flat. The Torah it conceals was always and still is the most sacred thing to the Jews. The curtain should therefore be of the most precious material. Naturally this depended on the wealth of the donor, for synagogue curtains were always the gift of pious members of the congregation. The earliest curtains to survive in Prague date from the sixteenth century, which was the time of velvets, often threaded with silver or gold, of silken damask and silver and gold brocades. The Jews traded in these luxury goods and were aware of their value. Brocades and velvets were mostly imported from Italy, and later from Spain. There was no flighty change of fashion either during the Renaissance or in the Baroque period, clothes and lengths of valuable cloth were handed down from one generation to another. Both the donors and the people who worked on these synagogue curtains were well aware of the real value of their material, whether brocade or velvet. The actual piece of cloth used to make a curtain could be a hundred or more years old; what counted was how precious the material was.

Most curtains are not a single piece of cloth. They have a design, or one might say a structure. The earliest Prague curtains can truthfully be described as architectonic in their character. A band at the bottom forms a base, or plinth; it may be embroidered so, or it may be formed by a separate piece of cloth. Embroidered plinths rise on each side, bearing columns worked in varied styles of embroidery and representing different architectonic styles. The shaft of these columns is usually embroidered with arabesques of foliage, most frequently vine leaves. The columns bear a horizontal beam on which a dedicatory inscription is often embroidered. This embroidered 'architecture' frames the rare damask, brocade or velvet of the central panel of the curtain; there is no decor here, the glory of the rare cloth suffices. The woven motifs varied, but from Gothic to the Renaissance the classical motif of the pomegranate and its innumerable variations held sway. The central motif of the fruit was often replaced by a vase, a crown, or a stylized bouquet. The pattern was woven strictly symmetrically, but in the Baroque period asymmetry came in, often diagonal in pattern. In some curtains this central panel displays a chessboard pattern of red, blue and gold rosette-embroidered squares, the embroidery using different types of rosette. For the oldest Prague curtain, dating from 1592 and believed to be the oldest synagogue curtain in existence, this pattern has been used. It was donated to the Old-New Synagogue by Salomon Perlstücker. This architectonic style persisted through the late Renaissance and into the Baroque period, incorporating changes in contemporary taste with a certain degree of latency. A similar structure can be seen in the ornaments on the title pages of both Hebrew and Christian printed works of the time.

In the course of time this architectural framework became less popular. The shafts of the side columns were exchanged for vertical bands of embroidered ornament, ending in a crown or other motif instead of a classical capital. The panel bearing the embroidered inscription is no longer a pediment, but is placed lower, between the two bands of ornament at the sides. During the seventeenth cen-

151/
The Torah 'cloak' dedicated by Mordechai Meisl in 1593. It is of greenish brown velvet, with the inscription in gold thread.

152/
The curtain dedicated to the Old-New Synagogue in 1609, of dark red velvet and red brocade with gold thread woven into it, and embroidered with gold.

153/
A curtain from the Pinkas Synagogue, 1693. Originally the velvet was pink, but it has faded to brown; the brocade is woven in vertical stripes of gold, pink and blue.

154/ ▷
A curtain from the Pinkas Synagogue, 1689. The dark red velvet is embroidered in relief.

נ״י הנעלה כה״ה חיים פריינד ז״ל
בן האלוף הה״ר יוסף יהודה נתן פריינד
ז״ל וזוגתו מרת אסתר בת הנעלה
כה״ר משה

155/
A curtain from the Old-New Synagogue, 1697. The dark red velvet is embroidered in appliqué, the red brocade is threaded with gold, and the dedication is embroidered on blue satin.

156/
A curtain from the Pinkas Synagogue, 1697. Dark red velvet, silver and gold brocade, with silver thread embroidery.

193

157/
A curtain from the Pinkas Synagogue, 1717. Red velvet, gold thread brocade, with gold lace.

tury a different type of curtain gradually became popular. Attention was centred on the main panel of precious cloth, which was surrounded on all four sides by a border of either plain coloured velvet, or of material distinctly different in colour and quality. The upper band of this border usually bears the dedicatory inscription.

A third type of synagogue curtain is the 'inscription curtain', a one-coloured curtain on which the inscription occupies the centre, surrounded by an ornamental embroidered frame. There are also gobelin type curtains, and some which are composed of an upper oblong section bearing an inscription, and a lower section of plain or patterned cloth. The Italian and Spanish brocades of the Renaissance and early Baroque used rich dark colours—crimson, dark green and violet or deep blue. From the end of the seventeenth century they were gradually replaced by French brocades which also employed pastel shades. Their patterns were smaller and finer, usually of flowers, brightly coloured, on a background of diagonal or vertical lacey ribbons against white, rose, salmon-pink or silver-gold. Where an architectonic scheme was still used, spiral columns were embroidered in bas-relief. Often nothing remained of the original structure but a centre panel with a border of varying width, sometimes a mere hem. The upper band with its inscription is usually preserved, however, the inscription either in a cartouche or an ornamental embroidered frame, sometimes with independent ornamental motifs at each side, a vase of flowers, or pomegranates. Some curtains were provided with a separate upper section to cover the pole on which they were hung — unless of course there was a firm decorative cover for the pole. This separate section was usually of the same material as the border of the curtain, and was embroidered. Symbolical motifs often appear here: the tablets of the Law, a *menorah,* a sacrifical altar, a table with sacrifical loaves, a crown, and so on.

Unlike the sequence of frontals used in a Catholic church, the colour of the curtain was not liturgically prescribed. It was only later that it became the custom to choose a curtain of a certain colour for specific festivals — so

158/
A curtain from the Klaus Synagogue, 1733. Dark red velvet embroidered in gold and silver thread.

159/
A curtain from the Old-New Synagogue, 1738. Dark red velvet with gold lace appliqué.

long as the synagogue possessed them, of course. On the Day of Atonement, for instance, *Yom Kippur,* a white curtain was hung, while a black one was chosen for the anniversary of the destruction of the temple in Jerusalem.

Satin stitch and closely executed stem stitch were the most widely used embroidery techniques. Lettering was usually embroidered in the seventeenth and eighteenth centuries by a satin stitch in diagonally placed squares. Appliqué techniques were also used, and there are some curtains entirely composed of different-coloured artfully shaped patches of silk. During the Renaissance tiny pearls were sewn on as an ornament. Tassels and fringes, and even silver and gold lace, were added as decoration. Tiny metal bells were sometimes sewn on the lower edge of the band bearing the inscription.

No less important a part of the appointments of the Ark of the Torah, although much smaller, was the cloak which covered the Torah itself, wound on its two rods. The Torah was said to be 'clothed' in its cloak. The front part of the cloak is ornamented, the back part usually plain. In form the cloak is not unlike the Catholic chasuble, though simpler and of course smaller. It is simpler because unlike the chasuble (if we except its Gothic form) it is not rounded at the bottom but made up of two oblong pieces of cloth of the same size, pulled over the rolled-up scrolls of the Torah and sometimes tied firmly. Other types of cloak existed, but this Ashkenazi type was the only one known in Prague or in Bohemia. Like the synagogue curtains, the front section of the cloak of the Torah was made of precious materials and often richly ornamented. There are cloaks that are replicas of the architectonic structure of curtains, and display a centre panel framed by columns with plinths and capitals, and with a dedicatory panel above. The back section of the cloak may be of the same material, or (when this is a rare brocade or gold and silver threaded velvet) of some less valuable cloth. As with the curtains, the architectonic structure of the cloaks is simplified, and reduced to a centre panel with a border and a section bearing the inscription, or to a single panel of rare cloth, framed in a

160/
A Torah cloak from the Pinkas Synagogue, 1740. Gold brocade with silver, gold and embroidery on dark red velvet.

161/
A Torah cloak from the Pinkas Synagogue, 1754. Emerald green brocade with interwoven threads of gold, silver and other colours.

162/
A curtain from the Klaus Synagogue, 1781. Green brocade with a multi-coloured pattern; the dedicatory inscription is embroidered in gold and silver thread on dark green velvet.

163/
A Prague curtain, 1850, from the State Jewish Museum. Green brocade.

fringe or tassels, and an upper panel bearing the inscription. There are also cloaks of one-coloured cloth, often velvet, where the front panel is embroidered with a symbolic motif and an inscription, usually in the centre. It does not seem that the form of the Torah cloak developed from the more elaborate to the reduced, simpler form. One of the earliest surviving examples in Prague, a cloak presented by Mordechai Meisl in 1593, is simple in design. It is entirely made of brownish-green velvet, the upper section bearing the dedication inscription separated from the lower by a gold braid. On the other hand, many Baroque cloaks show the complex architectonic design carried out in all detail. Embroidered symbols are frequent: a crown, the Star of David, or symbols derived from the donor's tribe or family or corresponding to his name. The stitches used in this embroidery are of course the same as those seen on curtains.

The scrolls of the Torah were prevented from unrolling by a textile attachment resembling a swaddling band. This was made

164/
Bands for the Torah, with a painted dedication.

165/
Bands for the Torah, with the dedication embroidered in different colours and different stitches.

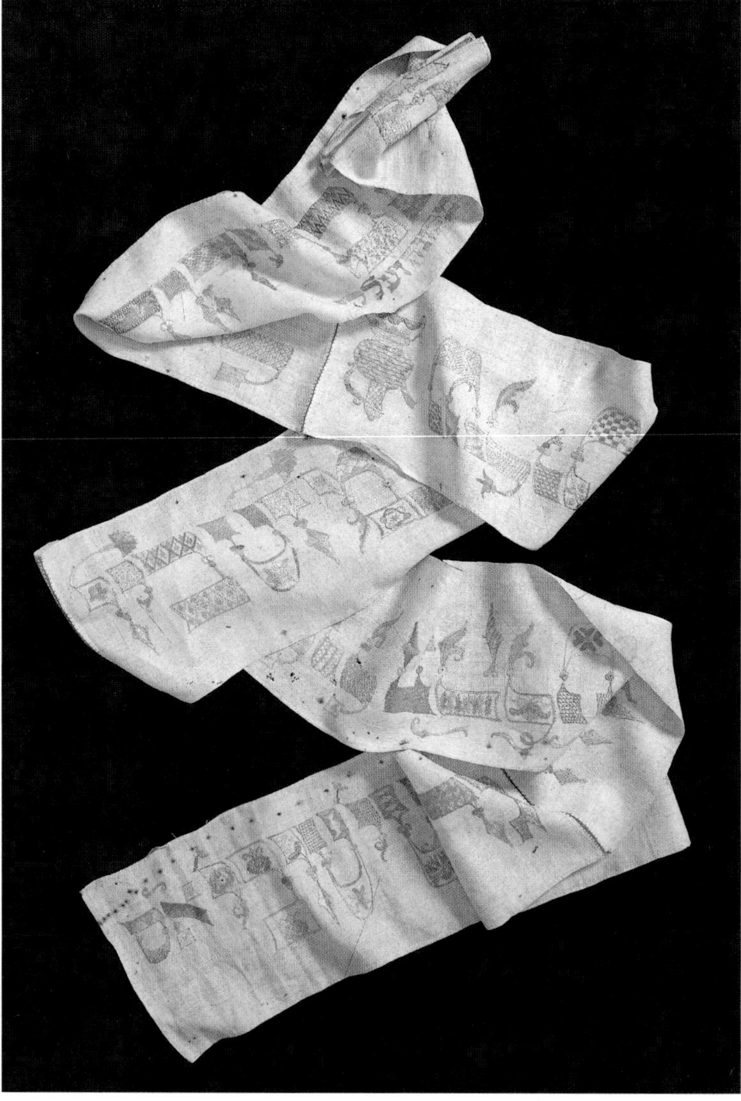

from the real swaddling band wrapped round a boy at circumcision, and on his first visit to the synagogue (usually at the age of three) the child presented this band to the synagogue. They are narrow strips of linen, or sometimes of more precious material, and are usually made of four pieces sewn together. The only decoration is the dedicatory inscription, embroidered or more rarely painted, and sometimes combined with an ornament or figural design. These bands seem to have been made by the mother or other relatives of the newborn, and are often more or less reminiscent of folk art. Other bands, especially made for the Torah, were also used; these were oblong pieces of cloth about 50 cm by 30 cm, fixed to the scroll by laces or buttons. They might be of velvet, silk, woollen or cotton cloth.

The last textile attribute of the Torah is the cloth which covers the lectern or the table on which the Torah is laid for reading, and on which it is unrolled. This cloth, too, was often of precious material.

We come now to the metal accessories of the Torah. As we have said, the scrolls on which the Torah is written are wound towards the centre on two wooden rods whose length depends on the width of the parchment. These rods end at the top and bottom in handles to help in unrolling and rolling the scrolls; the rods were made by turners. In Jewish symbolism the Torah is the Tree of Life, and so the upper handles of both rods ended in a beaten and sometimes gilt silver representation of a pomegranate (Lat. *malum punicum* or *malum granatum*), in Hebrew *rimonim.* This is the commonest type in Prague synagogues. The term *rimonim* was still used for these ornaments even after other symbols had taken the place of the pomegranate. There developed an architectonic design featuring a tower of several storeys and decorated with little bells that tinkled as the Torah was carried to and from the Ark. Some *rimonim* took the form of a small crown. Later, in the Classicist period, a composite type emerged, combining the tower with the crown. An openwork gallery often hung with bells was placed beneath the crown. The lower part of this handle, bearing the symbols, showed the most

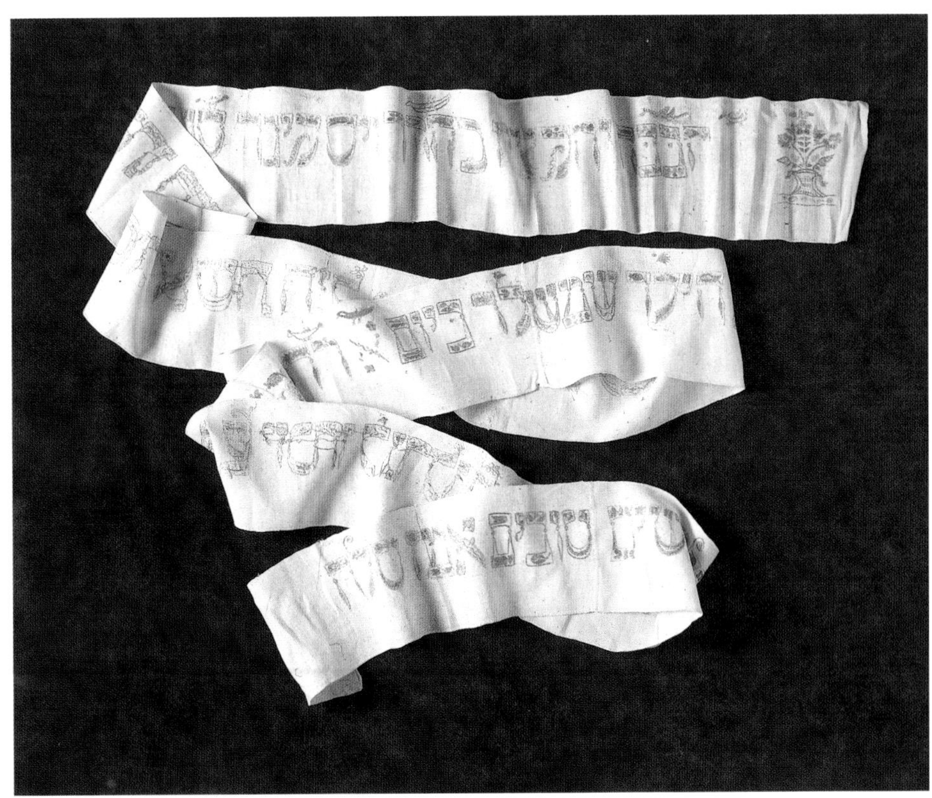

166/
Bands for the Torah, with a coloured embroidered dedication.

167/
Bands for the Torah, with an embroidered dedication and simple leaf pattern.

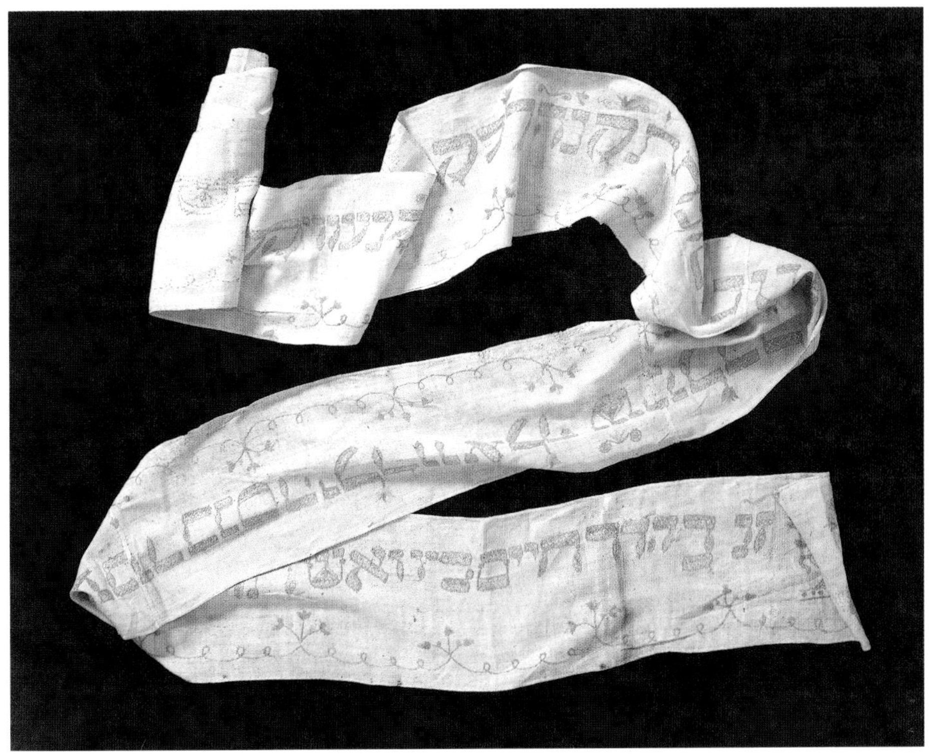

168/
A *rimonim* (handle ornament) for the Torah, in the shape of a crown borne by two seated lion cubs. Beaten and engraved silver, partly gilt. Moravia, 1805.

marked influence of contemporary taste. It often takes the form of spiral columns, or recalls the stem of a goblet or candlestick. This part of the handle is often richly adorned in relief ornament of beaten metal, Baroque, Rococo or Neo-Classical in style. No Renaissance *rimonim* have come down to us in Prague.

A more precious symbolical adornment of the Torah is the crown, an attribute of great significance since biblical times. The epitaphs in the Old Jewish Cemetery of Prague often repeat the saying: 'The crown has fallen from our heads', particularly in the epitaphs of learned rabbis. Here the crown is clearly identified with the great learning of the deceased. In Ashkenazi communities, the scrolls of the Torah were adorned with a pomegranate on the Sabbath, but with a crown on holy days. There are far fewer crowns than *rimonim,* however, and very few synagogues possessed this ornament in their treasury. They were certainly modelled on the crowns of ruling princes; usually they were of beaten silver, sometimes silver-gilt. The ornament was determined by the time at which the crown was made. Sometimes the metal was enriched with semi-precious stones, or cut glass of different colours. Some crowns have a little bell attached above.

169/
A *rimonim* for the Torah, in the shape of an openwork crown borne on slender columns with a gallery below, and openwork balustrades. There are small bells attached below. Beaten and engraved silver. Bohemia, 1860.

170/
One of a pair of Torah handles, shaped like a crown. Beaten and engraved silver. Moravia, 1810.

When the Torah was being read it was forbidden to touch the parchment with the hand — that would be a desecration. Probably, of course, this prohibition was intended to preserve the parchment from sullying, and from wearing out too soon. A pointer, *yad,* was used; a slender rod ending in a miniature hand with the first finger outstretched. It was attached to the Torah by a chain. Most pointers are of silver, some are of ivory, or wood, but sometimes a combination of materials was used: a silver pointer with a coral hand, or a wooden pointer with the hand of ivory or tortoiseshell. The pointers are variously shaped: a slender column with a ring about half way up, a spiral column, shaped like a sceptre or like a slim balustrade. Usually circular in section, there are some polygonal examples. The ornament, which is often combined with a dedicatory inscription, is either beaten or engraved, and sometimes worked in filigree. This ornament, again, depends on contemporary taste.

The last of the metal accessories to the Torah is the *tas,* or shield. It reminds us of the pectoral worn by the High Priest in biblical times, which was adorned with many-coloured stones. It is not impossible that Egyptian influences were at work in Palestine in biblical times. In Egypt the pectoral was an exclusive adornment worn only by the monarch. Egyptian pectorals had a long tradition, and they too were ornamented with coloured semi-precious stones or glass paste. The shield of the Torah was made of beaten silver, and hung on a chain of considerable size. Oblong, usually long rather than broad, but sometimes square, they were usually architectonic in design, and richly ornamented. The architectonic design was sometimes merely ornamental, but always strictly symmetrical. It incorporated different columns, in appliqué or freestanding, or grouped in twos. These columns may have had a symbolical significance, recalling the two legendary pillars of the Temple in Jerusalem, *Jachin* and *Boaz.* Popular motifs were the crown, the Tablets of the Covenant, and the hands raised in blessing. Frequent animal motifs were two lions, and a two-headed eagle. It is rare for a human figure to appear on this shield, but a richly ornamented one from the Meisl Synagogue at the beginning of the eighteenth century portrays Judith with the head of Holofernes, and Aaron. A pair of chimaera on a shield dating from 1831 is most unusual. The rest of the ornament, tendrils, festoons of flowers and fruit, acanthus and rocaille, all correspond to the period when the shield was designed. In the central axis, below, above or in the middle, there is usually a frame to hold changeable panels bearing the name of the festival being celebrated, or a large cartouche with a dedication. Small pendants hang from the lower edge of the shield, in the shape of little medallions hung on short chains or on a simple hook; these pendants, too, usually bear dedicatory inscriptions. It is worthy of interest that the pectorals worn by the pharaohs of Egypt also bore pendants.

An ‘eternal’ light hangs before the Ark of the Torah (in Hebrew *ner tamid*). The lamps were wrought in beaten or chiselled silver, and usually hung from three chains. In form they are completely dependent on contemporary taste, and do not really differ from the ‘eternal light’ lamps hanging in Catholic churches.

Among the precious vessels we must mention the bowls and pitchers used for the washing of hands before prayers. These ‘Levite vessels’ were often elegantly wrought in beaten silver, sometimes ornamented with engraved motifs. Some of them recall contemporary Christian vessels for the Mass, which is not surprising, for well-known Prague goldsmiths and silversmiths often worked for both Catholic and Jewish customers, and the same was true of those artisans who made vessels commissioned abroad.

Collection boxes were usually made of less precious materials, of wood or brass. Some were hung on the wall near the entrance to the synagogue, others were carried round among the congregation. The former were usually shaped like a small chests, the latter like jugs with a hole in the cover for coins, or simply dish-shaped. Both pitchers and dishes were of wood, or copper covered with silver, and of silver, decorated with beaten or engraved motifs. The dishes were usually patterned round the edge, and in the centre. On one side

171/
A crown for the handle of the Torah. Silver gilt, beaten and engraved, set with coloured stones. Prague, 1817.

172/
A Torah shield, oblong, segmented, ornamented with pairs of twisted columns in relief, their capitals shaped like crowns. A large crown is placed between the columns, at the top, with shells beneath it, and completed with a pattern of foliage. Beaten silver. Rokycany, 1762.

173/
A Torah shield, oblong, higher than broad, with an indented edge. The ornament consists of two spiral columns bearing a large crown, with typical Rococo ornament. Beaten silver. Prague, 1784.

174/
A Torah shield, broader than high, with a horizontal bar below, ornamented with scroll pattern and completed by a large crown, with festoons of laurel. The two panels of the Covenant occupy the centre. Beaten and engraved silver. Prague, late eighteenth century.

they had a handle, and on the other a tiny candlestick.

In synagogues following the traditonal orthodox rite, the *shofar* is used in the liturgy. This is a ram's horn which is blown at the New Year and on the Day of Atonement. This primitive musical instrument has preserved its natural form and has never been adorned in any way. In the nineteenth century reformed synagogues introduced music into the liturgy, and some synagogues were then equipped with an organ.

The textile accessories to the Ark of the Torah and for the synagogue were mostly made in special Jewish embroidery workshops. This is confirmed, too, by the fact that they had their own guild, which marched alongside that of the tailors in the ceremonial procession organized in 1741 — as well as by the frequency of names like Perlstücker or Goldstücker, derived from their professions. It may well be that less difficult work was done as a cottage industry, which is certainly the case for most of the bands to hold the Torah firmly rolled.

On the other hand, we know for certain

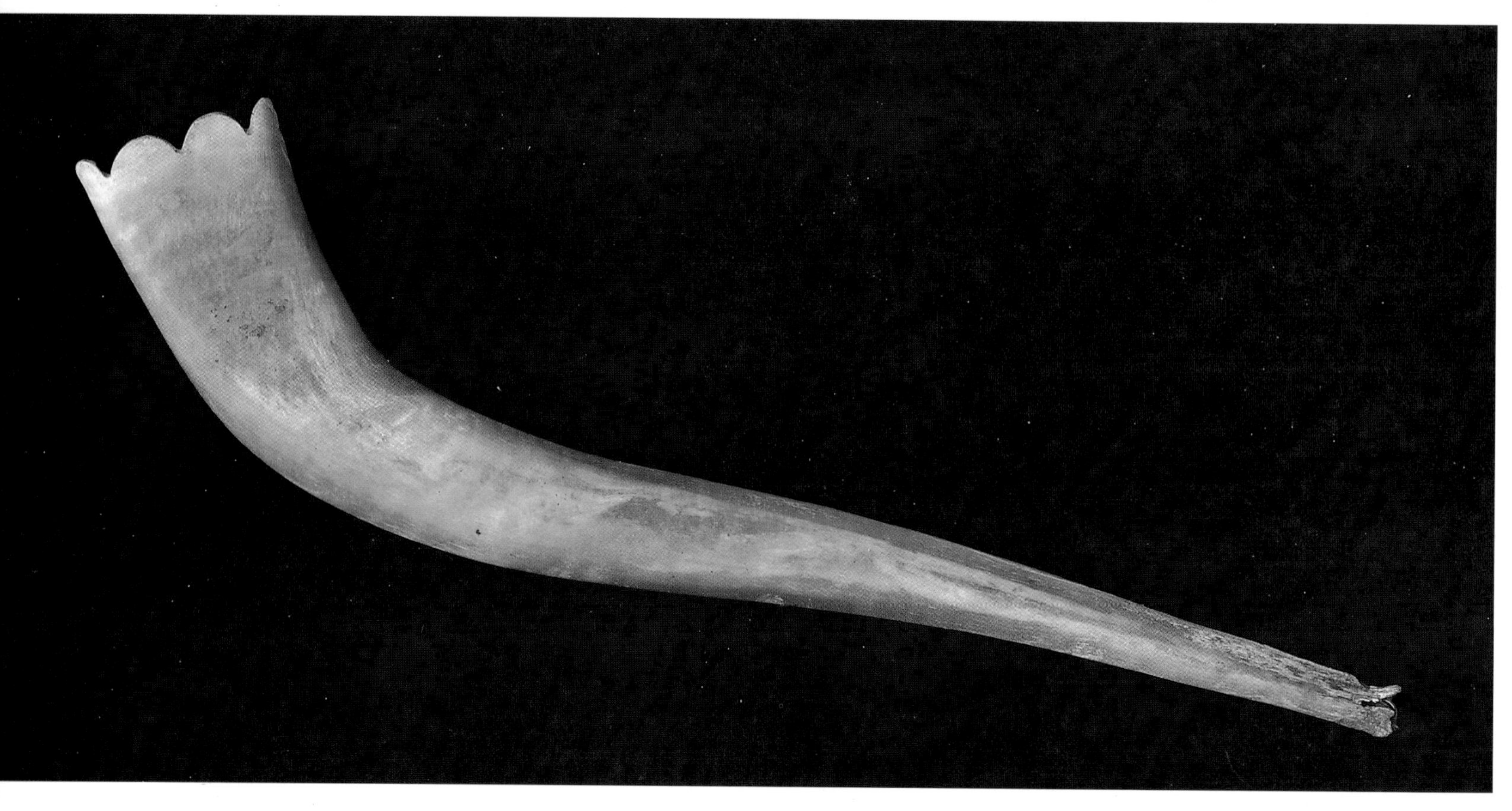

175/
The *shofar,* the ram's horn blown on holy days, at the New Year and on the Day of Atonement.

from the hallmarks of the goldsmiths' guilds, that silver vessels were commissioned from both Jewish and Christian smiths, and not only in Prague itself but abroad, in Germany, especially in Nuremberg, Augsburg and Vienna. This in spite of the fact that there were quite a number of gold and silversmiths in the ghetto itself. In 1729, for instance, there were twenty. The name Goldschmied, in Hebrew *Coref,* attests a trade handed down by generations. Nevertheless it would seem that those articles which show the highest artistic achievement were made in Christian and not in Jewish workshops. This was probably due to the fact that the Jews were long forbidden to learn a trade, and their work did not attain the desired standard.

The other sphere in which special vessels and special cloths were used for religious purposes was the Jewish home, the family. The Jewish festivals, taking place in the home, required these special articles. The Jewish home was marked out and at the same time protected, by the *mezuzah,* a strip of parchment on which a Hebrew prayer is written (a quotation from Deuteronomy 6, 4—9 and 11, 13—21). It is placed in a special little box which is fixed to the right door-post at the entrance. The *mezuzah* box was made of metal or wood, and usually decorated with a carved or engraved ornament.

The day-by-day rhythm of the week was broken by the Sabbath. The commandment to keep the Sabbath day holy dates back to Biblical times, and in the Babylonian exile the Sabbath became a sign of the Covenant, just as

176/
Torah pointers (*yad*), from right to left:
a) A two-part pointer, ellipsoid in the middle and upper part, the latter square in section, the lower part circular, encircled with an engraved pattern. Beaten and engraved silver. Velhartice, 1810.
b) A two-part pointer with a ball at the top and in the middle; the upper part square in section; the lower part has a relief ornament in triple moulding. Engraved and chased silver. Český Brod, 1800.
c) A two-part pointer, ending and divided in the middle with a ball; the upper part square in section, the lower twisted. Silver. Kolín, 1814.
d) A two-part pointer, both parts circular in section, ending and divided by an ellipsoid; the lower part is twisted and ends in a cuff. Silver. Louny, 1884.
e) A two-part pointer, the upper part square and the lower circular in section, separated by a ring; a twist pattern is engraved on the lower part. Silver. Prague, 1832.
f) A two-part pointer, the upper part square in section and the lower circular, both parts connected by a ring; the lower part encircled with an engraved pattern. Silver.

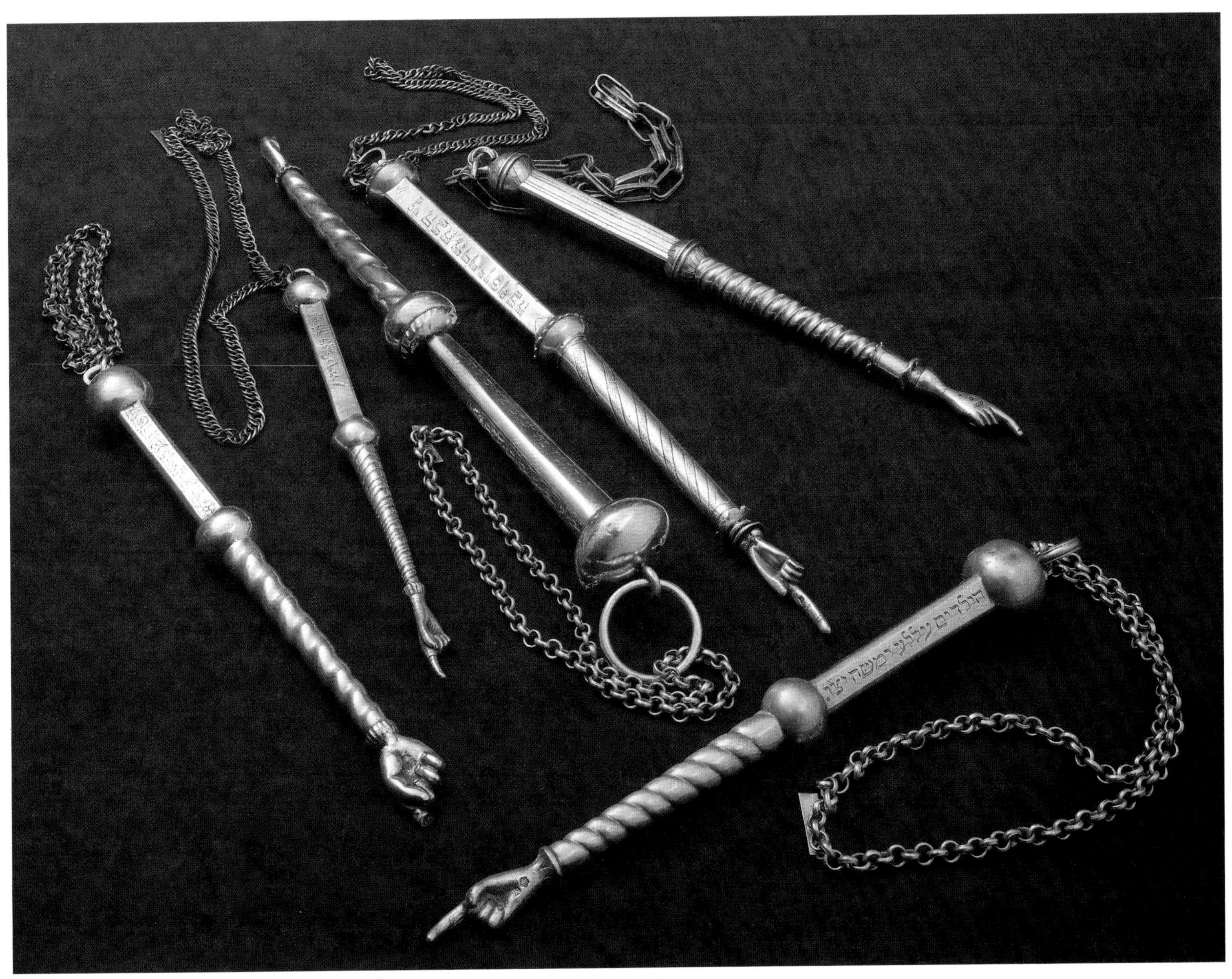

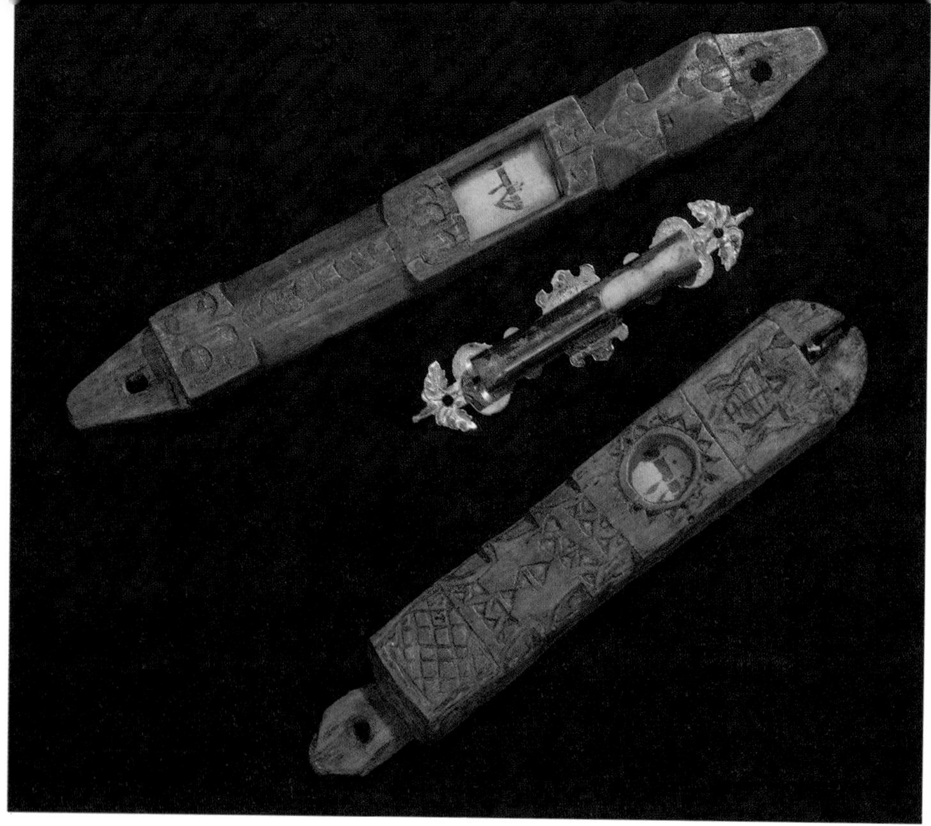

circumcision was. The rules for the Sabbath concerned both sexes, and were strictly kept. Saturday, the seventh day in the week, was a day of rest on which it was forbidden to work, to trade, to travel or to take arms. This last was allowed only in cases of mortal danger. The Sabbath was devoted to religious tasks and works of charity. The community met in the synagogue for prayers, and individuals performed acts of charity by visiting the sick. In Jewish households the arrival of the Sabbath was celebrated after sunset on Friday, by lighting at least two candles fixed in special candlesticks, either a matching pair, or one with two branches. They were usually cast of brass or silver, with an engraved ornament. A hanging Sabbath lamp was also lit; filled with oil, it burned throughout the Sabbath. Part of the Sabbath ritual were the blessings — *kiddush* — pronounced over a goblet of wine.

177/
The *mezuzahs*, tiny caskets holding a strip of parchment inscribed with sentences from the Scriptures, is affixed to the right door-jamb at the entrance to a Jewish home. First half of the nineteenth century.
a) A wooden *mezuzah*, with carved ornament.
b) A silver *mezuzah* shaped like a tube lying on a design of foliage.
c) A wooden *mezuzah*, with carved ornament.

178/
A pewter *seder* dish with an engraved inscription and symbolic crown. Prague, 1850.

179/
A *kiddush* goblet, over which the Sabbath blessing is pronounced. Silver gilt with beaten, engraved and chased tendril ornament. Central Europe, seventeenth century.

These goblets were also among the ritual vessels kept in Jewish households. Because the blessing was said over them they were called *kiddush* goblets, although they were also used on other occasions. Their form varied a great deal. They might have a stem, or not; usually they were of silver with a modest engraved inscription, sometimes magnificent in the style of the times, with beaten and engraved ornament. Glass *kiddush* goblets are rare.

Towards the end of supper, after the arrival of the Sabbath, sweet spices were burned. However, this oriental custom did not persist after the late Middle Ages. The spices were then kept in special caskets, and were merely sniffed at. As a rule these caskets were in filigree silver, shaped like little towers and of varying style according to the time they were made. Silver spice boxes shaped like fruit, or animals, are rarer. In all cases a filigree technique is used, for only thus could the scent of the spices spread round the box. Spices, wine, and light — usually in the form of a plaited braid of tapers — were essential for the ceremonial farewell to the Sabbath, the *Havdalah.*

The ceremonial inauguration of the Spring

180/
A Hanukkah candlestick of the 'bench' type. Filigree silver. Prague, *c.* 1800.

182/
A spice-box shaped like a small tower supported by a lion cub, with a shield. Silver openwork. Prague, late nineteenth century.

181/
A dish for the 'etrog', the citrus fruit which was one of the symbols used in celebrating the festival of Succoth. Wrought and beaten silver, engraved. Prague, 1820.

festival of *Pesach* also required special vessels. There was a flat dish on which symbolical food was placed, recalling the exodus from Egypt. This dish was called *seder,* from the 'order' or *seder* with which the evening begins. Seder dishes of the eighteenth and nineteenth century are mostly of pewter, with an engraved inscription or ornament, or decorated with figural scenes recalling the exodus from Egypt. Later these dishes were made of pottery or porcelain, and did not differ from normal dishes used for food. An egg was needed for the *seder,* and placed in a small oval dish, or an egg-cup. Either special bags, or a long napkin, were used for the unleavened bread, the *matzoth*; in the napkin the three pieces symbolizing the three groups of the Jewish people lay carefully separated, the priestly Cohens *(cohanim),* the Levites *(leviim),* and the rest of the people of Israel *(am).* The dish on which the mixture called *charoseth* was placed, symbolizing by its colour the clay from which the Jews had to make bricks in Egypt, was sometimes shaped like a brick-

layer's hod, or was decorated with that motif. The vessels are completed by a bowl with salt water, *mej melach,* for the tears shed by the enslaved Jews in Egypt. Sprigs of parsley, or radishes — also symbolical plants — are dipped into the water.

For the festival 'under the green', when

meals were eaten in special booths set up for the occasion *(succoth)*, replaced in the Prague ghetto by attics opening up in the roof, two things were required: a special citrus fruit called *etrog*, similar to a lemon, and called in contemporary Czech sources Paradise or Jewish apple, and the bunch of palm, willow and myrtle twigs known as *lulav*. The citrus fruit was laid in a special oval dish, often beautifully ornamented; it was usually of beaten silver, or filigree, decorated in the taste of the time. Sometimes the etrog was simply placed in a sugar basin, but this was then set aside only for that purpose.

On the feast of *Hanukkah*, commemorating the delivery of Jerusalem by Judas Maccabaeus and the reconsecration of the Temple, eight candles are lit, an additional one each day while the festival lasts. There are special candlesticks for this festival, either shaped like the *menorah*, the traditional seven-branched candlestick of the Temple in Jerusalem, or a horizontal bar with eight candle-holders on a high stem, or a bar resting on two supports, and bearing candlesticks backed by a panel variously shaped and ornamented. This candlestick is usually a symmetrical composition incorporating an inscription and some symbolic motif. The material is usually brass or silver, pewter being rare. This type of Hanukkah candlestick could be hung on the wall.

183/
An 'etrog' dish shaped like a sugar-basin. Beaten silver. Prague, 1860.

At the festival of *Esther (Purim)* the narrative was read from a special scroll, the *Megillah Esther*. Unlike the Torah, this scroll is wound only on one rod, but often clothed in a special ornamental cover of leather, ivory or silver.

Besides these festivals celebrated by all Jewish families on the same date, there were purely family events. The first centred around the birth of a son, and his circumcision, the second around a wedding. Circumcision was and still is a fundamental Jewish commandment, and commenced with a solemn celebration in the synagogue on the eighth day of the boy's life. In ancient synagogues there was a special double seat for the ceremony; on one half the *sandak* sat and held the child during the circumcision ceremony, while the other was left for the invisible Prophet Elijah, actually there in the minds of those present. In old synagogues this seat was of stone, later of wood, and was provided with a cushion, ei-

184/
A pocket watch with a Hebrew dial. Engraved silver, traces of gilt.

ther embroidered, or covered with precious cloth. There were four items required for the ceremony: a special knife with a rounded tip, and sharp along both edges of the blade; the handle was usually of semi-precious stone (crystal, agate, jasper or smoke quartz) or of ivory, or the exceptionally hard wood of the box tree. Metal handles are extremely rare. Sometimes the handle was inlaid with silver. A popular motif was the Sacrifice of Isaac. A special bowl usually of beaten silver was ready to receive the foreskin. Then there was the metal pincers to hold the foreskin during the operation; and finally a vial containing the antiseptic used. There was also a special wine goblet which was blessed by the *mohel*, especially trained for the circumcision, who then sprinkled a few drops of wine on the child's face and on the wound. These requisites could be the property of the synagogue, or of the *mohel*. The bands holding the child's shawl usually had an embroidered (or more rarely painted) wish that the child may 'enter into Torah, into marriage (the *chuppah*) and into good deeds', together with the name of the child and his parents. These bands were later dedicated to binding the Torah.

There were certain items required for a wedding, too. The ceremony took place under the baldaquin, or *chuppah*, which stretched over the couple and the rabbi. The *chuppah* was usually square, fixed to supports at each corner. The cloth was ornamented, as a rule with embroidered texts on the subject of marriage, and symbols of fertility, especially the pomegranate. The *chuppah* could be re-

185/
J. Minařík: The Old-New Synagogue and Jewish Town Hall. Oil on canvas, early twentieth century.

186/
J. Minařík: The Old Jewish Cemetery with the tomb of Rabbi Loew in the foreground. Oil on canvas, early twentieth century.

187, 188/
Unknown artist: Anton Weiss, leather merchant (1782—1832), and his wife Therese, née Fogesová (1793—1863). Oil on canvas, *c.* 1810.

placed by a *tallit,* the striped shawl with fringes at the corners, used during prayers.

The marriage was finalized when the marriage contract was read and the bridegroom slipped the ring on to the bride's finger. This ring was not allowed to be set with precious stones, or to bear an inscription. The ring itself was often given a tiny house, as a symbol of setting up one's own household. Sometimes special dishes appeared, usually of pewter, and inscribed with the bridegroom's name. These were usually wedding gifts from one of the organizations the new husband belonged to.

The last things of man, death, and the preparation of the body for burial, also called for special accessories, usually the property of the Burial Society. These included a comb, a flat instrument for cleaning the nails, and a special dish to receive the combed-out hair and cut nails. These things were made of silver and decorated only with inscriptions. The round dish resembled the alms dish with its handle and tiny candlestick, but it was divided into three parts, one taking up half the dish, the others smaller.

The work of the Burial Societies led to other needs, and many types of jugs or pitchers were created, either of pewter or of glass. The latter were often engraved or painted with scenes from funeral processions led by the Society. Towards the end of the eighteenth century the Prague Burial Society, the *Chevra kaddisha,* had its activities illustrated in a series of pictures, showing the members of the Society visiting the sick, watching over the dead, and then at various stages of preparation for the burial. This series of pictures was later supplemented by one of the annual banquet of the Society, and their traditional prayers at the tomb of Rabbi Loew, one of their founders.

Works by Jewish writers and especially those printed by the Prague Hebrew press inspired many prints and engravings, especially the woodcuts on the frontispieces of the books which were issued in Prague from 1513 onwards. Hebrew calligraphy itself is an art, whether in manuscripts, the scrolls of the Torah, or on some gravestones. The human figure first appeared in *Haggadah* manuscripts, illustrating the excerpts from the Pentateuch read on the festival of Pesach. The second work printed by the Prague Hebrew press and illustrated in 1514 is the liturgical *Seder zemirot u-birkat ha-mazon,* a collection of hymns and prayers of thanksgiving after food. The frontispiece of the Prague edition of the Pentateuch, printed in 1518, and that of the *Haggadah* of 1526, have an ornamental frame in which decorative motifs — especially the grotesques popular at the time — mingle with the figural. On the whole these frontispieces are similar to those of contemporary Czech works in their ornament. The architectonic frame is characteristic of both. It rests on a base, columns or pilasters are drawn on each side, bearing a simple architrave above. Ornamental borders often incorporating biblical figures, or simply decorative, were also popular. This type of frontispiece persisted in Hebrew books until the late Renaissance. It is possible that this architectonic design used in Prague Hebrew editions may have influenced the design of the Prague Renaissance synagogue curtains.

The Prague ghetto was not only the producer but also a purchaser of works of art of a specific type, for the whole of its existence, of objects of purely religious significance. From the seventeenth century we can trace a growing interest in portraiture, particularly portraits of important members of the community. Only a few modest engravings have survived, since the ghetto was twice burned down, and we cannot imagine what may have hung on the walls of Jewish homes, especially those of the wealthy. From the early nineteenth century on, it certainly became the fashion in wealthy families to commission portraits, as we can see from the portraits of married couples and of important figures like Rabbi Rapoport or Eleazar Fleckeles. Engraved portraits were also popular, especially that of the author — more or less well-known — on the frontispiece of his books.

Lastly, the ghetto itself became a source of inspiration. The crooked lanes and picturesque architecture of some of the houses and nooks in the ghetto attracted the Romantic painters of the nineteenth century. The stern sobriety of the Old-New Synagogue drew many, and also the huddled gravestones of strange shape and with incomprehensible lettering, in the Old Cemetery. Few painters of the time passed through the ghetto without finding a theme. Many Prague artists painted and drew scenes from the Prague ghetto — Karel Postl, Karel Würbs, Vincent Morstadt, Josef Mánes, and later Jaroslav Čermák, Zdenka Braunerová, Václav Jansa, Jan Minařík, Jan Skramlík, Emil Orlík. Thanks to these nineteenth century artists the ghetto has been preserved for us in paintings and engravings, with all the specific atmosphere that attracted each of them.[1)] The ghetto inspired foreign artists, too. In 1847 George Gilbert Scott painted it, and in the fifties it inspired Henri Leysse, the Belgian painter of historical themes, and the well-known German realist Adolf Menzel.

Abbreviations

I Institutions

AMP — Archiv hlavního města Prahy (Archives of the City of Prague)
SUA — Státní ústřední archiv (Central State Archives, Prague)
SUPPOP — Státní ústav památkové péče a ochrany přírody (State Institute for the Care of Historical Monuments and the Preservation of Nature, Prague)
SŽM — Státní židovské museum (State Jewish Museum, Prague)
ASŽM — Archiv Státního židovského musea (Archives of the State Jewish Museum, Prague)
MMP — Museum hlavního města Prahy (Municipal Museum, Prague)

II Sources (manuscripts)

SM — Stará manipulace (Old Cataloguing)
NM — Nová manipulace (New Cataloguing)
ČG Camerale — České gubernium, Camerale (Gubernium bohemicum camerale)
JS — Jesuitica

III Source editions

BD — Bondy, Bohumil—Dvorský, František, *K historii židů v Čechách, na Moravě a ve Slezsku, 906—1620* (The Jews in Bohemia, Moravia and Silesia, 906—1620), I, II, Prague 1906

IV Periodicals

ČŽK — Českožidovský kalendář (Czech-Jewish Calendar)
JB — Judaica Bohemiae
PA — Památky archeologické (Archeological Monuments)
RKDU — Ročenka Kruhu pro pěstování dějin umění (Yearbook of the Society for Art History)
RSDŽ — Ročenka Společnosti pro dějiny židů v ČSR (Yearbook of the Society for Jewish History in Czechoslovakia)

Notes

Chapter I

1) H. Volavková, *Zmizelá Praha* (Vanished Prague) 3, pp. 59 f., 66 f.
2) H. Volavková, *Zmizelá Praha* 3, p. 66.
3) S. Steinherz, *Die Einwanderung der Juden in Böhmen,* in: *Die Juden in Prag,* pp. 7 f.; H. Volavková, *Zmizelá Praha* 3, p. 7.
4) BD no. 1.
5) BD nos. 2, 3.
6) BD no. 4.
7) BD no. 1108.
8) V. Ryneš, *L'incendie de la synagogue du faubourg du château de Prague* (further: *L'incendie*), in: JB I, pp. 9 f., pp. 18 f., p. 20, note 33.
9) BD nos. 6, 8, 16.
10) J. Čarek, *Románská Praha* (Romanesque Prague), pp. 246 f.; map on p. 249.
11) BD no. 9.
12) BD no. 10; S. Steinherz, *Kreuzfahrer und Juden in Prag (1096),* in: RSDŽ 1929, pp. 1 f.
13) BD nos. 13, 1106.
14) BD no. 97.
15) BD nos. 273, 274; V. Ryneš, *L'incendie,* in: JB I, p. 17, note. 27.
16) V. Ryneš, *L'incendie,* in: JB I, p. 21.
17) BD no. 24.
18) BD no. 97.
19) BD no. 123.
20) BD no. 125.
21) BD nos. 160, 170, 178, 1131, 1132.
22) BD no. 187.
23) BD nos. 211, 232.
24) W. W. Tomek, *Základy starého místopisu pražského* (Materials for the Early Topography of Prague) I, pp. 20, 21, 46, 47, 211 f., 214 f., 218 f., 228 f.
25) W. W. Tomek, *Dějepis Prahy* (History of Prague) II, pp. 215 f.
26) W. W. Tomek, *Dějepis Prahy* II, pp. 216—18.
27) W. W. Tomek, *Dějeis Prahy* VIII, pp. 143 f.; in his placing of the house 'At the Coats of Arms', however, Tomek was mistaken. He identified it with the Jewish number 113 close to the gate by the Holy Spirit Church, at the further end of what was then Jewish Street. It is clear from later sources that the house stood in the same block as the Pinkas Synagogue.
28) BD no. 1150.
29) W. W. Tomek, *Dějepis Prahy* VIII, p. 146.
30) V. Vojtíšek, *Židovské ulice v Novém Městě pražském* (Jewish Streets in the New Town of Prague), in: ČŽK 1913, pp. 152 f.; J. Heřman, *La communauté juive de Prague et sa structure au commencement des temps modernes* (further: J. Heřman, *La communauté*), in: JB V, p. 32.
31) J. Heřman, *La communauté,* in: JB V, p. 33.
32) BD no. 312.
33) BD nos. 329—31, 333, 337, 342.
34) BD nos. 347, 351, 352, 355, 363.
36) J. Heřman, *La communauté,* in: JB V, p. 60.
36) BD nos. 306, 407, 408, 436, 1134, 1243—6, 1251, 1257.
37) ND nos. 405, 434.
38) BD no. 410.
39) BD nos. 459, 460, 463—5, 469, 471, 472, 479, 493, 498, 502, 514, 1274, 1278, 1279.
40) BD no. 40.
41) BD no. 533.
42) BD nos. 554, 556, 557, 560, 561, 1284.
43) BD nos. 577, 579—81, 584, 586—8, 590—2, 595, 596, 600, 601, 605, 609, 611, 612, 619, 621, 628—32, 635, 641, 645, 649, 1292, 1298, 1300—2, 1305, 1306.
44) J. Heřman, *La communauté,* in: JB V, pp. 61—3.
45) BD nos. 685, 687, 698.
46) BD nos. 706, 709—15, 794, 799.
47) BD nos. 765, 828, 834, 856, 880, 924, 1016.
48) BD no. 975.
49) AMP, *Libri albi Judaeorum,* MS no. 2169, fol. 33 v., fol. 135, fol. 219, fol. 366, fol. 370.
50) BD no. 978.
51) BD no. 1037.
52) BD no. 1040.
53) BD no. 1055.
54) BD no. 876; J. Heřman—M. Vilímková, *Pražské synagogy* (The Synagogues of Prague); H. Volavková, *Zmizelá Praha* 3, pp. 28 f.
55) J. Prokeš—A. Blaschka, *Úřední antisemitismus a pražské ghetto v době pobělohorské* (Official Antisemitism and the Prague Ghetto after the Battle of the White Mountain) (further: *Úřední antisemitismus,* in: RSDŽ 1929, pp. 41 f. (*Pražské ghetto a křesťanská společnost v době od bitvy na Bílé hoře do velkého moru v roce 1680* — The Prague Ghetto and Christian society from the Battle of the White Mountain until the Great Plague of 1680); K. Spiegel, *Die*

Prager Juden zur Zeit des dreissigjährigen Krieges, in: *Die Juden in Prag,* pp. 107 f. It had long been the duty of the Prague Jews to help put out fires; the regulations of 1611 and 1619 (BD 1047 and 1097) were undoubtedly based on existing practice. The earliest documentary evidence that the Jews helped to extinguish fires dates from 1607, when fire broke out in the Castle area (Hradčany) in the big house 'At the Moor' (no. 72-IV) and spread to neighbouring houses. The house was the seat of the Spanish ambassador, and the fire was caused by rockets fired in honour of the patron saint of Spain, St James. On that occasion the Jews were paid for their assistance (AMP, MS no. 123, fol. 123).

56) J. Prokeš—A. Blaschka, *Úřední antisemitismus,* l.c.; V. Vojtíšek, *O rozšíření židovského města pražského 1622 a 1623* (Enlargement of the Prague Jewish Town in 1622 and 1623), in: ČŽK 1915, pp. 154 f.
57) SUA, no. SM — J 4/7.
58) SUA, no. SM — J 4/7.
59) C. Straka, *Plán Starého Města pražského z r. 1641* (Plan of the Old Town of Prague in 1641), in: PA XXIX, pp. 242 f.; V. Sádlo, *Pohled na část Starého Města pražského z počátku 1. poloviny XVII. století* (View of Part of the Old Town of Prague, Early 17th Century), in: RKDU 1939—40, pp. 33 f.
60) B. Nosek, *Die jüdische Kultusgemeinde in Libeň,* in: JB XVI, pp. 103 f.
61) SUA, nos. NM — P 1 — 7/2; SM — J 4/18.
62) BD nos. 624, 1344; SUA, nos. SM — J 4/21, 22; NM — P 1 — 7/27; NM — P 1 — 3/11; J. Prokeš—A. Blaschka, *Úřední antisemitismus,* pp. 111 f.; V. Vojtíšek, *Po ohni židovského města pražského r. 1689* (After the Fire in the Jewish Town of Prague of 1689), in: ČŽK 1914, pp. 61 f.
63) V. Vojtíšek, *Staré plány židovského města* (Early Plans of the Jewish Town), in: ČŽK 1911, pp. 28 f.; SUA, no. SM — J 4/26.
64) SUA, no. SM — J 4/1; J. Prokeš—S. Blaschka, *Úřední antisemitismus,* in: RSDŽ (in German), pp. 236 f.; J. Prokeš, *Soupis pražských židů z roku 1729* (Census List of Prague Jews, 1729), in: RSDŽ 1933, pp. 309 f.; H. Volavková—V. Lorenc, *Dientzenhoferovo zaměření starého židovského města* (Dientzenhofer's Survey of the Old Jewish Town), in: *Kniha o Praze* 1958, pp. 145 f.
65) SUA, no. SM — J 4/1; J. Bergl, *Das Exil der Prager Judenschaft von 1745—48,* in: RSDŽ 1929, pp. 225 f.
66) B. Nosek, *Die jüdische Kultusgemeinde in Libeň,* in: JB XVI, pp. 103 f.
67) SUA, ČG Camerale, no. T 13, cart. 59; V. Žáček, *Po požáru pražského ghetta r. 1754* (After the Fire in the Prague Ghetto of 1754), in: RSDŽ 1934, pp. 157 f.
68) SUA, ČG Camerale, no. T 13, cart. 59.
69) SUA, ČG Camerale, no. T 13, cart. 59.
70) SUA, ČG Camerale, no. T 13, cart. 59.
71) H. Volavková, *Zmizelá Praha* 3, pp. 43 f.
72) H. Volavková, *Zmizelá Praha* 3, pp. 50 f.; F. Roubík, *K dějinám židů v Čechách v první polovici devatenáctého století* (The Jews in Bohemia in the First Half of the 19th Century), in: RSDŽ 1934, pp. 281 f.; R. Roubík, *Tři příspěvky k vývoji emancipace židů v Čechách* (On the History of Emancipation of the Jews in Bohemia), in: RSDŽ 1933, pp. 305 f. (further: F. Roubík, *Tři příspěvky*).
73) F. Roubík, *Tři příspěvky*; AMP, MS 242, Judenstadt 1826—35.
74) H. Volavková, *Zmizelá Praha* 3, pp. 59 f.; pp. 66 f.

Chapter II

1) I. Epstein, *Judaism*; R. Krüger, *Die Kunst der Synagoge; The Precious Legacy, Judaic Treasures from the Czechoslovak State Collections*; relevant entries in the *Encyclopaedia Judaica* and *The Jewish Encyclopaedia.*
2) J. Janáček, *The Prague Jewish Community before the Thirty Years War,* in: *Prague Ghetto in the Renaissance Period,* p. 48.
3) BD no. 24.
4) BD nos. 21, 26.
5) BD nos. 178, 230, 292, 298, 303, 305, 312, 313, 337, 342.
6) BD nos. 282, 288, 341, 347, 451.
7) SUA, no. SM — J 4/7.
8) SUA, nos. SM — J 4/5; SM — J 4/7; NM — P 1 — 7/1.
9) SUA, nos. SM — J 4/5; SM — J 4/7; NM — P 1 — 7/1.
10) BD nos. 609, 617, 625, 1293; SUA, no. SM — J 4/9.
11) SUA, nos. JS — L/1a-d, L/2a, cart. no. 91; no. SM — J 4/24. The proceedings of the trial were published in Latin and German in 1698 and again in German in 1728 (O. Muneles, *Bibliografický přehled židovské Prahy* — Bibliographic Survey of Jewish Prague [further: *Bibliografický přehled*], nos. 184, 186, 187, 241).
12) SUA, no. SM — J 4/16; JS cart. no. 143.
13) SUA, no. SM — J 4/16.
14) SUA, nos. SM — J 4/16; NM — P 1 — 7/27.
15) SUA, no. SM — J 4/2; J. Prokeš — A. Blaschka, *Úřední antisemitismus,* in: RSDŽ 1929 (in German), pp. 95 f., 184 f., 236 f.
16) SUA, no. J 4/8.
17) BD nos. 292, 302, 341, 347.
18) BD nos. 312, 313, 347.
19) SUA, no. SM — J 4/3; *The Prague Ghetto in the Renaissance Period,* ill. 19.
20) BD nos. 434, 719.
21) BD no. 837.
22) BD nos. 888, 906, 908.
23) BD no. 1091; SUA, no. SM — J 4/17.
24) SUA, no. SM — J 4/17.
25) SUA, no. SM — J 4/7; NM — P 1—7/2; T. Jakobowitz, *Die jüdischen Zünfte in Prag,* in: RSDŽ 1936, pp. 57 f.
26) AMP, MS no. 3724, fol. 26; G. Kisch, *Die Prager Universität und die Juden,* in: RSDŽ 1934, pp. 47 f.; J. Prokeš, *Soupis pražských židů z roku 1729* (Census List of the Prague Jews in 1729), in: RSDŽ 1932, pp. 309 f.
27) SUA, no. NM — M 1 — 1/3.
28) SUA, no. NM — P 1 — 7/5.
29) J. Heřman, *Das Steuerregister der Prager Juden aus dem Jahre 1540 (1528),* in: JB I, pp. 28 f., Table I, p. 32; SUA, no. SM — J 4/17.

Chapter III

1) O. Muneles, *Die hebräische Literatur aus dem Boden der ČSR* (further: *Die hebräische Literatur*), in: JB V, pp. 109 f.
2) O. Muneles, *Die hebräische Literatur,* in: JB V, p. 113; O. Muneles, *Die Rabbiner der Altneuschul* (further: *Die Rabbiner*), in: JB V, p. 95; O. Muneles, *Starý židovský hřbitov* (The Old Jewish Cemetery), MS, commentary on the epitaph of Rabbi Abigdor Kara.
3) O. Muneles, *Die Rabbiner,* in: JB V, p. 97 f.
4) O. Muneles, *Die hebräische Literatur,* in: JB V, pp. 114 f.; O. Muneles — V. Sadek, *The Prague Jewish Community in the Sixteenth Century (Spiritual Life)* (further: *The Prague Jewish Community*), in: *Prague Ghetto in the Renaissance Period,* pp. 67 f.
5) O. Muneles, *Bibliografický přehled,* pp. 15—16.
6) O. Muneles, *Die Rabbiner,* in: JB V, p. 106; O. Muneles,

Die hebräische Literatur, in: JB V, pp. 116 f.; O. Muneles, *Bibliografický přehled,* pp. 19—22.

7) O. Muneles, *Die Rabbiner,* in: JB V, pp. 103 f.; O. Muneles, *Die hebräische Literatur,* in: JB V, pp. 117 f.; O. Muneles — V. Sadek, *The Prague Jewish Community,* pp. 71 f.
8) O. Muneles, *Die hebräische Literatur,* in: JB V, p. 121; O. Muneles, *Starý židovský hřbitov,* MS, commentary on the relevant epitaphs.
9) G. Alter, *Two Renaissance Astronomers,* pp. 14 f.; O. Muneles, *Die hebräische Literatur,* in: JB V, p. 121.
10) O. Muneles — M. Vilímková, *Starý židovský hřbitov v Praze* (The Old Jewish Cemetery in Prague), pp. 245 f.; O. Muneles, *Die hebräische Literatur,* in: JB V, p. 125.
11) O. Muneles, *Die hebräische Literatur,* in: JB V, p. 123.
12) O. Muneles, *Die hebräische Literatur,* in: JB V, pp. 124 f.
13) O. Muneles, *Starý židovský hřbitov,* MS, commentary on the epitaphs of individual members of the Horowitz family; O. Muneles—M. Vilímková, *Starý židovský hřbitov v Praze,* commentary on epitaphs nos. 10, 18, 62, 71, 76, 79, 114; cf. Chapter I, note 36.
14) O. Muneles, *Starý židovský hřbitov,* MS, commentary on the epitaph of Mordechai Meisl; BD nos. 753, 789, 803, 866, 871, 876, 886, 896, 928, 934, 962, 966—72, 997, 1054, 1310, 1316, 1321, 1323, 1339.
15) O. Muneles, *Starý židovský hřbitov,* MS, commentary on the epitaphs of the family of Jacob Bashevi buried in the Old Cemetery; BD nos. 947, 1037, 1043; *Encyclopaedia Judaica,* Bashevi.
16) O. Muneles, *Starý židovský hřbitov,* MS, commentary on the epitaphs of the rabbis Reuben Hoschke, Ahron Simon Spira, Gabriel of Eltsch and Elijah Spira; SUA, no. SM — J 4/23.
17) O. Muneles, *Die hebräische Literatur,* in: JB V, pp. 126 f.; G. Alter, *Two Renaissance Astronomers,* pp. 45 f.
18) O. Muneles, *Die hebräische Literatur,* in: JB V, pp. 126 f.
19) O. Muneles, *Die hebräische Literatur,* in: JB V, pp. 127 f.; O. Muneles, *Starý židovský hřbitov,* MS, commentary on the epitaph of Rabbi David Oppenheim.
20) O. Muneles, *Die hebräische Literatur,* in: JB V, pp. 129, 130.
21) O. Muneles, *Die hebräische Literatur,* in: JB V, pp. 131 f.; V. Sadek, *La synagogue réformée de Prague,* in: JB XVI, pp. 129 f.
22) O. Muneles, *Die hebräische Literatur,* in: JB V, pp. 131 f., 138, 139; V. Sadek, *La synagogue réformée de Prague,* in: JB XVI, pp. 129 f.; V. Sadek — J. Šedinová, *Petr Beer (1788—1838),* in: JB XIV, pp. 7 f.

Chapter IV

1) R. Krautheimer, *Mittelalterliche Synagogen*; R. Wischnitzer, *The Architecture of the European Synagogues*; J. Heřman — M. Vilímková, *Pražské synagogy* (The Synagogues of Prague); V. Ryneš, *L'incendie,* in: JB I, pp. 9 f.
2) Z. Münzerová, *Staronová synagoga* (The Old-New Synagogue), p. 37; SUA, no. SM — J 4/21; NM — P 1—7/27.
3) J. F. Schor, *Plán pražského ghetta po požáru v r. 1754* (Plan of the Prague Ghetto after the Fire of 1754), SUA, in: *Sbírka map a plánů* (Map Collection), cat. no. 2394 .
4) J. Heřman — M. Vilímková, *Pražské synagogy,* p. 14.
5) Z. Münzerová, *Staronová synagoga*; M. Vilímková, *Seven Hundred Years of the Old-New Synagogue,* in: JB V, pp. 71 f.
6) W. W. Tomek, *Dějepis Prahy* (History of Prague) VIII, p. 143; AMP, MS nos. 2106, fol. 490, 491; 2107, fol. 28; 2108, fol. 151 r., 209; 2109, fol. 85; 2111, fol. 211; 2117, fol. 358; 2118, fol. 139; 2169, fol. 241 v., 292, 332, 374; 2170, fol. 19, 106.
7) H. Volavková, *Pinkasova škola, památník minulosti a našich dnů* (The Pinkas Shul, a Memorial of the Past and Present) (further: *Pinkasova škola*), pp. 21 f. The author believes that a Romanesque synagogue already stood on the site of the later Pinkas Synagogue; we would point out, however, that the historical name of the house 'At the coats of Arms' itself does not suggest that it had always been Jewish property. Further, the name does not necessarily mean that any coats of arms were painted on the house; in the sixteenth century the word 'erb' was a synonym of 'heir'. The remains excavated beneath the floor of the synagogue, said to be Romanesque, could equally well be the remains of a secular structure.
8) H. Volavková, *Pinkasova škola,* pp. 51 f.
9) H. Volavková, *Pinkasova škola,* pp. 79 f, 95 f; AMP, MS 2169, fol. 374; 2170, fol. 106.
10) H. Volavková, *Pinkasova škola,* pp. 108 f.
11) A. Pařík, *Pražské synagogy v obrazech, rytinách a starých fotografiích* (The Synagogues of Prague in Pictures, Engravings and Early Photographs), SŽM 1986.
12) J. Heřman — M. Vilímková, *Pražské synagógy,* pp. 41 f; A. Pařík, *Pražské synagógy v obrazech.*
13) SUA, no. SM — J 4/21; NM — P 1 — 7/27; J. Heřman — M. Vilímková, *Pražské synagógy,* pp. 44 f.
14) SUA, no. SM — J 4/21; NM — P 1 — 7/27; J. Heřman — M. Vilímková, *Pražské synagógy,* p. 48; the almemor can still be seen on the engraving of 1870 in the book by B. Foges — D. Podiebrad, *Altertümer der Prager Josefstadt.*
15) J. Teige — I. Hermann — Z. Winter, *Pražské ghetto* (The Prague Ghetto), p. 122.
16) J. Heřman — M. Vilímková, *Pražské synagógy,* p. 53; A. Pařík, *Pražské synagógy v obrazech;* H. Volavková, *Zmizelá Praha* (Vanished Prague) 3, pp. 40, 42; SUA, nos. SM — J 4/21; NM — P 1 — 7/27.
17) J. Heřman — M. Vilímková, *Pražské synagógy,* p. 53; H. Volavková, *Zmizelá Praha* 3, pp. 40, 42; A. Pařík, *Pražské synagógy v obrazech.*
18) SUA, no. SM — J 4/21; NM — P 1 — 7/27.
19) H. Volavková, *Zmizelá Praha* 3, p. 51.
20) J. Heřman — M. Vilímková, *Pražské synagógy,* pp. 56 f; A. Pařík, *Pražské synagógy v obrazech.*
21) K. Guth, *Židovská radnice v Praze* (The Jewish Town Hall in Prague), in: ČŽK 1915, pp. 164 f; H. Volavková, *Zmizelá Praha* 3, p. 46; AMP, MS 2118, fol. 199; 2182, fol. 46.

Chapter V

1) This chapter is based partly on the book by O. Muneles and M. Vilímková, *Starý židvoský hřbitov v Praze* (The Old Jewish Cemetery in Prague) and partly on the manuscript by O. Muneles, *Starý židovský hřbitov* (The Old Jewish Cemetery), supplemented by important epitaphs of the 16th, 17th and 18th centuries. The excerpted texts were translated from Hebrew into German by O. Muneles. On the purchase of land to extend the cemetery: BD nos. 1150, 1229, 1324, 936, 968, 771.
On the part of the cemetery which was destroyed: O. Muneles — M. Vilímková, *Starý židovský hřbitov v Praze,* p. 95; H. Volavková, *Zmizelá Praha* 3, pp. 66 f.
2) AMP, MS no. 5724, *Mistrovská kniha cechu kameníků z r. 1741* (The Master Stonecutters' Book of 1741), fol. 26; record of work done for the Prague Jewish Cemetery.

Chapter VI

1) All existing monographs and synthetic studies of synagogue art cited in the Select Bibliography have been consulted for this chapter.

Source Materials

Státní ústřední archiv (Central State Archives, Prague) — SUA

Stará manipulace (Old Cataloguing), no. SM — J 4/1—52 (the Jews).

Nová manipulace (New Cataloguing), nos. NM — P 1 — 7/1 — 60 (the Jews),
NM — P 1 — 3/11 (fires in Prague),
NM — M 1 — 1/3 (the painters' guild).

Jesuitica, nos. JS — L/1a—d; KS — L/2a; JS cart. no. 143 (censorship of Jewish books).

České gubernium, Camerale (Gubernium bohemicum camerale), ČG Camerale, no. T 13, cart. 59 (fire in the Jewish Town in 1754).

Archiv hlavního města Prahy (Archives of the City of Prague) — AMP

Libri contractuum Starého Města pražského, MS nos. 2106 — 2118 (these manuscripts were destroyed when the Old Town Hall was burned down in 1945; our data were taken from extracts made earlier by J. Teige, and now preserved in the State Jewish Museum).

Libri albi Judaeorum od r. 1577 (from the year 1577), MS nos. 2169, 2170.

Tzv. Liechtenštejnské domy (The Liechtenstein Houses), MS no. 177.

Judenstadt, seznam domů z let 1826—35 (A List of Houses Standing in 1826—35), MS no. 242.

Mistrovská kniha cechu kameníků z r. 1741 (The Master Stonecutters' Book of 1741), MS no. 5724.

Liber Proventum et Expensarum Reg. Urb. Prag. Hradschanensis 1599—1627, MS no. 123.

Source Editions

Tomek, Wácslaw Wladiwoj, *Základy starého místopisu pražského* (Materials for the Early Topography of Prague) I, Prague 1872.

Bondy, Bohumil — Dvorský, František, *K historii židů v Čechách, na Moravě a ve Slezsku 906 — 1620* (The Jews in Bohemia, Moravia and Silesia), I, II, Prague 1906.

Select Bibliography

Alter, George, *Two Renaissance Astronomers, David Gans, Joseph Delmedigo,* in: *Rozpravy Československé akademie věd* (Treatises of the Czechoslovak Academy of Sciences), 68, 1958.

Bergl, Josef, *Die Ausweisung der Juden aus Prag im Jahre 1744,* in: *Die Juden in Prag,* Prague 1927, pp. 187 f.

Bergl, Josef, *Das Exil der Prager Judenschaft von 1745—1748,* in: RSDŽ I, 1929, pp. 225 f. (in German, pp. 263 f.).

Čelakovský, Jaromír, *Příspěvky k dějinám židů v době Jagellonské* (The Jews in the Jagellonian Period), in: *Časopis Českého Musea* (Journal of the Czech Museum), 1898, pp. 385 f.

Čermáková, Jana, *The Synagogue Textiles,* in: JB XVI, pp. 54 f.

Doleželová, Jana, *Die Sammlung der Thorawickel,* in: JB XVI, pp. 60 f.

Doleželová, Jana, *Binders and Festive Covers from the Collection of the State Jewish Museum in Prague,* in: JB X, pp. 91 f.

Doleželová, Jana, *Wedding Dishes and Plates,* in: JB XIII, pp. 29 f.

Doleželová, Jana, *Thoraschilder aus der Werkstätte der Prager Silberschmiede, aus Sammlungen des Staatl. Jüdischen Museums,* in: JB XIX, pp. 22 f.

Epstein, Isidor, *Judaism,* in: *A Historical Presentation,* London 1968.

Guth, Karel, *Židovská radnice* (The Jewish Town Hall), in: ČŽK 1915, pp. 164 f.

Heřman, Jan, *Das Steuerregister der Prager Juden aus dem Jahre 1540 (1528),* in: JB I, pp. 26 f.

Heřman, Jan, *The Prague Jewish Community before the Expulsion of 1541,* in: *Prague Ghetto in the Renaissance Period,* Prague 1965, pp. 27 f.

Heřman, Jan, *La communauté juive de Prague et sa structure au commencement des temps modernes,* in: JB V, pp. 31 f.

Heřman, Jan — Vilímková, Milada, *Pražské synagogy* (Prague Synagogues), Prague 1970.

Horák, František, *Česká kniha v minulosti a její výzdoba* (Czech Books in the Past and their Ornament), Prague 1948.

Hrázský, Josef, *La corporation juive d'orfèvres à Prague,* in: JB II, pp. 19 f.

Hrázský, Josef, *Sixteenth and Seventeenth Century Items in the Collections of the State Jewish Museum,* in: *Prague Ghetto in the Renaissance Period,* Prague 1965, pp. 103 f.

Jakobovits, Tobias, *Das Prager und Böhmische Landesrabbinat Ende des siebzehnten und Anfang des achtzehnten Jahrhunderts,* in: RSDŽ 1933, pp. 79 f.

Jakobovits, Tobias, *Die jüdischen Zünfte in Prag,* in: RSDŽ 1936, pp. 57 f.

Janáček, Josef, *The Prague Jewish Community before the Thirty Years War,* in: *Prague Ghetto in the Renaissance Period,* Prague 1965, p. 43.

Jeřábek, Luboš, *Starý židovský hřbitov pražský* (The Old Jewish Cemetery in Prague), Prague 1903.

Jeřábek, Luboš, *Stará Pinchasova škola* (The Old Pinkas Shul), in: ČŽK 1907, pp. 110 f.

Kisch, Quido, *Die Zensur jüdischer Bücher in Böhmen,* in: RSDŽ 1930, pp. 444 f.

Kisch, Quido, *Die Prager Universität und die Juden,* in: RSDŽ 1934, pp. 1 f.

Krautheimer, Richard, *Mittelalterliche Synagogen,* Berlin 1927.

Krüger, Renate, *Die Kunst der Synagogue,* Leipzig 1966.

Kybalová, Ludmila, *Die Thoramäntel aus den Textilsammlung des Staatl. Jüdischen Museums in Prag, 1750—1800,* in: JB X, pp. 69 f.

Mann, Vivian B., *Symbols of the Legacy. Community Life, Family and Home, The Precious Legacy, Judaic Treasures from the Czechoslovak State Collections,* ed. by David Altschuler, New York 1983, pp. 110 f., 164 f.

Muneles, Otto, *Bibliografický přehled židovské Prahy* (Bibliographic Survey of Jewish Prague), Prague 1951.

Muneles, Otto — Vilímková, Milada, *Starý židovský hřbitov v Praze* (The Old Jewish Cemetery in Prague), Prague 1955.

Muneles, Otto, *Zur Prosopographie der Prager Juden im 15. und 16. Jahrhundert,* in: JB II, pp. 64 f.

Muneles, Otto, *Zur Namengebung der Juden in Böhmen,* in: JB II, pp. 3 f.

Muneles, Otto — Sadek, Vladimír, *The Prague Jewish Community in the Sixteenth Century (Spiritual Life),* in: *Prague Ghetto in the Renaissance Period,* Prague 1965, pp. 67 f.

Muneles, Otto, *Die Rabbiner der Altneuschul,* in: JB V, pp. 92 f.

Muneles, Otto, *Die hebräische Literatur auf dem Boden der ČSR,* in JB V, pp. 108 f.

Münzerová, Zdenka, *Staronová synagóga* (The Old-New Synagogue), Prague 1932.

Münzerová, Zdenka, *Staronová synagóga ve světle dosavadních názorů* (Earlier Views on the Old-New Synagogue), in: RSDŽ 1932, pp. 63 f.

Neher, A., *Le puits de l'exil. La théologie dialectique du Maharal de Prague, 1512—1609,* Paris 1966.

Nosek, Bedřich, *Die jüdische Kultusgemeinde in Libeň im 16. —19. Jahrhundert,* in: JB XVI, pp. 103 f.

Pařík, Arno, *The Topographics of the Picture Collection of the State Jewish Museum,* in: JB XIX, pp. 99 f., and in: JB XX, pp. 97 f.

Polák, Josef, *Nápisy pražských Peroches* (Epitaphs of the Peroches of Prague), in: *Kniha o Praze* (Book on Prague) 1931, pp. 25 f.

Polák, Josef, *Židé v Libni v XVI. století* (Jews in Libeň in the 16th Century), in ČŽK 1912, pp. 62 f.

Prokeš, Jaroslav — Blaschka, Antonín, *Ústřední antisemitismus a pražské ghetto v době pobělohorské* (Official Antisemitism and the Prague Ghetto after the Battle of the White Mountain), in: RSDŽ 1929, pp. 41 n.

Prokeš, Jaroslav, *Soupis pražských židů z roku 1729* (Census List of the Prague Jews in 1729), in: RSDŽ 1933, pp. 309 f.

Roubík, František, *Tři příspěvky k vývoji emancipace židů v Čechách* (The Emancipation of the Jews in Bohemia), in: RSDŽ 1934, pp. 305 f.

Roubík, František, *Z dějin židů v Čechách v devatenáctém století* (Jews in Bohemia in the 19th Century), in: RSDŽ 1935, p. 291 f.

Sadek, Vladimír, *Rabbi Loew, sa vie, son héritage pédagogique et sa légende,* in: JB XV, 1979, pp. 27 f.

Sadek, Vladimír, *Social Aspects in the Work of Prague Rabbi Loew Maharal (1512—1609),* in: JB XIX, 1983, pp. 3 f.

Sadek, Vladimír, *L'Argenterie des synagogues,* in: JB XVI, p. 68.

Sadek, Vladimír, *Goblets and Jugs of Czech and Moravian Burial Brotherhoods,* in: JB XVI, pp. 79 f.

Sadek, Vladimír, *La synagogue réformée de Prague,* in: JB XVI, pp. 112 f.

Sadek, Vladimír — Šedinová, Jiřina, *Petr Beer (1788—1838), penseur éclairé de la vieille ville juive de Prague,* in: JB XIV, pp. 7 f.

Sádlo, Vojtěch, *Pohled na část Starého Města pražského z počátku druhé poloviny XVII. století* (View of Part of the Old Town of Prague in the mid 17th century), in: RKDU 1939, Prague 1931, pp. 33 f.

Šedinová, Jiřina, *Old Czech Legends in the Work of David Gans,* in: JB XIV, 1978, pp. 89 f.

Šedinová, Jiřina, *Czech History as Reflected in the Historical Work by David Gans,* in: JB VIII, 1972, pp. 74 f.

Spiegel, Käthe, *Die Prager Juden zur Zeit des dreissigjährigen Krieges,* in: *Die Juden in Prag,* Prague 1927, pp. 107 f.

Steinherz, Samuel, *Die Einwanderung der Juden in Böhmen,* in: *Die Juden in Prag,* Prague 1927, pp. 7 f.

Steinherz, Samuel, *Die ältesten Wohnstätte der Juden in Prag,* in: *B'nai B'rith Monatsbilder,* 1927, pp. 433 f.

Steinherz, Samuel, *Kreuzfahrer und Juden in Prag (1906),* in: RSDŽ 1929, pp. 1 f.

Teige, Josef — Hermann, Ignát — Winter, Zikmund, *Pražské ghetto* (The Prague Ghetto), Prague 1903.

Thiberger, F., *The Great Rabbi Loew of Prague,* London 1954.

Tomek, Wácslaw Wladiwoj, *Dějepis Prahy* (History of Prague) II, 2nd ed., Prague 1892; VIII, Prague 1891.

Vilímková, Milada, *Seven Hundred Years of the Old-New Synagogue,* in: JB V, 1969, pp. 72 f.

Vojtíšek, Václav, *Po ohni židovského města pražského r. 1689* (After the Fire in the Jewish Town of Prague of 1689). *Příspěvek k dějinám židů pražských* (History of the Prague Jews), in: ČŽK 1914, pp. 61 f.

Vojtíšek, Václav, *Staré plány židovského města* (Early Plans of the Jewish Town), in: ČŽK 1911, pp. 28 f.

Vojtíšek, Václav, *Židovské ulice v Novém Městě pražském* (Jewish Streets in the New Town of Prague), in: ČŽK 1913, pp. 152 f.

Vojtíšek, Václav, *O rozšíření židovského města pražského r. 1622 a 1623* (Enlargement of the Jewish Town of Prague), in: ČŽK 1915, pp. 32 f.

Volavková, Hana, *Zmizelá Praha* (Vanished Prague) 3, *Židovské město pražské* (The Jewish Town of Prague), Prague 1947.

Volavková, Hana, *Grafické portrétní dokumenty pražského ghetta z počátku 19. století* (Graphic Portrait Evidence for the Prague Ghetto in the Early 19th century), in: *Hollar, Sborník grafického umění* (Graphic Art Miscellany) 28, pp. 156 f.

Volavková, Hana, *The Synagogue Treasures of Bohemia and Moravia,* Prague 1949.

Volavková, Hana, *The Jewish Museum of Prague, A Guide to the Collections,* Prague 1948.

Volavková, Hana, *Pinkasova škola, památník minulosti a našich dnů* (The Pinkas Shul, a Memorial of the Past and Present), Prague 1954.

Volavková, Hana, *Průvodce po státním židovském museu v Praze: I, Klausová synagoga; II, Museum pražského židovského města* (Guide to the State Jewish Museum im Prague: I, The Klaus Synagogue; II, Museum of the Prague Jewish Town), Prague 1956.

Volavková, Hana — Lorenc, Vilém, *Dientzenhoferovo zaměření starého židovského města* (Dientzenhofer's Survey of the Old Jewish Town), in: *Kniha o Praze* (Book on Prague) 1958, pp. 145 f.

Žáček, Václav, *Po požáru pražského ghetta r. 1754* (After the Fire in the Prague Ghetto in 1754), in: RSDŽ 1934, pp. 157 f.

List of Illustrations

123 The tombstone of Ahron Meshullam, son of Jeshaja Horowitz the Levite, known as Zalman Munka, 1545.
124 The tombstone of Shabbatai, son of Jeshaja Horowitz the Levite, 1554 or 1555.
125 The Old Jewish Cemetery in spring, looking south-east.
126 The tombstone of the martyred Rabbi Chayyim, son of Rabbi Jizchak Cohen, 1576.
127 The tombstone of Sheindl, wife of Gabriel, 1583.
128 The tombstone of Levi Cohen, son of Alexander, 1585.
129 The tombstone of Moshe, son of Rabbi Jacob, and his wife Kresl, 1585.
130 The tombstone of Mordechai Meisl, 1601.
131 The tombstone of the first Jewish woman writer in Prague, Rivka, daughter of the rabbi Meir Tikotin, 1605.
132 The tombstone of David Gans, chronicler and astronomist, 1613.
133 The tombstone of Jehuda Loew, son of Bezalel, and his wife Perl, 1609.
134 The Old Jewish Cemetery in summer. View of the cemetery around the grave of Mordechai Meisl.
135 The tombstone of Hendl, wife of Jacob Bashevi, 1628.
136 The tombstone of the Chief Rabbi of Prague, Simon Wolf Auerbach, 1632.
137 The tombstone of the rabbi Nehemiah, called Feiwl Duschenes, son of Abraham the Levite, 1648.
138 The Old Jewish Cemetery in autumn, looking towards the Pinkas Synagogue.
139 The tombstone of the Chief Rabbi of Prague, Ahron Simon Spira, 1679.
140 The tombstone of the son of Rabbi Spira, the regional rabbi Benjamin Wolf Simon Spira, 1715.
141 The tombstone of the Chief Rabbi of Prague, David Oppenheim (often written as Oppenheimer), 1736.
142 The tombstone of Simon, son of Jehuda Lejb Kuh the Levite.
143 The Old Jewish Cemetery in winter, looking south-east, towards Široká Street.
144 Celebrating the festival. An illustration in the liturgical book *Seder zemirot u-birkat ha-mazon,* printed in Prague, 1514. SŽM, Prague.
145 Hunting the hare. A mnemotechnical device illustrated in the Prague edition (1514) of the *Seder zemirot u-birkat ha-mazon.* SŽM, Prague.
146 The tombstone of Joseph Shelomo del Medigo. An engraving by Václav Popelík, *c.* 1860. (B. Foges — D. Podiebrad: *Altertümer der Prager Josefstadt,* Prague, 1870).
147 The tombstone of the Chief Rabbi of Prague, David Oppenheim. An engraving by Václav Popelík, *c.* 1860. SŽM, Prague.
148 K. Würbs — S. Langer: The Old-New Synagogue. An engraving dating from the second quarter of the nineteenth century. SUPPOP, Prague.
149 The early Gothic *ahron ha-kodesh* in the Old-New Synagogue with the curtain drawn back (thirteenth century), completed in the Renaissance.
150 The early Baroque *ahron ha-kodesh* in the High Synagogue dating from the end of the seventeenth century.
151 The Torah cover dedicated by Mordechai Mesil in 1593. SŽM, Prague.
152 The curtain dedicated to the Old-New Synagogue in 1609. SŽM, Prague.
153 A curtain from the Pinkas Synagogue, 1693. SŽM, Prague.
154 A curtain from the Pinkas Synagogue, 1689. SŽM, Prague.
155 A curtain from the Old-New Synagogue, 1697. SŽM, Prague.
156 A curtain from the Pinkas Synagogue, 1697. SŽM, Prague.
157 A curtain from the Pinkas Synagogue, 1717. SŽM, Prague.
158 A curtain from the Klaus Synagogue, 1733. SŽM, Prague.
160 A Torah cloak from the Pinkas Synagogue, 1740. SŽM, Prague.
161 A Torah cloak from the Pinkas Synagogue, 1754. SŽM, Prague.
162 A curtain from the Klaus Synagogue, 1781. SŽM, Prague.
163 A Prague curtain, 1850. SŽM, Prague.
164 Bands for the Torah, with a painted dedication. SŽM, Prague.
165 Bands for the Torah, with the dedication embroidered in different colours. SŽM, Prague.
166 Bands for the Torah, with a coloured embroidered dedication, SŽM, Prague.
167 Bands for the Torah, with an embroidered dedication. SŽM, Prague.
168 A *rimonim* (handle ornament) for the Torah, in the shape of a crown borne by two seated lion cubs. Beaten and engraved silver, partly gilt. Moravia, 1805. SŽM, Prague.
169 A *rimonim* for the Torah, in the shape of an openwork crown, beaten and engraved silver. Bohemia, 1860. SŽM, Prague.
170 One of a pair of Torah handles, shaped like a crown. Beaten and engraved silver. Moravia, 1810. SŽM, Prague.
171 A crown for the handle of the Torah. Silver gilt, beaten and engraved, set with coloured stones. Prague, 1817. SŽM, Prague.
172 A Torah shield. Beaten silver. Rokycany, 1762. SŽM, Prague.
173 A Torah shield. Beaten silver. Prague, 1784. SŽM, Prague.
174 A Torah shield. Beaten and engraved silver. Prague, late eighteenth century. SŽM, Prague.
175 The *shofar,* the ram's horn blown on holy days. SŽM, Prague.
176 Torah pointers (*yad*), SŽM, Prague.
a) A two-part pointer, beaten and engraved silver. Velhartice, 1810.
b) A two-part pointer, engraved and chased silver. Český Brod, 1800.
c) A two-part pointer, silver. Kolín, 1814.
d) A two-part pointer, silver. Louny, 1884.
e) A two-part pointer, silver. Prague, 1832.
f) A two-part pointer, silver.
177 The *mezuzahs*, tiny caskets holding a strip of parchment inscribed with sentences from the Scriptures. First half of the nineteenth century. SŽM, Prague.
a) A wooden *mezuzah,* with carved ornament.
b) A silver *mezuzah* shaped like a tube on a leaf pattern.
c) A wooden *mezuzah,* with carved ornament.
178 A pewter *seder* dish, with an engraved inscription and symbolic crown. Prague, 1850. SŽM, Prague.
179 A *kiddush* goblet. Silver gilt beaten, engraved and chased tendril ornament. Central Europe, seventeenth century. SŽM, Prague.
180 Hanukkah candlestick of the 'bench' type. Filigree silver. Prague, *c.* 1800. SŽM, Prague.
181 A dish for the 'etrog'. Openwork beaten silver, engraved. Prague, 1820. SŽM, Prague.
182 A spice-box. Silver openwork. Prague, late nineteenth century. SŽM, Prague.
183 An 'etrog' dish shaped like a sugar-basin. Beaten silver. Prague, 1860. SŽM, Prague.

184 A pocket watch with a Hebrew dial. Engraved silver, traces of gilt. SŽM, Prague.

185 J. Minařík: The Old-New Synagogue and the Jewish Town Hall. Oil on canvas, early twentieth century. MMP, Prague.

186 J. Minařík: The Old Jewish Cemetery with the tomb of Rabbi Loew in the foreground. Oil on canvas, early twentieth century. MMP, Prague.

187, 188 Anton Weiss, leather merchant (1782—1832), and his wife Therese, née Fogesová (1793—1863). Oil on canvas, *c.* 1810. SŽM, Prague.

(Endpapers) The Old Jewish Cemetery in autumn. Gravestones to the west of the main gateway.

Acknowledgements

The publishers wish to express their thanks to all the Prague institutions and museums which were kind enough to permit the photographing and reproduction of their exhibits:

the State Institute for the Care of Historical Monuments and the Preservation of Nature, Prague,
the State Jewish Museum, Prague,
the Municipal Museum, Prague,
and the Jewish religious community.

The archive photographs reproduced here give the name of the author in the List of Illustrations. The remaining black and white photographs are the work of

Vladimír Uher (nos. 4—6, 10—12, 15, 17, 18, 20, 23—27, 57—62, 64—71, 74—80, 82, 86—93, 96, 98, 99, 101, 104—106, 108, 113, 114, 116, 118—126, 128—133, 135—137, 139—142, 144—148), and the colour photographs are by

Miroslav Fokt (nos. 7, 9, 28, 29, 31, 35, 111), and

Pavel Štecha (nos. 1, 19, 22, 32—34, 36—38, 47, 48, 55, 56, 72, 73, 81, 83—85, 94, 95, 97, 100, 102, 103, 107, 109, 112, 115, 117, 127, 134, 138, 143, 149—188).

Index

Page numbers in *italic* indicate captions to illustrations.